SUSHI A...

Michael Booth is a travel writer and journalist who contributes regularly to *Condé Nast Traveller*, the *Independent on Sunday* and *Monocle*, among many other publications at home and abroad. His last book, *Doing Without Delia*, was Book of the Week on Radio 4.

www.michael-booth.com

ALSO BY MICHAEL BOOTH

Just as Well I'm Leaving:
To the Orient with Hans Christian Andersen

Doing Without Delia:
Tales of Triumph and Disaster in a French Kitchen
(also published as *Sacré Cordon Bleu*)

MICHAEL BOOTH

Sushi and Beyond

What the Japanese Know about Cooking

VINTAGE BOOKS

London

Published by Vintage 2010

8 10 9 7

Copyright © Michael Booth 2009

Michael Booth has asserted his right under the Copyright,
Designs and Patents Act 1988 to be identified as the author
of this work

This book is a work of non-fiction based on the experiences and
recollections of the author. In some cases the names of people, places
and sequences have been changed solely to protect the privacy of
others. The author has stated to the publishers that, except in such
minor respects not affecting the substantial accuracy of the work,
the contents of this book are true.

First published in Great Britain in 2009 by
Jonathan Cape

Vintage
Random House, 20 Vauxhall Bridge Road,
London SW1V 2SA

www.vintage-books.co.uk

Addresses for companies within The Random House Group
Limited can be found at: www.randomhouse.co.uk/offices.htm

The Random House Group Limited Reg. No. 954009

A CIP catalogue record for this book
is available from the British Library

ISBN 9780099516446

Typeset in Garamond MT by Palimpsest Book Production Limited,
Grangemouth, Stirlingshire

The Random House Group Limited supports The Forest Stewardship
Council® (FSC®), the leading international forest-certification organisation.
Our books carrying the FSC label are printed on FSC®-certified paper.
FSC is the only forest-certification scheme supported by the leading
environmental organisations, including Greenpeace. Our
paper procurement policy can be found at
www.randomhouse.co.uk/environment

MIX
Paper from
responsible sources
FSC® C016897

Printed and bound in Great Britain by Clays Ltd, St Ives plc

To Asger and Emil

JAPAN

日本

Sapporo

Minamikayabi-chō

Kyoto

Osaka

Tokyo

Yaizu

Hiroshima

Noda

Shimonoseki

Kobe

Yokohama

Fukuoka

Izu
Peninsula

Matsusaka

Koya
San

Osatsu

Higashikagawa

Okinawa

Chapter 1
Toshi

'Ha! You so fat you not see your dankon for years! You pants too small. You so fat, sun go down when you bend over!'

It was a characteristically abusive and, I should stress, not entirely accurate conclusion to what had started off as a perfectly temperate discussion about the relative merits of French and Japanese cuisines.

I had recently had dinner at the feted French restaurant, Sa.Qua.Na, in Honfleur on the Normandy coast. The chef, Alexandre Bourdas, is a fast-rising culinary star in France and I had innocently remarked on his lightness of touch, and the freshness of his raw ingredients, drawing what turned out to be a rash comparison between his food and Japanese cooking. I knew that Bourdas had worked in Japan for three years, so it didn't seem too outlandish to suggest that his cooking had been influenced by the food he had eaten there.

I ought to have known this would be a red rag to my friend Katsotoshi Kondo.

'What you know about Japan food, huh?' he snapped. 'You think you know anything about Japan food? Only in Japan! You can not taste it here in Europe. This man is nothing like Japan food. Where is tradition? Where is seasons? Where is meaning? *Tu connais rien de la cuisine Japonaise. Pas du tout!*' From experience I knew that this sudden switching of languages was a bad sign, as was the pouting. I had to get my retaliation in before he detonated fully.

'I know enough about it to know how dull it is,' I said. 'Japanese

1

food is all about appearance, you don't know anything about flavour. Where's the comfort, the warmth, the hospitality? No fat, no flavour. What have you got? Raw fish, noodles, deep-fried vegetables – and you stole all that from Thailand, the Chinese, the Portuguese. Doesn't matter though does it? You just dunk it in soy sauce and it all tastes the same, right? All you need to make good Japanese food is a sharp knife and a good fishmonger. What else is there? Ooh, don't tell me, cod sperm and whale meat. Mmm, got to get me some of those.'

I had met Toshi while training at the Cordon Bleu cooking school in Paris a couple of years earlier. A tall, austere half-Japanese, half-Korean man in his late twenties, he was wrapped in many layers of inscrutability, but had a subversive, dry sense of humour lurking behind the gruff, Beat Takeshi facade.

While the rest of us would wear our chef's whites for days until we looked like a walking Jackson Pollock, Toshi was always immaculately turned out. His plates were always perfect: his food presented just so, with ample white space surrounding it: his knives always fearsomely sharp. But he had clashed with the French chefs who taught us. They invariably marked him down because he refused to cook fish for more than a few seconds, and he served vegetables with a crunchy bite, rather than soft all the way through as they preferred. This seeded in Toshi a lingering resentment towards the French and their cuisine but still he stayed on in Paris, partly, I suspect, out of a sheer bloody-minded determination to single-handedly educate the locals in the superior ways of Japanese cooking.

'The French know Japan food like she know sex,' he once told me, pointing to a passing nun.

After graduating, Toshi went to work in a Japanese restaurant in the sixth arrondissement, the kind of thoroughly authentic place – virtually invisible from the street but a haven of serenity within – that registered only on the radar of Japanese tourists. We kept in touch and met up from time to time to eat and talk food, our get-togethers usually descending into a childish rally of insults.

But this time things ended slightly differently. 'OK, just shut up, OK?' Toshi said, his head disappearing beneath the table as he fished around in his satchel. 'I have something for you. You stupid, you read.'

He handed me a large hardback with a blurry painting of a leaping fish on the cover. Momentarily taken aback, I promised to read it and thanked Toshi. This was embarrassing. He had never given me anything before. It had taken me some time to explain to him the concept of buying a round of drinks, for instance. It was clearly an expensive book too and, though it sounds ridiculous given the times Toshi had ranted at me and called me a 'no-brain-whitey-*gaijin*', for the first time, as I held the book on my lap on the bus home, I began to understand how keenly he must have felt the slights from me and our teachers at Le Cordon Bleu.

The book was *Japanese Cooking: A Simple Art*, by Shizuo Tsuji, a new edition of the original published in 1979. Introductions by Ruth Reichl, the editor of *Gourmet* magazine, as well as the legendary US food writer, the late M. F. K. Fisher, served notice that this was no ordinary food book. As I would later discover, it is still the pre-eminent English-language Japanese food reference source, the bible of Japanese cooking for a generation of Japanophile food lovers throughout the world.

'This is much more than a cookbook,' writes Reichl. 'It is a philosophical treatise.'

There are recipes, of course, over two hundred of them covering grilling, steaming, simmering, salads, deep frying, sushi, noodles and pickling – many of the dishes unfamiliar to me – but along the way Tsuji also covers everything from the spiritual meaning of rice, to the role of tableware in Japanese cuisine. 'No Japanese, however humble, would think of serving food on just any old plate, relying on flavour alone to please,' he writes. Tsuji emphasises the fundamental importance of the seasons in Japanese food: in Japan ingredients with a particularly brief seasonal window are often celebrated with a quasi-spiritual verve by cooks and diners. I learned, too, that the Japanese employ a number of virtually flavourless ingredients – tofu, burdock and something called *konnyaku*, 'a dense, gelatinous, dark brown to hazy grey cake', made by peeling, cooking, pounding and coagulating a root called the 'devil's tongue' – purely for their texture and mouth feel. Others, such as 'steam-processed bonito filets, dried to wood-like hardness and shaved into flakes', or the fearful-sounding fermented soybean breakfast dish of *natto* were, to me, mystifying. There seemed to be a remarkable array of fermented foodstuffs – from miso to soy to *natto*, not forgetting (how could one?) fermented sea slug entrails – all of which belied the impression I had of the Japanese as being fussy about 'rotten' foods, like cheese or yoghurt.

I knew that the Japanese were wary of applying heat to their food, but Tsuji writes breezily about a dish in which 'chicken is tinged with pink near the bone' (in fact, it turns out that chicken sashimi – *raw* chicken – is not uncommon in Japan), and more generally of an overriding obsession with freshness and simplicity in cooking which mitigated against excessive application of heat.

At times I detected a note of condescension, albeit wrapped in a tissue of humility: 'Many of our foods may seem thin and lacking in substance,' he writes in his preface. 'But you must learn to look for the subtle, natural aroma and flavour of ingredients.' Occasionally subsequent developments in global food trends had rendered his concern for the squeamish sensibilities of the Western palate a little outdated: 'The best-loved food in Japan, sashimi – sliced raw fish – often seems unbearably exotic, almost bordering on the barbaric, and requiring a great sense of gastronomic adventure and fortitude to down!'

More troubling was the lack of desserts. There are literally none in *A Simple Art*. If this was a reflection of Japanese cuisine in general, it would be cause for more than a few moments of sombre reflection. It was like hearing about a people who never laughed. Perhaps Tsuji just didn't have a sweet tooth, I thought to myself, and read on.

Throughout five hundred pages of what Fisher calls the 'delicate pageantry' of Japanese cuisine, what struck me above all was how prescient so much of Tsuji's writing seemed. The mantra of local, fresh, seasonal food; a diet featuring less dairy and meat; more vegetables and fruit; all of it prepared with the minimum of meddling from the chef and a deep respect for the ingredients, resonated precisely with contemporary thinking in the West. Though written almost thirty years ago, this was still a thoroughly modern food book with important, perhaps critical, lessons for us all.

Reflecting on the eponymous simplicity of Tsuji's recipes, it seemed to me a colossal oversight that, while it is perfectly normal for us to cook Indian, Thai, Chinese, French, Italian and even Mexican or Hungarian food at home (I even made a German dish once), we hardly ever try to make Japanese food – and if we do it will most likely be a poor approximation of sushi. Even when we eat Japanese food in restaurants, it will be the inevitable nigiri and maki with the same half dozen toppings, or perhaps inexpertly cooked tempura. But, according to Tsuji, not only is Japanese food remarkably healthy and delicious, it is also a cinch to make. It doesn't rely on slow-cooked stocks or tricky sauces, nor does it require extensive preparation. According to Tsuji you don't even need to mix your tempura batter properly – it is *supposed* to be lumpy.

Though, of course, I could never admit as much to Toshi, Tsuji's writing had a profound effect on me. I had heard chefs waffle on about simplicity, and 'letting the ingredients speak for themselves', about how they only cook seasonal, local food, and so on – they all said the same thing. While conducting interviews for magazines and newspapers I had spent many a glassy-eyed hour listening to them

5

drone on – but their fussy, complicated food invariably undermined the platitudes. Yet here was a writer, and a national cuisine, that embodied all those sentiments.

There was another reason why *A Simple Art* fascinated me. Three years of committed eating in Paris had taken its toll. I had perilously high levels of cholesterol – for every Michelin star I had sampled, it seemed as if I had added one of the company's tyres to my waist. A flight of stairs left me winded and I was already beginning to worry about how, in the near future, I would be able to put my socks on in the morning. Toshi had taken to poking me in the belly, then pretending to have lost his finger. He, of course, was whippet slim and fit. His grandmother, he said, had recently turned ninety-seven and still tended her garden. Did I know the Japanese lived longer than any other race on earth? he asked. And did I know why? Diet.

'You know, you start eat Japan food now, maybe you live to sixty,' Toshi goaded. 'I live to one hundred because always eat tofu, fish, soy, miso, vegetables, rice.' He made outlandish health claims for various Japanese foodstuffs: shiitake mushrooms cured cancer, apparently, and daikon radish could prevent acne. Lotus root reduced cholesterol, he said, and, patting my barren forehead, I really should start eating more wakame seaweed as it was guaranteed to cure baldness ('You ever see bald Japan man? Huh?'). According to Toshi, soybeans were a miracle product that reduced cholesterol, prevented cancer and helped people live for ever.

I began reading more about Japanese food. Or, rather, I didn't. Because, astonishingly, though three decades have passed since it was published; as far as serious, authoritative English-language books on Japanese cuisine go, Shizuo Tsuji's is still pretty much the beginning and the end. There are dozens of books on sushi, of course (though, as I would discover, few that do justice to the true majesty of a master sushi chef); some writing on the health benefits of the Japanese diet; and a couple on Westernised Japanese cooking, known as *yoshuku* in Japan (*The Wagamama Cookbook*, for instance); but precious little about the current state of Japanese food, about what they are eating in Japan right now and the direction their cuisine is going in.

Troublingly, in the late seventies Tsuji was already observing the decline of traditional Japanese cuisine: 'I am sorry to say our own cuisine is no longer authentic. It has been polluted with frozen foods,' he writes, later adding that foreign influence had also had an insidious effect on the palates of the Japanese. In particular he bemoans their new found taste for frozen tuna which, he says, is 'ruining the tradition of Japan's cuisine'.

How had things developed since he wrote those words, I wondered? Was there anything left of the authentic Japanese cooking Tsuji described, or had his countrymen surrendered to the tyranny of the Colonel and the Clown with the rest of us?

Shortly after finishing the book, the same day Toshi had given it to me, I made a rash, impulsive and, it would turn out, life-changing decision. I decided I had no other choice but to go and see, and taste, for myself; to travel to Japan and investigate the state of Japanese food today, to learn as much as I could about their techniques and ingredients, and find out whether or not Tsuji's dire predictions had come true. Was there still much we could learn from the Japanese about cooking, or was *A Simple Art* now nothing more than an elegy for a lost culinary tradition? Were Toshi's claims about the longevity of the Japanese and the amazing health benefits of their diet true, and if so, would it be possible to introduce any of them into a Western life? Was Japanese cooking at all compatible with Western living? And did they really use sock glue instead of garters, as Toshi claimed?

I would travel to Japan, and slowly, methodically, greedily work my way from the northernmost island of Hokkaido, south to Tokyo, then on to Kyoto, Osaka, Fukuoka and the islands of Okinawa, eating, interviewing, learning and exploring along the way. I wanted to sample the indigenous ingredients, learn about the philosophy, the techniques and, of course, the health benefits of Japanese food. I badly needed to lose some weight too of course, and to start eating more healthily, but had found that the options for that in the West – low-fat yoghurts, Weight Watchers meals – held little appeal. Tsuji's book, on the other hand, had revealed a world of beautiful, healthy, simple food that I could easily envisage eating, if I could only learn to make it for myself.

Tentatively, I raised the idea with my wife, Lissen, that evening.

'God, that's a brilliant idea,' she said. 'I would love to go to Japan. Can you imagine how great it would be to travel there with the kids. It would be something they would remember for the rest of their lives. Imagine!'

'Wait, no. Ermm. I didn't really mean . . . you know, I don't really think . . . research . . . interviews and things like that . . .' I said.

But it was too late. I could tell by the way she was looking *through* me that her imagination was already elsewhere, captivated by visions of lavish kimonos; kneeling in contemplative Zen repose before an immaculately raked gravel garden; or staggering beneath the weight of gilded boxes through a never-ending Duty Free cosmetics bonanza. And I knew from experience that there was no use even trying to fight it.

Actually, that was fine by me. Like a lot of modern dads I suffer from a constant nagging guilt about the amount of time I spend – or rather don't spend – with my children. I don't have a proper job, which means I never really have proper holidays either. I hadn't taken such a thing for over five years. But the idea of a flaccid pool-side fortnight in some rented villa, or worse, a trip to Disneyland, made me feel itchy and depressed. Here, though, was a way I could combine work and family; a way for me to share a passion for food with my children and perhaps plant a spore of curiosity that would grow within them and bond us over the years to come. In truth, it was a selfish decision in so many ways, which is why it feels fraudulent to dress it up as some kind of noble parenting sacrifice. I was burning to spend time in Japan, but I crumble if I don't see my family for more than a few days.

*

That early August night I booked four open tickets to Japan, instead of one, and began to map out a workable route through what Toshi had assured me were the pulse points of Japan's culinary culture.

We would take a foodie family road trip lasting just under three months. We were going to fly to Tokyo, where we would spend three weeks gently acclimatising (an absurd notion, looking back). Tokyo was, Toshi told me, the restaurant capital of Japan with more, and more diverse, restaurants than anywhere else in the country. This was where we would find the best sushi, as well as the best tempura restaurants in Japan, along with numerous other surprises (he offered this last bit of information with a knowing smirk).

From there we would fly north to the island of Hokkaido, a place in utter contrast to the urban intensity of Tokyo, with wide open spaces, a far more relaxed vibe and stunning seafood. We would be based in its capital, Sapporo, for around ten days.

Then, we would head back to the island of Honshu, where Tokyo is, but this time go further south to Kyoto, the former royal capital and still the spiritual and cultural heart of Japan. This, Toshi said, was *kaiseki* country – the elaborate multi-course formal dinner, Japan's answer to haute cuisine, yet far more refined, far more complex and, according to him, leagues better. I should be sure to try the tofu, too, which was the finest and freshest in the world.

After three weeks in Kyoto, with day trips to various other places (we should make sure to visit the sacred mountain of Koya-san, Toshi said, and Kobe would offer some familiar Western comforts), a short train ride would take us to the modern metropolis of Osaka. I didn't need Toshi to tell me the food here was radically different from Kyoto. François Simon, the esteemed restaurant critic of *Le Monde*, had enthused about it when I'd interviewed him earlier in the year; he'd gone as far as to call it the most exciting food city in the world.

A much anticipated journey by bullet train would then take us further south-east to Fukuoka, on the island of Kyushu. Toshi didn't say much about Fukuoka, other than that we would love it and to make sure I tried the local ramen noodles, but he became truly enthused when talk turned to Okinawa, our last destination. This wasn't really Japan, he said, it was Japan but different, with a unique food culture and way of life. If I wanted to know the secret of how to live to a hundred, this was the place to find it – it has more centenarians than anywhere else in the world, apparently. We set aside another two weeks here.

From Okinawa, we would return to Tokyo for a few more days before flying home.

I had no idea whether it was realistic to attempt such a journey with young children in tow, but I knew I wanted them to see and experience as much as possible of Japan and the Japanese.

Asger, six, and Emil, four, had never travelled beyond Europe. Asger was as fussy an eater as I had been at his age, which meant his diet was restricted largely to potato-based foodstuffs shaped like dinosaurs. Meanwhile Emil was cursed with a hair-trigger oesophagus, to the point that we had all grown accustomed – blasé even – to the smell of aged vomit on clothing and furniture. What on earth were they going to eat?

I, meanwhile, had no definable image of Japan beyond the clichéd cinematic polarities of *Lost in Translation* and Kurosawa, and no grasp of the language beyond the few words of polite greeting Toshi had taught me, which I suspected were almost certainly rank obscenities (and, you know what? They were).

What was the real Japan like? Was it navigable? How did the Japanese live and, amid the liquid crystal canyons and the concrete, the geometric gardens and the snow-capped mountains, the Gothic Lolitas and the geishas, would there be space, let alone a welcome, for a small, curious (in both senses) family from the West?

Chapter 2

A Flaming Comet Over Braintree

We are sitting by the window on the wing of a 747. I turn idly from my video screen and look out to see vaporised liquid gushing from the far engine. My stomach summersaults.

Petrol.

I glance round. Asger is sitting beside me spellbound, his mouth gaping in front of a video screen which, I only now notice, he has somehow switched from cartoons to *Reservoir Dogs*. Emil is similarly entranced by the tray table in front of him, which he is opening and closing for the 827th time. Lissen is reading a book. Only I see the petrol. Perhaps I am imagining it. I look again. But it is still flowing. Should I alert the stewardess?

The captain's voice comes over the tannoy. 'Ladies and gentlemen, I am afraid we have a small problem with one of our engines. We are having to jettison our fuel in preparation for a return to Heathrow. This is normal procedure, so please don't be alarmed. I will let you know as soon as we have made arrangements for landing.'

Two hours into our twelve-hour flight to Narita International Airport and, at best, we will have to return to London and endure an interminable wait at an interminable terminal, at worst we will end our lives in a flaming comet of death over Braintree.

You will have deduced that we didn't die, but we endured something perhaps worse: five hours in the purgatory of Heathrow Terminal 4, rummaging like refugees for something edible to stave off our hunger, eventually making do with Pret A Manger sushi – wet, flavourless and indigestible. The memory of that sushi would at least be instructive by way of comparison with the sushi we would eat during the coming months, but at the time it really did seem as if our trip was cursed from the start.

'It's an omen,' I muttered glumly as I swallowed cold, nutty rice. 'If things have started to go wrong already, what hope have we got?'

'Michael, we haven't even left England yet,' said Lissen, calmly. 'I am sure everything will be fine.'

Chapter 3

The Pledge

Before we return our tray tables to the upright position and prepare to land in Japan, there are a few things I would like to clarify. I have been told that, occasionally, I am susceptible to making cheap jokes at the expense of others. I may also sometimes be guilty of casual racism (the Italians have suffered most from this, largely because Italian males are so preposterous); and am prone to knee-jerk prejudice; so I thought I had better lay down some ground rules, just a few guidelines for me really; things I am keen to avoid with this book, things we have all seen countless times before in depictions of Japan and the Japanese; lazy stereotypes, old jokes and insulting generalisations. With this in mind I have drawn up a list of pledges to which I hereby swear to adhere, for as long as I can.

I hereby pledge never to score cheap points at the expense of the Japanese people's confusion regarding the pronunciation of the letters 'r' and 'l'.

Neither will I make jokes about their height.

There will be no bemused riffs about the technological complexity of Japanese toilets.

However odd I may find certain aspects of Japanese culture, I will at no point refer to visiting Japan as 'the closest you can get to going to another planet while still on earth'.

I will not quote from badly translated menus (you want 'furenchi furais' with that?) nor mock the creative use of English in automobile names, like the Mazda Friendee Bongo, or T-shirt slogans or shop names (like the one called Nudy Boy I saw in Tokyo).

This isn't going to be easy, is it?

I will not sneak around photographing teenage girls dressed like Gothic Lolitas without them knowing.

At no point will I allow myself to descend into a kind of hushed reverence when confronted with examples of high Japanese culture I do not, and never will, understand (like, 'I don't really understand this kabuki/Zen garden/calligraphy, but I have a powerful sense that it is really deep so I am going to whisper and back away slowly').

I will not invoke the film *Blade Runner* when describing Japanese cities by night.

I will not make jokes about the war, kamikaze pilots, sumo wrestlers, the way I 'admire the Japanese for sticking with chopsticks even after they found out about forks', nor their uniformity of hair types.

Let's see how we get on, shall we?

Chapter 4

No Broccoli

Tokyo by night left us dumbstruck. We stepped out of our taxi into the warm, thick late August air to be swamped by the ceaseless tide of people that flows from Shinjuku station day and night. The four of us stood there for a few moments, floodlit and flabbergasted as thousands of people swarmed around us like swallows.

We had arrived in Tokyo a few hours earlier that evening, frazzled but, given the time difference, still frisky as our brains remained convinced it was early afternoon. The foreignness of Japan had become apparent before we had even cleared customs in the form of a 'NO BROCCOLI' sign – literally a silhouette of a head of broccoli with a red line through it – at the passport desk. Was broccoli smuggling an issue in Tokyo? Were other brassicas also prohibited?

As with anyone who travels from Heathrow, we embraced our luggage like lost relatives and headed out of the airport to find a way to our hotel. Though he would graciously change his opinion over the course of our journey, Emil was not immediately taken with Japan: 'It smells,' he said, as we waited outside for the airport bus. 'What of?' I asked. 'Everything,' he said, unfurling his bottom lip.

The bus carried us forty slow miles west through treacly traffic along the ten-lane Higashi Kanto Expressway, past mammoth sex hotels, malls and pachinko parlours. We caught a glimpse of the Tokyo Tower, taller than the Eiffel Tower but dwarfed by the buildings around it, before we came in to land for the second time that evening, spiralling downwards via several off-ramps into the centre of Tokyo.

Actually, Tokyo has no real centre. As our glimpses from the bus had indicated, the Japanese capital is an infinite urban maze, with tower blocks and freeways stretching to all four vanishing points and beyond. I imagine that people have driven themselves to the brink of madness looking for this city's centre, or even simply trying to make sense of Tokyo as a city in any conventional meaning of the word. Toshi told me it is better to think of Tokyo more as twenty or so smaller cities, wheels within a giant wheel, all connected by the circular overground Yamanote train line.

Once we had opened and closed all the cupboards and drawers in our self-catering apartment in Aoyama, we realised we were hungry and decided to dip our toes in Tokyo for the first time. But neither is Tokyo a toe-dipping kind of city. Step outside your door for a moment and it will overwhelm you like no other place on earth; it will sweep you off your feet in a tsunami of whelm, particularly if you choose, as we did, to alight from your taxi in Shinjuku, the largest nightlife centre in Japan.

Twelve million people live in this city: one tenth of the population of Japan inhabiting two per cent of its land. Every day two million of them pass through Shinjuku Station, said to be the busiest in the world. They were all there that night to welcome us; it was like finding ourselves amid a throng of migrating wildebeest, albeit more smartly accessorised.

Emil clung to my thigh for the first few minutes until it became apparent that the crowd was remarkably well ordered, its streams of commuters, shoppers and fun-seekers avoiding each other through the use of some kind of sonar, flowing in calm streams towards their destinations. Meanwhile, above us, a cliff face of liquid crystal broadcast the incongruous face of Tommy Lee Jones enjoying a canned coffee drink in alarmingly grizzled detail.

Emil soon retreated once more as he began to attract the attention of groups of giggling girls. Emil has his mother's charisma; he is a miniature rock star, one of those people who attract attention without effort or desire. Asger is more gregarious and his blond hair and brown eyes had also begun to turn heads; soon they were both being cooed over and photographed by polite young women bearing sweets and stickers, by fortuitous coincidence two of the things Asger and Emil cherish most in the world. It was our first taste of what we would come to think of as the Royal Walkabout Syndrome, the strange, thankfully benign, magnetic power our children – most Western children, from what we saw – had on a certain female, Japanese demographic. If they could have given autographs, Asger and Emil would have signed hundreds over the following months.

Shinjuku station is virtually a self-contained town in its own right with department stores, restaurants, offices and bars both above and below its tracks. You could spend a day there and never leave nor catch a train. We soon got lost in its labyrinth of walkways, serendipitously emerging into one of Japan's largest department store food halls, known as *depachika*.

Most of Japan's major department stores have these vast supermarket-come-multiple-takeaways in their basements, astonishing places selling just about every type of raw ingredient and processed food imaginable, and many beyond imagining, both Western and Asian. We wandered for a while, me in a pleasant food-induced trance, the others restless but impressed. There were freshly-made, restaurant quality packs of sushi; an array of tempura; tonkatsu (breaded pork cutlets); tofu; rice balls; grilled eels glistening beneath a dark, sweet basting sauce – a microcosm of modern Japanese eating habits. We saw the famously expensive fruit: immaculately veined, orange-fleshed yubari cantaloupe melons from Hokkaido, tied with red ribbons and sold in individual wooden boxes like Fabergé eggs, selling for 21,000 yen (over £100 – although the record is 1.25 million yen for one melon); mangos for 15,000 yen and apples tenderly packed with little square sponges protecting their stalks. There were barrels of tiny dried fish; deep-fried eel spines (well, you wouldn't want to waste them, would you?); and, in small, glassed-off kitchens, chefs busy making dim sum, fresh noodles and mochi cakes (from rice flour, typically stuffed with sweet, red adzuki bean paste). There was a display of French cheeses almost as comprehensive as the one at my local market in Paris, and not much more expensive; elaborate gateaux, Swiss rolls and macarons as good as – perhaps even more precisely fashioned than – those from Ladurée. Asger tugged on my sleeve, reminding me that we really needed to eat.

Shinjuku station acts as a buffer between two very different parts of the city – on its west side are office and hotel skyscrapers, with more going up amid the few spaces between. But we emerged on the eastern side in Kabuki-cho, a maze of restaurants, kaiten sushi joints, shops, bars and nightclubs.

Kabuki-cho and the nearby Golden Gai are about as sleazy as things get in Japan, housing lavish hostess bars with names like Vanity and Seduce, as well as bars hosted by young men for female clients, all crowded together over many floors of many high-rise buildings. Every single floor of every single building for several blocks around had a lit sign outside indicating the presence of some kind of restaurant, bar or karaoke joint. It is a staggering place, said – and this time it's true – to be the inspiration for the look of *Blade Runner*.

This may not seem a terribly appropriate place to take young children of an evening, but even though this is a yakuza heartland (or perhaps because it is), Kabuki-cho is clean, safe and, apart from the artfully highlighted Kajagoogoo haircuts of the gigolo bar touts, fairly restrained. Even if they were older, Asger and Emil would have been none the wiser regarding the – I've no doubt hair-raising – activities in the windowless salons around us. In Japan, anything 'pink' is 'blue' in Western porn parlance; a 'fashion massage' is a handjob; a 'fashion health' is a blow job (according to Toshi, at least). Legend has it the city's Turkish baths all had to change their name to 'soap lands' after the Turkish Ambassador was taken to one by mistake and a diplomatic incident ensued (that was his story).

A fair proportion of Tokyo's 300,000 or so restaurants are contained within this densely packed quarter. The majority of them specialise in just one style of cooking, or even just one dish. In Japan, the places you most often see one restaurant serving several different types of food tends to be the station restaurants, which everyone knows will only usually serve average food for low prices to people in too much of a hurry to care. And this is the key, I think, to the unparalleled wealth of Tokyo's dining scene. In Paris, one quite often sees individual 'Asian' restaurants serving Thai, Chinese, Vietnamese and Japanese food, all of which will be third rate at best, but in Tokyo chefs become attuned to every nuance and variation involved in the preparation of their chosen culinary genre, evolving over years into masters of tempura, sushi, teppanyaki, soba noodles, or whatever. And their customers, of whom they need but a handful of regulars as rents are not too high even here, know exactly what to expect and how to evaluate it in relation to other specialists in the same food.

The only problem, of course, is the choice, which is paralysing. I am terrible at choosing restaurants at the best of times. What's more, in Tokyo a novice can find it very difficult even to decipher what kind of restaurant they are looking at from the outside unless there are photo-menus. These are not necessarily the warning sign they might be in other countries, but this was our first night, and I wanted to sample something special.

Beside the railway tracks heading north out of Shinjuku, is a narrow alleyway of rather more human-scale *izakaya* (Japanese-style pub-diners), each of them with space for between six and ten diners. This is Shonben Yokocho ('Piss Alley'), a dark, shabby, downbeat remnant of late 1940s Tokyo, the kind of place Hawkeye used to go to on leave in *MASH*; a timeless sliver of old black-market Tokyo that has survived against the odds and in defiance of the developers right in the heart of one of the glitziest nightlife zones in the world.

The air was thick with the smoke and steam of charcoal grills and noodle cauldrons, and everything was covered in a thin film of transparent brown grease. In any other country the name and ramshackle appearance of a place like this would also serve as a deterrent, but

Toshi had assured me that not only was it perfectly safe and that its one-man owner chefs and their clientele were welcoming to strangers, but the food they served – ramen, yakitori (grilled skewers) and yakisoba (fried noodles) – was compulsively delicious and cheap.

We sidled up to a tiny, Formica-topped L-shaped bar, behind which an elderly lady, bent in the shape of a question mark, with tightly permed grey hair and a red apron was busy scraping at a hotplate with a metal spatula, tossing an unruly mound of ramen noodles (confusingly yakisoba is made with ramen noodles, not soba) beneath fluorescent tube lighting. She barely glanced at us, though we must have been an unlikely sight, so I just pointed to the noodles, raised two fingers and smiled. She nodded and set to work.

The place was designed for efficient consumption: Kikkoman bottles and jars of chopsticks stood on the bar; the menu, written in Japanese on wooden tabs, hung around the walls; red and white lanterns dangled from the ceiling; and we sat on red vinyl stools. We shared a couple of piles of yakisoba with a sweet, soy-based sauce (a strain of dark, tangy-sweet teriyaki-style sauce, that we would encounter in all sorts of dishes throughout Japan), and topped with bright red pickled ginger and little flakes of dried seaweed. It was clinically moreish.

The other diners – salarymen in dark suits, their ties loosened at the end of the day – toasted us with brown bottles of beer as big as their forearms, pouring little glass tumblers-full and offering them to me and Lissen with polite questions in disjointed English about where we were from, how long we had been in Japan, and what we thought about Japanese food. Seeing Asger and Emil struggle with their chopsticks, the owner rooted around and pulled out a couple of small forks and we all stuffed our faces contentedly.

It is usual to hop from one izakaya to another having a small plate of something in one and a few yakitori at another, so we did just that, settling in for a second helping in front of a smoking charcoal grill in another tiny cubicle. This time it was a young man with a wispy goatee stoking the flames and turning the skewers. We ordered by pointing at what others were having and at the raw skewers in the glass case that divided the counter from the kitchen.

Usually barbecues worry me. The meat is either overcooked, raw or charred, often all three, and usually inferior to anything that comes out of a normal oven. But the Japanese have mastered the charcoal fire better than any other nation thanks to one simple but characteristic innovation: they make the food smaller.

Yakitori literally means 'grilled chicken' but asparagus, quail eggs, tomatoes and various vegetables are also cooked this way. Crucially, the meat is cut into bite-sized pieces and skewered, three or so pieces at a time, along with short lengths of negi – very tender, small leeks. The skewers are grilled for a few minutes over a hot charcoal grill, and basted with sauce, then put back over the charcoal briefly before being served. It is not especially healthy but is as addictive as crystal meth and, short of administering a general anaesthetic – which is hardly cost effective, and besides Lissen says there are some ethical issues – there are few better ways to get children to eat vegetables.

Chicken livers, crunchy gizzards (lacking teeth, this is the muscle birds use to break down grains before digesting them), skin, and hearts are all yakitori menu staples but there was one skewer in the glass case I couldn't identify. I ordered one, just in case I was missing something. It had no discernible flavour beyond the sauce that covered it, but an unusual texture, like crunchy plastic.

It was cartilage – specifically the piece at the crown of the chicken's breast. It wasn't that appealing but Emil diligently gnawed his way through the rest of the skewer before polishing off some chicken livers – true testament to the power of sugary sauces.

Each yakitori chef will have his own recipe for this sauce, and they guard them fiercely. Shizuo Tsuji writes that serious yakitori chefs never let their sauce run out, but instead add more when it starts to get low, which means that as they have no water in them, some sauces can go on for years. The essential ingredients are the same as for so many Japanese basting sauces: soy, sake, mirin and sugar, in which you can also simmer chicken bones and add a thickener such as arrowroot or kuzu starch, which comes in the form of rocks and, unlike cornflour, is light and flavourless. Equal parts soy and mirin, with a little less sake and sugar is a good base.

Sitting wreathed in charcoal smoke watching my children happily munch chicken organs on sticks was a surreal way to end a day that had begun with cornflakes and toast on the other side of the world, but also, in a strange way, utter bliss. We had landed.

The next day was payback time for Asger and Emil following their stoic performance during the journey to Japan. In their minds Japan was synonymous with just one thing, and it had nothing to do with food. They had long been obsessed with Pokémon, the bizarre chimerical cartoon characters that inhabit the globally popular yet, to anyone over the age of eighteen, unfathomable animations. We had promised them a visit to the Pokémon store in Shinagawa, but had forgotten it was Saturday. By the time we arrived the shop was dense with seven-year-olds all clamouring for Pokémon T-shirts, figures, lunch boxes and key rings. Asger and Emil's eyes were on stalks and they soon commenced their own kind of pleading chant: 'I want, I want, I want . . .' filling their baskets as if preparing for a siege.

As far as I can understand, demand for Pokémon figures is entirely predicated on the mere fact of their existence, rather than, say, any inherent practical or artistic merit. They are, then, the perfect product, placing their addicts entirely at the mercy of the corporation that churns them out; and they don't get much less merciful than the Nintendo Corporation of Japan.

The next stop was Kiddiland, the surprisingly small, largest toy store in Tokyo. While we were browsing the Pokémon department there, a mother approached.

'How old is he?' she asked pointing to Asger.

'Six,' I told her. She looked aghast. I asked how old her boy was, he looked about four. 'Eight,' she said, looking at Asger. 'Is he normal?'

'Well, depends what you mean by normal.'

'Oh, *Daa-aad*.'

Across the way a small kiosk caught my eye. It was selling vinegar drinks, which I had heard were a current fad. I bought one – cherry vinegar flavour – and took a gulp. Initially all was well: there was a sweet, sugary cherry flavour, like old fashioned worm medicine but, good *grief*, the afterburn was horrific – pure vinegar. It could have been worse. Another recent Tokyo drink craze I'd heard about was for a zero calorie jelly drink, made with pig placenta.

In the Hello Kitty heartland of Harajuku a short walk away, we took sneaky photos of teenage girls dressed in lacy, stack-heeled, puffball-skirted Gothic Lolita costumes (I appear to be going through those pledges at quite a rate); as nurses complete with bloodstained aprons; favourite anime characters; French maids; and what you might call 'LA punks' (like the ones you see as extras in old Kiefer Sutherland movies).

We caught a cab back to the apartment. In Paris catching a cab is like trying to capture a wasp; requiring a great deal of patience, and you are likely to get stung. But Japanese cab drivers are a different breed, a super race of chauffeurs. Within seconds of standing by the kerb with our arms outstretched (or, in Asger's case, his light sabre illuminated), a boxy yellow Toyota had pulled up. The rear door opened automatically, prompting impressed gasps from the boys.

'Wha . . . wow! Did you see that!' said Emil.

'It was me! I was using the Force!' said Asger.

We climbed in the back and showed the white-gloved driver where we wanted to go on our map. He smiled, nodded and started to drive. Ten minutes later we paid the exact fare, the rear door opened automatically once more and we bundled out. 'Please remember to take any your belongings with!' he called after us.

It sounds so simple, doesn't it? A taxi driver takes you where you want to go, and you pay him the fare. But we were more used to myriad arbitrary additional charges, erratic driving, a random confrontation and, finally, a complaint about the lack of tip.

The experience inspired me to write a list as soon as we got in the door.

Great things about Tokyo in comparison to Paris, in the order they occurred to me:

There is no dog shit

No one expects a tip

There is no litter

Hold on, there are no litter bins either

I'm the tallest person here

People won't steal your stuff, try to cheat you, or be rude to you because you don't speak their language

How can so many restaurants make a living?

It really is great being taller than everyone for once

You can get a taxi

Even in the rain

You can be sure the driver will simply take you where you want to go without fuss or any funny business

People in shops act like they really want your business

I could probably have had quite a good basketball career in Japan

Back at our apartment complex the concierge told us that there was a typhoon on the way. 'What does that actually mean?' we asked. 'Big wind. Lain,' she said. We were a little nervous.

The next morning was blustery. The local supermarket – slogan: 'Delicious Foods Make Us Pleasant' – had set out its 'Typhoon Preparedness Kits' containing blankets, food and water for two days. This made us a little more nervous, but was surely an overreaction. By the afternoon, however, the wind and rain were bludgeoning the windows and objects were flying through the air. The problem was, we had nothing for dinner. I would have to go out.

Outside the rain was horizontal. The streets were empty. There were no cars, no people. This was madness, I thought to myself as I leaned into the wind and battled onward. A bicycle outside a shop was blown over and began to move slowly down the street on its side. I was forcing myself forwards like a bad mime. A single taxi drove by. A shopkeeper, his face pressed up against his window, looked genuinely alarmed to see someone on the street. By now I was soaked to the skin but I eventually made it to the supermarket.

Inside, tinkly muzak played as if all was normal. I stood bewildered by the unfamiliar packaging and lack of any English wording, in awe of the perfection of the fruit and vegetables on display. The Japanese are clearly very finicky about their fresh produce. There was not a blemish on anything. The apples were air-brushed rosy red, the aubergines glossy and lacquered. Even the potatoes were uniform; everything looked new and freshly plucked. I noticed that the only other customer in the shop was waving her mobile phone close to a curious looking barcode on a burdock root: the phone screen was filled with a picture of a farmer, presumably the farmer who had grown the root. I later found out the system also tells customers when the produce was harvested – to the hour – so they can be sure it was Japanese-grown and organic, this following a number of food scares linked to Chinese produce.

I filled up my basket with noodles and sushi and a few other items, humming along to a muzak version of 'Smells Like Teen Spirit', paid and left.

Back outside Armageddon raged. I took a deep breath, leaned into the wind again and forged onwards, but after fifty metres it was too much for me. I panicked and dived into the first open door I passed, a ¥100 shop. Everything inside was for sale at ¥100 (50p), from umbrellas to underwear to clown costumes. I bought a Hello Kitty umbrella but no sooner had I left the shop than it was carried off on the wind like a dandelion spore.

Eventually, I clawed my way back to the apartment where we watched on the news an entire house being blown away, *Wizard of*

Oz-style; boats being washed up on the coast south of the city; and *Mr Bean*, in Japanese.

The concierge assured us the storm would die down by the next morning, which was fortunate as we had rather a special lunch date planned.

Chapter 5

Sumo Size Me

'Are sumos people?' Emil whispered to me, his hands covering his ears as two mammoth mounds of nappied blubber collided before us with a sickening crack.

It was a fair question. Sumo wrestlers did not resemble any of the varieties of human life Emil had encountered so far in his four years on earth, particularly not in Japan where, as his brother had already pointed out, there was 'no one here as fat as you, Dad'.

The Japanese could hardly have picked a national sport less suited to their physique, but sumo has been it for more centuries than anyone knows, having emerged from the rituals of Shintoism to become an imperial spectator sport in the eighth century. Though in something of a decline these days, it is still watched by millions on TV, its protagonists unlikely sex symbols inspiring David Beckham-style mania among their adoring female fans.

I was curious to know how it was that, in a country of almost uniformly slender people with a diet so low in fat, rikishi ('strong men'), as the wrestlers are called, manage to turn themselves into these colossal walrus-people. If I wanted to sumo size me, how would I go about it? I had always assumed their diet was made up of fatty meats, ice cream, chips and chocolate and heard that they slept after meals. It had been a strange source of comfort to know that someone, somewhere, had been living my dream life.

Toshi had warned me that getting access to a sumo stable would be difficult. 'No way, no chance you get there,' were his exact words.

27

He had described sumos as famously arrogant, dim and overly concerned with expensive perfume and hair tonics, laughing scornfully when I had described them as 'the last real samurai'. But he had given me one important tip before we left for Japan: I would need a Japanese fixer, someone who would know how to make the formal approaches to the people I wanted meet, and who understood the protocol of dealing with the gatekeepers of Japanese society.

That someone was Emiko Doi, or Emi, a researcher for an American newspaper group with an office in Tokyo, who I got in touch with via a mutual acquaintance. Out of a population of a hundred and twenty-seven million, I don't believe I could have found anyone more suited to the task, not least because Emi was a knowledgeable food lover and, unlike many Japanese women, an enthusiastic eater.

We met Emi for the first time that day (our third in Japan), outside Ikegami station. I was nervous; it felt a little like a blind date – albeit with my wife and kids, which was even more peculiar, but Emi's warm greeting soon put us at ease. Emi was a slim, elegant, single woman a couple of years older than me with a penchant for dangly jewellery and pearls. I had been nervous about how she might react to the fact that I had my family in tow – hardly normal for a supposed professional journalist – but she scooped Emil and Asger up in her arms with genuine eagerness.

Emi had spent some time in Canada during her teens and so had an understanding of the quirky ways of Westerners that would prove useful over the coming months. She was also astonishingly efficient and, from the initial email approach earlier in the year onwards, somehow always 'got' what it was I was after, even though most of the time I didn't really know myself. Though occasionally I would sense her disapproval of my chaotic approach to the project, as well as my many etiquette lapses (the pursed lips on the various occasions I forgot my business cards, for instance), Emi would prove to be a remarkably tolerant and knowledgeable guide.

It was Emi who had miraculously arranged access to a stable, or *heya*, a semi-sacred place – the rikishi's home as well as their training camp.

The Onoe stable is situated in the quiet residential suburb of Ikegami, a dense grid of low-rise houses with tiny front gardens and no pavements. The stable itself was small, home to just eight rikishi, their trainer (a former wrestler of some note), his wife and their two small sons. The building was makeshift; a single-storey, corrugated warehouse with chipboard walls. From the outside, sitting amid the neat little concrete houses, each with a cigarette paper's space between them, it looked little more than a self-storage centre. Inside there was just enough room for the brown clay ring, or dohyo, and the raised wooden dais where we sat. In one corner were some weights, but other than that there was no visible training equipment.

On our way there, on a crowded Yamanote Line train sitting with dozens of commuters' bottoms in our faces, Asger on my lap, Emil on Lissen's, trying our best not to take up too much valuable space. I had tried to explain to Asger and Emil about sumo and their sport.

'OK, so, it's like, you have two really, really fat men, you know like Monsieur Laurent at the patisserie, but bigger.'

Emil's eyes widened. 'Bigger?'

'Yes, bigger, *really* fat. Basically, they throw salt around and slap their thighs for a bit. Then a bell rings and they have to push each other over. The one that does this first, wins. Then they bow and say thank you to each other. Oh yes, and they are naked, except for a, well, it's a kind of nappy thing I suppose.'

This last bit of information prompted disbelieving giggles. They weren't falling for it for a minute. Dad was up to his tricks again, no doubt (like that time he said cars ran on the power of singing).

So it was with some satisfaction that I was able to present the real thing, very much in the flesh. We sat on a tatami covered dais beneath a large, flat screen TV – the area also served as the rikishi's living room, dining room and bedroom. Asger and Emil cowered behind us with their fingers in their ears as the wrestlers continued their training. One or two of them had noticed us, and exchanged glances with one another, but remained focused on their routines, as the trainer, Keishi Hamasu, in polo shirt and shorts, paced outside the ring.

'They are actually quite beautiful, in a strange way,' Lissen whispered to me. I gave her a funny look. 'They must get the most appalling wedgies,' I whispered, but she wasn't listening; she was watching, rapt, at their bending, stretching, pushing and shadow-sumo-ing. For one exercise, called butsukari-geiko, one rikishi would stand still while the other tried to push him across the ring as if he was a large wardrobe. It was horribly gruelling and the pusher would invariably end up on the floor coughing up his lungs and crying out in pain.

There are no weight divisions in sumo, all sizes and shapes compete against each other. But weight superiority is no guarantee of a win, as was the case when a smaller rikishi sent his opponent, a two-hundred-and-thirty-kilo wrestler nicknamed Sumo Monster, hurtling from the ring into the wall with a terrifying crash.

A twenty-three-year-old Estonian took his place. Kaido Höövelsen, nicknamed Baruto (a mangled Japanese phonetic interpretation of his home region, the Baltic), is a rising star of sumo and was clearly a cut above the rest of the stable, despite weighing a mere one hundred and seventy-five kilos. He dispatched five of his Japanese stablemates without losing breath. At one point he pushed a rival all the way across the dohyo, out of the open, garage-style doors and onto the street where a small crowd had gathered to watch the session. Asger could hardly believe his eyes. 'Wow, did you see what he did?'

With the training session at an end, the rikishi washed their hands with a long-handled ladle at the corner sink and began to waddle up to introduce themselves, clearly intrigued by Asger and

Emil. Emil hid behind my legs, but Asger offered his hand to the sweaty, pink giants. Baruto lifted him up on to his shoulder and then, as Emil emerged, he lifted him with another great, meaty palm up on to the other shoulder. Sumo Monster also introduced himself. 'Heaviest sumo in world,' he said, proudly in English.

Baruto had been in Japan for four years, he told me. 'It must have been quite a culture shock to come here while still a teenager,' I said. 'I did struggle when I first arrived in Japan,' he said. 'The food, I couldn't eat it. It is the same for all foreign sumo.' It is also quite normal for young rikishi to be physically beaten by the senior rikishi. That week, the Japanese newspapers had been full of stories about a seventeen-year-old trainee, Tokitaizan, who had been beaten to death in a hazing incident that went badly wrong in a Nagoya stable. The story had given a rare and, to many, shocking glimpse into stable life where younger wrestlers wake at four in the morning to begin cleaning and preparing breakfast, rarely seeing the outside world throughout the day, and get to bed after midnight, their lives consumed by the duties of the stable.

Tokitaizan had died of heart failure after a prolonged training session that culminated in a half-hour butsukari-geiko. The autopsy revealed that he was severely bruised, had a fractured nose and ribs, and was marked with so-called 'tolerance burns' from cigarettes. He had tried to escape the stable three times in the last month but his father had sent him back.

It can't have been much easier for Baruto, who had the added burden of being a foreigner. The influx of foreign wrestlers – mostly from countries with a similar wrestling tradition such as Mongolia, Bulgaria and Greece – has been the single greatest change to sumo since the sport began, and the source of great controversy. The first to break through was a 284kg Samoan, Konishiki, who began fighting in 1982 and achieved the second highest rank in the sport. He was said to be able to consume a hundred beers and seventy nigiri at one sitting) and retired a few years ago suffering from gout, a stomach ulcer and knee problems. Later, a Hawaiian rikishi, Akebono, surpassed Konishiki's achievements to achieve the highest rank of yokozuna, but the sumo establishment still has trouble accepting that foreigners can make as good, or as is more often the case, superior wrestlers to the home-grown talent, and overseas champions can find rules mysteriously changed to prevent them from dominating. Watching sumo on TV in Japan you notice, too, how the camera never lingers on foreign victors. That week the most famous sumo of all, a Mongolian called Asashoryu, had done little for the overseas wrestlers' cause when he had been caught on YouTube playing football in his home town, Ulan Bator, when he should have been undertaking various duties in Japan (he had claimed he had to return home to treat an injured leg). But still they come, like Baruto, drawn by annual earnings of up to and over half a million dollars a year for top-flight wrestlers.

It was lunch time: what I had been waiting for. Each day the rikishi take turns to make the food for the rest of the stable. Today was Sumo Monster's turn and, as he went off to the kitchen to prepare our lunch, still wearing nothing but his *mawashi* (the 'nappy'). 'Come on, would you like to see where we fight?' asked Baruto, inviting Asger and Emil down to the ring. Emil scuttled behind Lissen, but Asger followed tentatively, removing his shoes. To his astonishment, Baruto squatted down into position in the ring, ready for a bout, inviting Asger to do likewise. Asger glanced nervously towards us, but I smiled and nodded that it was OK. He hurled himself at the Estonian who fell obligingly onto the dusty brown clay flinging his legs up in the air for good measure. Asger stood with his mouth open, stunned by his own strength as Baruto dusted himself off, shaking his head in shock at his defeat at the hands of a six-year-old. As he sat at the edge of the dohyo he did the splits, a reminder that suppleness is also an important trait for a rikishi. Meanwhile, outside in the street was a sight that will, I suspect, remain indelible even in Emil's vague recollections of his trip to Japan in future years: a sumo wrestler riding in circles on a bicycle, like a circus elephant.

I followed Sumo Monster's (real name Yamamotoyama) dimpled, spotty thighs into the small kitchen, most of it taken up with two fridge freezers. My heart was actually racing in anticipation of finally learning the secrets of the sumo diet. Amused at my interest in his lunch plans, Sumo Monster explained that he was making a chanko nabe, the traditional sumo hotpot. 'There are lots of different kinds,' he said. 'Maybe as many as ten. We all take turns to make it and each of us has a speciality. This is a chicken and soy sauce one.' He chopped daikon radish then carrots into a pot of simmering water seasoned with soy, as if sharpening a pencil (a cut known as sogi giri). He then added half a ladle of salt. Did he have a recipe? 'No, this is man's cooking, we don't really worry about the details. The important thing is that there is enough – this is how the chanko nabe developed. Sumo stables used to be much larger, up to a hundred wrestlers, and they needed a dish that could be cooked in one pot but feed many.'

With Sumo Monster engrossed in his chanko nabe I took my chance to sneak a look into the fridges. Instead of the cakes and chocolates I was hoping to find, they were full with sweetcorn, tofu, chicken and other vegetables – a veritable showcase of healthy eating. I was a little crestfallen.

Sumo Monster had been studying economics before becoming a pro sumo, he told me. I asked him if there were riches to be made in the ring. 'Only seventy or so rikishi make much money out of nine hundred. I still worry about the money.' He chopped some chicken pieces and added them to the pot. They cooked for a few minutes before he threw in some Chinese cabbage and then the tofu. 'You must cut tofu in your hand like this,' he said, using his broad palm as a chopping board, before swiftly adding shiitake and enoki mushrooms. 'It is the only way, otherwise it falls apart. You cook the hardest things first, and then work your way to the softer things.'

Back in the training room, Lissen had got us all an invitation to lunch from the stable master, Keishi Hamasu, and his wife. As we sat down on the floor by the low dining table, Oyakata-san, as Hamasu is addressed at the stable, beckoned for me to sit with him.

'They are kind of like my sons,' he explained, gesturing to the rikishi who were milling around the room. One was watering the dohyo, the others were waiting, I later realised, for us to eat so they could come to the table and eat themselves. 'Expensive sons! We live like a family, my wife does their washing, they sleep right here, my own children are like siblings to them. I tell my [actual] sons that we eat because of their work.'

I told him I was disappointed not to see more chocolate in the fridges. He laughed. 'For us, carbohydrate is the best way to make our size, along with meat and fish, but it has to go hand in hand with training. We have got to build muscle that won't get damaged, not fat. But the sumo diet has changed. We get many more imported things now, like sausages. It used to be more fish-orientated.'

Rikishi begin their careers in their teens and tend to finish in their early thirties, although there is a forty-seven-year-old sumo still fighting. Oyakata-san had retired only three years ago aged thirty-six but already seemed relatively slim. He told me he had lost almost thirty kilos since he stopped. Only a cauliflower ear betrayed a lifetime of combat at the highest level. How had he lost all that weight? 'When I stopped I just ate less, particularly less carbohydrate, my appetite died down naturally because I was using less energy. But I have diabetes from the time when I was a rikishi.'

Diabetes is just one of the illnesses to which rikishi are prone, along with high cholesterol, high blood pressure and heart problems. In the nineties the sport's governing body implemented a regime of medical checks to try to control wrestlers' health, and things have improved. Many of the problems rikishi suffer from in later life arise through the use of performance-enhancing drugs: there is no testing in the sport, and use of steroids and similar drugs is apparently rife. As with pro-cyclists, rikishi will, it seems, put their bodies through almost any stress to achieve success. They used to have a similar life expectancy to normal Japanese, but as the rest of the population started living longer, their average life expectancy remained at around the mid-fifties to early sixties. That said, recent studies have shown that wrestlers don't have *absurdly* high body fat levels and are remarkably fit, with fairly normal levels of uric acid and glucose – usually high among us bona fide fatties.

The lunch spread, though relatively healthy, was on an impressive scale. As well as the protein-rich chanko nabe, there was omelette, rice, cocktail sausages and, of all things, fried spam (traditionally sumo wrestlers don't eat four-legged animals because a rikishi on all fours is a loser, but processed pork apparently doesn't count). We barely made an impression on the amount of food at the table, and left them to enjoy their well-earned feast and afternoon beauty nap.

The training at the Onoe stable had been particularly intensive that day as the September Grand Tournament was starting the next day, the first week of the month. We rose early and took the train across the river to Ryogoku in eastern Tokyo, for 300 years the traditional sumo quarter and home of the national sumo stadium, Kokugikan. Outside the stadium were rows of flagpoles with multicoloured banners. Crowds of fans swarmed over the rikishi as they arrived. As we queued for tickets, four wrestlers climbed out of a visibly sagging taxi, dressed in kimonos with bold floral patterns, their hair heavily oiled and perfectly arranged. They looked like a Hawaiian welcoming committee made up of silverback gorillas.

I had never been especially taken by the sumo I had seen on TV – the small screen seems to render sumo even more ridiculous somehow. But watching real, live bouts inside the stadium, sat cross-legged on red cushions, it all made sense. The preamble was the best bit as the wrestlers waddled into the ring, clutching the sticks that dangle in front of their crotches, slapping imaginary mosquitoes on their thighs and belts and cocking their legs. Next comes one of the most bewildering rituals in sport: the pre-bout jockeying for psychological advantage during which each wrestler will start to bend down as if readying for action. The knuckles of one hand might even touch the clay, but just as you think the other is about to touch down, signalling the start of the fight, one of the wrestlers will apparently have second thoughts, feign indifference to the whole affair, stand up, turn his back on his opponent and launch into the whole face wiping, salt scattering, thigh slapping rigmarole once again. They can go on like this for minutes with five or more false starts, during which a knowledgeable audience will applaud eagerly at a particularly audacious sumo tease.

Though the bouts themselves usually last mere seconds, there are few more thrilling moments in sport. Two great fatties slapping each other, then tumbling on top of each other in a great blubbery heap? Bring it on! (Although I can't help thinking some stout ropes around the ring might be a good idea.) Techniques for winning varied from frenzied, girly slapping to locking horns and standing in stalemate until one began to flag. One sumo, who would go on to win the tournament outright, simply picked up his opponent and dumped him out of the ring like a large barrel.

Afterwards Asger, Emil, Lissen and I retired to a sumo restaurant around the corner for lunch. Yoshiba is housed in a former sumo stable – much larger than the one we had visited the day before – and staffed by ex-sumo wrestlers, some of whom were engaged in what I presume was sumo stand-up comedy when we arrived. Several diners shoved 1000 yen notes into their *mawashi* belts as if they were lap dancers. Our still-simmering chanko nabe arrived within minutes. It was a more refined version of the one we had tried the day before, with shiitake mushrooms, prawns, red snapper, scallops, pork, chicken, tuna dumplings, potato noodles, fried tofu and omelette. It was terrific, though in the manner of all *nabemono* and *saimono* dishes

(Japanese 'one-pot' and 'soups') screamingly hot. Long after the others had eaten a seemly amount, I was still forcing down mouthfuls, my stomach stretched like a haggis skin. I was determined to finish the lot, but as I did, the waitress arrived with a vast mound of noodles which she added to the pot, before giving it all a quick stir with her chopsticks.

Reluctantly, I had to draw the line. That was enough for me. I was as sumo-sized as I was going to get, for now.

Chapter 6

World Famous in Japan

I am shaking hands with one of the five most famous people in Japan. His name is Takuya Kimura.

No, me neither.

Close by, in the same TV studio, designed in a kind of Disney-baronial style with fake stone walls, pastel colours, extravagant floral displays and stained glass windows, are the four other most famous people in Japan, known to every school child, parent and grand-parent from Hokkaido to Okinawa. Their names are Masahiro Nakai, Goro Inagaki, Tsuyoshi Kusanagi and Shingo Katori. Ring any bells?

This was the day after the sumo championship. We had only been in Tokyo a few days but once again Emi had somehow known what I wanted to see, even when I didn't really know it myself. I had expressed a vague interest in trying to get to the bottom of the Japanese TV food show obsession which, to judge by the sheer volume of programmes about food, cooking, restaurants or food producers, surpasses even that of the British and Americans. According to some estimations, over forty per cent of all Japanese television output can be categorised as 'food TV' – whether it is serious programmes in search of obscure artisanal producers, or the crazy campery of the world famous cook-off, *Iron Chef* (sadly no longer in production but still repeated). Certainly, my own empirical research during our first few days in Japan had confirmed that, if you turn on the TV, you will come across something to do with food within two or three clicks of the remote.

I had a vague idea that I might like to talk to some programme makers, perhaps on a minor cable channel, and maybe watch a recording or two, but Emi had more ambitious plans for me, which is how I found myself standing in the wings, the only non-crew member in the studio during the recording of Japan's most popular TV show of the last decade.

I had heard neither of *SMAP* – for 'Sport, Music, Assemble People' – nor its constituent elements: five former boy band singers, now in their early thirties, turned TV chat show interviewers, cooking show hosts and movie stars, but they are, without rival, the biggest TV stars in Japan. Over the last dozen years these five young men have conquered every entertainment sphere, whether it was J-Pop (execrable Japanese pop music aimed at – presumably lobotomised – teenage girls), TV or, latterly, their own individual film careers. Along the way they have amassed unfathomable fortunes; millions of devoted, obsessive fans; and a level of fame that exceeds even that of the Hollywood stars who make sure *Bistro SMAP*, as their food show is called, is the first stop on their Japanese publicity junkets (recent guests had included Matt Damon, Madonna, Cameron Diaz and Nicolas Cage). *Bistro SMAP* is not just the number one food programme in Japan, as a segment of the band's main variety show, *SMAP × SMAP*, it is the number one TV show in Japan full stop, with up to thirty million tuning in most weeks – a position it has held on and off for over ten years. You can't travel for more than a few minutes in Tokyo without seeing the band's faces promoting the unappealingly named sugary 'sports' drink Pocari Sweat on the metro; Japan Airlines, on a four-storey billboard beside the Mori Tower; or their latest movies and TV series just about everywhere.

I always think that domestic-only stars reveal far more about a country's tastes and aspirations than those who go global – just think about Claude François or Norman Wisdom. So what does SMAP tell us about the Japanese? Most obviously that they like pretty, polite and apparently wholesome young men who conform to just about every boy band stereotype, right down to their hurt puppy faces during ballads and Bronx-pimp moves in the rap bits.

But SMAP have done more than just polish their Backstreet Boys moves in their bedroom mirrors. Through *Bistro SMAP* they have done nothing less than overturn centuries-old conventions about who wears the aprons in Japanese households. Thanks to this show, and its seven spin-off cookbooks which, I should add, are the best-selling celebrity cookbooks in the world, these five performers have managed to convince the Japanese male that it is OK to cook at home, that there is no shame in a man frying noodles or taking time to slice sashimi and present it just so on a bed of grated daikon. Today more Japanese men than ever cook at home, and the boys from SMAP are one of the main reasons. Indeed, you could argue that they are the most influential people in contemporary Japanese food culture.

So what is the televisual magic that has almost a quarter of the Japanese population glued to their boxes every Monday night at ten? I was about to find out.

Band member Masahiro, the maître'd and non-cooking host, enters through the upper floor of the horseshoe-shaped, two-storey, faux-bistro set, dressed in black waistcoat, white shirt and black trousers. The rest of the band, wearing Western-style chef's uniforms and toques, take their places in the kitchens below, two per team. I take an instinctive step backwards behind the central camera, and trip over some cables, prompting a look from the stage manager. Shingo, the 'funny one' waiting in the wings, shoots me a quizzical glance – I am the only Westerner in the studio – but then winks and waves as the stage manager starts his countdown. I smile back. Even though I had no idea who he was until fifteen minutes earlier, celeb whore that I am, this contact with Japanese light entertainment royalty makes me unaccountably happy.

Masahiro introduces this week's guests, a Japanese husband and wife acting couple, who enter through the upstairs door and are shown to their table. Masahiro's opening remarks prompt exaggeratedly loud laughter from the crew. (There is a man standing next to me whose job, it seems, is to laugh as loudly as he can at every comment or gesture.) It turns out that the host is friends with the couple and has visited their house. 'I remember when we were just getting famous,' he says, 'and we came round your house to watch porn!' Everyone laughs; the wife giggles coquettishly. Following the same routine as every week, Masahiro asks the guests what they want to eat. 'We have no menu so you can order anything you like!' They order 'Chinese food with lots of vegetables'. All the ingredients have already been prepared and set out in the kitchens below for the other four SMAP boys to cook.

More hard-hitting questions – 'Do you love your wife?' – are interspersed with shots of the boys cooking. Off-stage professional chefs prompt them from time to time, but I can exclusively reveal that the SMAP boys really do cook the food and with impressive confidence and skill.

'Well, they have made over 6,500 dishes over the last twelve years,' the show's producer tells me as we chat in the studio canteen after recording has finished, adding that the band themselves create the menus. What do the American and English guests make of it? I ask (the show is very much in the tradition of wacky Japanese TV). 'They love it. Nicolas Cage said the food was better than Wolfgang Puck's. Cameron Diaz has been on twice, she was singing and dancing! Madonna loved Shingo's *shabu shabu*. When we started none of them could cook, but they wanted to challenge themselves. They'd done singing and dancing, now they wanted to do cooking. At the beginning they just learned how to wash the rice and cut the cabbage. They weren't trying to impress anyone, they just wanted a challenge but now they are really involved in creating the menus; they love to make new dishes. They have shown the same type of creativity they did with their music. We didn't know it at the time but this was the beginning of a whole new trend of getting boys to cook. There used to be a Japanese proverb about how a man should never enter a kitchen, SMAP changed all that.'

So what is the secret of their success? 'First, they are like the

Beatles! They each have distinct characters that everyone can relate to [the boy next door, the class clown, the older brother, the rebel, and the pretty one]. The second and most important thing as far as the show is concerned is the energy of hospitality they show to the guests in the studio. They really want the guests to enjoy it and the audience can sense that. This is the real secret of the programme. SMAP communicates though food, and that is becoming a bigger and bigger way of communicating around the world.'

Back in the studio, the host takes the guests on a walkabout downstairs in the kitchens, where the other four are busy cooking. More anodyne barter ensues. Returning upstairs, the food – a cream lobster chow mein with pork-bone broth from the Red Team, and fried rice with tofu, beef tongue, shark fin, onion sauce, spinach and lettuce from the Yellows – is brought up for the guests to judge. Everything is pronounced *oishii* (delicious), but the Yellow Team are this week's winners.

Suddenly, Shingo appears in drag, wearing a short tartan skirt and long wig and sings a song that, apparently, the wife once sang in her days as a young pop star. Everyone laughs hysterically and, I must admit, he is funny, even though I understand nothing of what he is saying. He has touches of Buster Keaton about him, a great face-puller. Masahiro is also charismatic, a wiry ball of energy who reminds me of a young Billy Crystal, but as for the other three's talents, they seem limited to either smouldering, scowling, or looking blank.

As usual with TV cookery shows, the minute the cameras stop, the crew descend on the leftovers, and the talent leaves as quickly as possible. All except Tsuyoshi, the boy next door, who sits quietly in a corner finishing a bowl of rice as the crew begin to clean up around him. I approach and introduce myself, and he smiles warmly. 'Great show,' I say. He smiles again. I am not sure he understands English and, anyway, I feel guilty about interrupting his meal and leave him be.

I squeeze my way through the hundred or so fans waiting outside the Fuji TV studios that evening and make my way back to the apartment. Lissen, Asger and Emil, who have spent the afternoon playing in Yoyogi park and visiting temples, are underwhelmed by my new celebrity name drops but I can't help thinking Japan could have worse teen idols than this. Can Busted make shabu shabu? I very much doubt it.

Chapter 7
Tempura Master Class

The business district of Tokyo is a bustling, frenetic hive of activity; a maze of corporate canyons buzzing with the industrious clamour of people doing deals, making and losing millions. At least it is on weekdays. At weekends it is desolate. There might as well be tumbleweed. There actually *are* giant jungle rooks, wheeling in the sky like vultures. All of which means there is no one to ask for directions. When you get lost. And can't find what you have been assured by your friend Toshi is the best tempura restaurant in the city. And your wife and children are wilting in the midday heat. And you have been walking for an hour promising them that it is 'Not far now . . .' or 'Just around this corner . . .' and for the last half hour you have been buckling under the burden of a drowsy four-year-old who weighs roughly the same as an air conditioning unit and is sitting on your shoulders.

Street numbers in Tokyo are, famously, not arranged according to any logical order but awarded as and when the buildings are constructed, so that 1 Yoko Ono Avenue, might be halfway up, right next to 3005, and handy for 80 across the way. How anything gets delivered is one of the great inscrutable mysteries of the East but I do know that if you are trying to find the anonymous doorway of a small, one-room local restaurant, that has no external number or sign, not even a kanji character that you might match to the one on a crumpled piece of paper in your hand, or indeed any evidence that it is a restaurant of any kind, then you might as well go whistle.

We were about to give up hope. Looking back, I don't know how that would have manifested itself as our situation had been pretty hopeless anyway but, suddenly, seemingly from nowhere, a tiny, wizened old man, bent almost double, with close cropped grey hair and a knobbly walking stick appeared in front of us. Quickly, I shoved my crumpled note under his nose. He took it with a shaky hand, spent some minutes examining it from all angles, then eventually turned and beckoned us to follow. A left turn, a right turn and across a street: he stopped in front of a doorway concealed by various pot plants and a beaded curtain and gestured towards it with an open palm. Holding my breath, for I dared not believe this was our tempura Valhalla, I parted the curtain and waved the piece of paper at a passing waiter. He nodded and handed me a menu. Lissen and the kids had started to follow me into the restaurant. I turned to thank the old man, but he had completely disappeared from view. Had he been a phantom? Was he a mere apparition, a Fata Morgana somehow conjured by our collective desperation? Had we *willed* him into existence?

No. I looked down, and there he was, smiling. I thanked him, attempted to bow even lower than he, and invited him in to join us. He shook his head vigorously, waving his hands as if I had invited him to an opium den, and we parted.

We had just made the end of the lunch-time service and there was only one other diner, a woman in a business suit sitting at the counter being served directly from the chef's station in the tiny open kitchen. We were shown to a small side room where we sat down on the tatami floor, accompanied by what would over the next couple of months become my customary crescendo of ageing bone crunches.

We ordered whitebait, squid, eel and shrimp, the latter's heads served separately, much to Asger and Emil's consternation. It was exquisite, all of it: the crunchy, gnarled batter glistening yet virtually greaseless; the fish cooked to moist, still-steaming perfection within. The meal ended with a lip-smackingly savoury miso soup with minis-cule clams floating on the surface and a crispy-sweet, raggedy fritter of scallops each the size of Emil's fingernail, called kakiage no tendon, held together with a nut-brown batter and served on rice to indicate the end of the meal. Even Asger and Emil agreed it had been worth the walk. Tempura had shot to the top of their list of favourite dinners, edging out pasta and ketchup.

Toshi had assured me that if I mentioned his name the chef might talk to me.

This seemed generous of him, but I had learned to be wary of Toshi's assistance. Back in Paris he had helped me to write a Japanese business card, a *meishi*, as I knew that they were essential for almost any kind of social interaction in Japan. It was only when another Japanese acquaintance of mine had chanced to see the dummy of the card, a day before I was due to take it to the printer, that I learned that, instead of 'Michael Booth, Journalist, England', Toshi had in fact written 'Please help me, I have learning difficulties'.

Still, I took the chance and mentioned his name to the waiter, who passed it on to the chef, who soon appeared by the entrance to our room. Some more diners had arrived, would I like to come and watch him work in the kitchen?

I was dying to know the secret of great tempura with that crispy, light carapace, craggy with nodules of light brown, deep-fried batter, like a fat twig, with just-cooked vegetables or fish within. Why was it so different from British fish and chip batter, which tends to be smooth and heavy with oil, its interior often overcooked?

'It is all about your knowledge of the fish,' the chef explained in his cramped open kitchen, our faces burning in the heat from the shimmering oil. 'And the vegetables. And the seasons. And the oil. And the batter. I trained for ten years. It was one year before they allowed me to mix the batter.'

Clearly, I was going to struggle to master this during a lunch sitting. As Shizuo Tsuji writes in *A Simple Art*, 'Although the technique of deep-frying was originally introduced to Japan centuries ago by Europeans and Chinese, the Japanese have elevated it to its very apogee of refinement.' He then offers elaborate instructions on how to fold the paper on which you present the tempura. Quite. But the chef did let me in on a few secrets: first, the batter. This was made from just flour, water and egg, but the water was ice cold; he used his own special blend of tempura flour which also included a little baking powder and rice powder; and the eggs were ultra rich, as Japanese eggs usually are. You add them to the bowl in the order of flour, water and egg, so that the food gets coated egg first, flour last, and use immediately (there is no resting in the fridge as you do with traditional beer batter). The next secret is that you must, at all costs, resist the urge to overmix the batter, or *koromo* (clothing). The chef used chopsticks to give it just the most cursory of swirls.

'But you've got great lumps of flour sticking around the side of the bowl,' I said. This unmixed batter made me feel tense. I wanted to give it a good whisk. He smiled enigmatically, 'Yes. Lumps are good. Now, you need one pair of chopsticks to mix and cover with the batter, another to fry. Next test the oil.' Most books say tempura oil should be at around 180°C, but an expert tempura chef will modify the temperature depending on what is being fried. He explained why: though the oil is one 180°C, most of the items within the batter have a large water content which will mean it won't cook beyond 100°C — the water sets a ceiling on the temperature it can reach, which is also why the items you are frying should be as dry as possible before you start. The skill of the chef — and it is a highly specialised skill, good tempura chefs don't cook anything else — is to know when the tempura is cooked to perfection inside. This depends on the ingredient being fried, of course, and on the batter but also on how the batter is applied. With eel, for instance, the chef showed me how, after coating the eel with batter, he scraped the skin side so that the batter was thinner there where the heat has to penetrate the skin.

I made an exasperated face, and the chef conceded that 180°C is fine for home cooking. In other words, a piece of bread should come fizzling to the surface almost immediately when you drop it in (although, should you find yourself cooking tempura for Japanese people, be warned that those from eastern Japan — the Kanto region

– like theirs golden brown, while those from the west – Kansai – prefer their tempura pale and interesting).

He deftly lifted a shrimp with his extra-long chopsticks, placing it in the ceramic batter bowl which was tilted at an angle for ease of access, before lowering it into the oil. After a few seconds he moved it around in the oil, then took it out again. 'Is that it?' I asked. He nodded. 'What exactly is the oil? Just vegetable?' 'Well, in Kanto we put a little sesame oil in, but in Kansai they don't. The important thing is not to put too many vegetables into the oil at the same time, or it will cool the oil and the batter won't crisp.'

I have learned to my cost that such impatience is my most common failing, that and the fact that I usually get carried away and cook too much. After all, the human body can take, only so much deep-fried food. The Japanese always serve tempura with grated daikon mixed in with the dipping sauce (made from a base of dashi, the Japanese 'stock' made from seaweed and dried bonito filet shavings, with mirin and light soy added – although tempura purists dip only in fine salt), because it is said to help the digestion of oily foods. The so-called 'Father of Japan', the legendary shogun Tokugawa, is said to have died from eating too much tempura, and the Japanese remain wary of overindulgence to this day.

I tried to describe to the chef the concept of a deep-fried Mars Bar. He squinted sceptically. I drew a picture in my notebook, he looked more dubious and called another chef over. They conferred and looked at me expectantly, awaiting further clarification. 'In Scotland – you know, haggis. Sean Connery?'

'Besides guns and the Bible, they brought tempura,' writes old Japan hand Donald Richie of the European missionaries who came to Japan in the mid-sixteenth century.

Clearly, thankfully, there were no Scots among them.

Chapter 8

A Tale of Two Cooking Schools: Part One

There is a vacancy at the pinnacle of the Japanese food scene, a vacuum that no one seems able to fill. Since the death of Shizuo Tsuji in 1993, there has been no obvious figurehead, no unimpeachable authority on culinary matters, someone to whom everyone turns for a definitive answer on what to dip your soba in if you live in Fukuoka, the correct expression to adopt when grilling eel, and suchlike. No one has managed to replace Tsuji, though several have tried.

Today, there are perhaps two clear contenders who, fittingly, represent the two main rival culinary camps that divide Japan: Kanto, the area of eastern Japan with Tokyo at its centre, and Kansai, in the western part of Japan, centred on Kyoto and Osaka.

As we continued on our travels through Japan it became increasingly apparent that virtually every type of Japanese food had a Kanto and a Kansai method of preparation and, needless to say, each group devoutly believes theirs is the superior method, the other's barbaric. This great Japanese food schism encompasses everything from how to fillet an eel, to whether to eat your noodles hot or cold, to how sweet you prefer your sushi rice.

Each of these two rival regions boasts two large, state-of-the-art cooking schools – bastions of their respective culinary traditions: in Osaka, there is the Tsuji Culinary Institute which Shizuo founded in 1960, and is currently run by his son, Yoshiki Tsuji. In Tokyo the Kanto school of cooking is championed by the Ecole de Cuisine et Nutrition Hattori, founded in 1939, and currently run by Dr Yukio Hattori, also the son of the founder.

Today, if any two men can claim to be the torch bearers for contemporary Japanese cuisine, it is Yukio Hattori and Yoshiki Tsuji. As I would discover, there is little love lost between these two: each of them is wealthy, highly educated, urbane and, face to face, not a little intimidating. Each is vying for the papacy of Japanese cuisine, a position of obvious cultural, quasi-spiritual significance in a country that venerates its food to such a degree as Japan.

The future of Japanese food in the early twenty-first century is, then, encompassed by a tale of two cooking schools. Hattori's first.

Of the two men, Dr Yukio Hattori is by far the better known in Japan. He is a major-league celebrity thanks to his starring role on Japan's – and my – favourite cooking show, *Ryori no Tetsujin*, or *Iron Chef*. If you have never seen an episode of *Iron Chef*, nothing I can do short of setting fire to myself and turning the lights on and off rapidly will be able to convey the hysterical fervour of this pioneering cook-off show, in which a professional chef challenges one of the in-house panel of Iron Chefs, each of them experts in French, Japanese, Chinese and Italian cooking. Hattori, nicknamed 'Doc' (he is a qualified medical doctor), helped to develop the series, devised the menus and acted as on-screen commentator each week, passing judgement on the gladiatorial goings on from a balcony above the lavish set, like a one-man Stadler and Waldorf. Sadly, the Japanese version of *Iron Chef* finished in 1999 (although the US version continued until 2001 and made a star of, among others, Matsuhisa Nobu), but Hattori remains very much in the public eye, appearing regularly on a number of Japanese TV food shows, including the evocatively titled *Apron of Love*, as well as in major advertising campaigns for a variety for food products (his face is almost as common on Tokyo's trains as the boys from SMAP on whose show he has, of course, also appeared).

In a recent profile the *Japan Times* called Hattori 'Japan's busiest man'. As well as running his media career and the school (which has over 1,800 students), Hattori writes regular food columns in the press and has written dozens of food books. Also, for the last fifteen

years or so he has been at the forefront of the Shokuiku movement, a food and health education programme run by the Japanese
government designed to reverse the national trend away from the
Western diet.

All of which made him the perfect man to give me an insight
into contemporary Japanese eating habits. Emi had made the neces-
sary arrangements and so I took the metro a couple of stops from
our apartment to Hattori's school, leaving Asger, Emil and Lissen
to relax with a Pokémon DVD marathon.

The Hattori school is based in a large office-style building in a
well-to-do district of central Tokyo, close to Yoyogi park. Outside
is a large poster showing Hattori shaking hands with a beaming Joël
Robuchon, the celebrated French chef, currently the holder of more
Michelin stars than any other, and in whose Paris restaurant I had
worked a couple of years earlier (though he is probably less well
known for this).

Hattori himself met me in reception, a dapper man in a Mao suit
made from the deepest black, seemingly frictionless silk. His silver
hair was oiled and combed in a meticulous arc above his rimless
glasses. His shoes alone looked like they cost more than my annual
clothing budget, as did his tan.

He led me through the school to a large door decorated with the
cartoon bulldog logo of El Bulli, the famous Spanish restaurant,
which led into the kitchen-boardroom 'atelier' overlooking tree-lined
Meji Avenue. Within seconds of us sitting down, two cups of green
tea and a small plate of cookies had arrived on the table.

I wanted to know where it had all gone wrong for the Japanese
diet. Though the situation isn't nearly as bad as in the West, I had
been reading in the local English-language press that the Japanese
are getting fatter, eating more processed foods, more dairy, more
sugar, more fat and fewer vegetables and fruit, and the popularity
of traditional foods is on the wane. Even consumption of rice, that
most sacred of Japanese foodstuffs, is down, from one hundred and
fifty kilos per person a year a century ago, to sixty kilos today.

Meanwhile, their consumption of fish has more than halved, and their meat intake more than doubled.

Hattori blamed the Americans.

'The Japanese had huge respect for Americans after the war. They saw their physical strength, saw that they ate bread and potatoes and steaks as thick as the soles of their shoes, and copied them,' he told me. 'They felt a huge pressure to be physically stronger, so started eating more butter, milk and flour to be like Americans. The lunch menus at school changed from rice to bread overnight; out went the balance of Japanese food, the soy, seaweed, cooked vegetables, rice and fish: in came the fat and the diabetes and heart problems which are all increasing. We had the ideal diet. We got our protein from soy, fish and tofu but young people today eat junk food, they buy ready-made meals, bad-quality food.'

Hattori explained that the problem was compounded by the physical differences between the Japanese and Westerners. Remarkably, the Japanese intestine is on average 60–70cm longer. This has obvious implications. Genetically programmed to having to maximise the nutritional yield from healthy foods due to a historical paucity of domestic produce and frequent famines, the Japanese are now paying the price for withholding all the fat, additives and sugar from their newly adopted Western diet in their bodies that bit longer. 'We have a long history of starvation and harvest crises in Japan,' Hattori said. Deep in our DNA is the fear that we may not eat again within the next week or month so we hold food in our bodies longer.' Which is why, when the Japanese move to, say, Hawaii, and adopt the local diet, they actually get fatter than the locals. No mean feat.

Hattori was not terribly impressed by the younger generation. 'Young people are not prepared to work as hard in the kitchen,' he told me. 'The quality of cooking is declining. If you work so hard, so that you are almost dying, you learn a lot but, when you look at Japan today, discipline is running out at school and in the home. People give up too easily, they get too much praise and can't take criticism. My students here in this school, they can't take criticism.'

(According to the *Japan Times* Hattori advocates a good smack on the hand or behind for disobedient children. 'Leave it too late and their character will be fixed!' he told the paper.)

Clearly, Hattori's attitudes to discipline and education were a product of immediate post-war Japan – he is sixty-four – which made it all the more surprising that he had chosen to be involved with populist shows like *Iron Chef*, and now *Apron of Love*.

But he was proud of *Iron Chef*. 'Before *Iron Chef* young people were not so interested in becoming chefs. *Iron Chef* created the superstar chef. Young people saw that and it motivated them. Before *Iron Chef* the job of chef was ranked thirty-fifth most popular in Japan among elementary school children. After *Iron Chef* it became the number one, and even now it is number five.'

Hattori had just returned from a trip to the UK. I asked him what he thought about British food, and about the Japanese food available in the UK. 'Japanese food in other countries is getting better,' he said diplomatically. I knew that he had been involved in a recent move by the Japanese Ministry of Agriculture to award authenticity certificates to Japanese restaurants overseas, but I suspect he was too polite to tell me what he really thought. 'I loved the Fat Duck,' he continued. 'Why has molecular cuisine not caught on in Japan?' I wondered. 'Especially in Tokyo where they seem to love innovation and play.'

'Hah!' Hattori laughed, dismissively. 'We have had molecular cuisine for forty years or more. You know the fake caviar they make with tomato juice, or whatever? That was in Japanese markets forty years ago [he is right, a similar gelling agent is used to make tofu]. Ferran [Adrià, the head chef of El Bulli] loves it here, he buys so many things when he comes. When I introduced him to yuzu six years ago he really went crazy for it, and miso, fresh wasabi and katsuobushi.' It turns out, too, that many of the other clever thickening compounds used in molecular cuisine are Japanese, such as kuzu and agar agar.

Hattori was now glancing impatiently at his watch, the interview was clearly drawing to a close. There was one last, crucial question I wanted to ask him. What was the best restaurant in Japan?

'Ah, the best restaurant? Regular people can't go there. It is not open to the public,' a beatific smile spread across his face. 'You can not make a reservation, it is not even in the phone book. You have to know someone who is a member. I am a member. Every year the chef sends me a reservation card and I can choose one day a month to eat there and he sends me back a confirmation. I took Ferran there. He cried when he ate the food. I took Robuchon there, he cried too. You should see the faces of people who eat there. They just smile naturally when they taste the food. The chef makes the most of each ingredient, he is amazing. A master of dashi. I have been going there for fifteen years.'

'Wow,' I said. 'It is now my greatest ambition to eat at that restaurant!'

Hattori looked me in the eye, and then looked down at his hands for a moment, considering. He looked back up.

'You will come with me,' he said.

'What? You mean to see the restaurant?'

Hattori took out a small black notebook.

'No. To eat. October 30th, 6:30 in the evening. Meet me outside the Sony building in Ginza. The restaurant is called Mibu.'

'Thank you, thank you so much. I will look forward to it.' I could scarcely believe what I was hearing. Japan's leading food authority (clearly this swung it for Hattori as far as I was concerned) was inviting me to dinner at the restaurant he held to be the finest in all of Japan, a dinner date with destiny.

Meanwhile, Hattori had another invitation to extend – the reason he had been looking at his watch. That afternoon, the school would be hosting the Tokyo round of the first ever national Chef of the Year competition, founded by the Japanese Culinary Association to find the best professional chef currently working in Japan. Hattori was the head judge of the competition. Would I like to come along and watch?

I arrived back at the school a couple of hours later to find the dozen contestants, all men (female chefs are even more rare in Japan than they are in the West), already at work in two vast and sparkling kitchens. I was the only Westerner among several Japanese journalists covering the event and I seemed to be the only one allowed to roam freely among the chefs – or perhaps it was just that no one could pluck up the courage to stop me. Either way I took full advantage of my stupid foreigner status. I love watching chefs work, their dexterity, speed and commitment is to me hypnotic.

Each chef had three hours to complete three dishes for four people – one each for the three judges and one for the display table. The chefs ranged in age from thirty to fifty, and each had a minimum five years' professional cooking experience. Only one would go through to the final in Kyoto in early 2008 where the winner would receive one million yen (£5,000) and, more importantly, go on to represent Japan in the Culinary Olympics in Frankfurt in October 2008.

The tension in the air was palpable, as was the rich aroma of dashi. I was slowly coming to appreciate that dashi is one of the major elements of Japanese cooking, in the same way as veal stock or tomato sauce is the basis of much classical French and Italian food. But dashi and *fond de veau* are very different substances, not least because dashi takes just a few minutes to make, as opposed to the six hours or so that it takes to roast and then simmer veal bones.

In the basic recipe for Ichiban – or Number One – dashi you slowly bring a postcard-sized piece of dried konbu seaweed almost to the boil, remove it before the water actually boils, (otherwise the smell can be off-putting), add a handful of katsuobushi flakes (the smoke-dried, fermented filets of the bonito fish, shaved on a special plane), leave them to infuse for a minute or so, then strain. And that's it. There are many other optional ingredients – other dried fish, different varieties of seaweeds, dried mushrooms – but this basic dashi is the foundation for a vast array of Japanese dishes, from miso soup to tempura dipping sauce.

I watched one competitor make dashi with several handfuls of katsuobushi. He let it infuse for some minutes, which I thought was a no-no; another was using chicken wings and spring onions for a more French-influenced stock, which smelled heavenly but most un-Japanese.

The rest chopped, stirred, primped and fried with intense focus beneath the watchful gaze of the kitchen-based judges who were observing how well the contestants organised themselves, their processes, and hygiene. 'To be a good chef you must have the entire process in your mind from the beginning,' one judge whispered to me. 'You have to be clear about your goals. We have different judges for tasting because we don't want them to be influenced by having seen the chef working in the kitchen. If you see really good process you can become a fan of them but if you go to a restaurant you don't see the process.'

One chef took a small head of raw wheat and deep fried the whole thing – the seeds exploding like popcorn – which he used for decoration. Clearly of an avant-garde bent, the same chef left the scales on a fish filet before grilling so that, beneath the heat, the scales threw spectacular shapes, like quartz crystals.

Some ingredients were unfamiliar to me. One chef was cooking with mugwort; another was working with konnyaku, the clear, flavourless, jelly-like substance made from the 'devil's tongue' tuber, said to be good for the digestion. Another had Cape jasmine seeds, lilyroot bulb, sake lees (a by-product of sake brewing) and 'Jew's Ear' mushrooms on his counter top.

I asked contestant number thirteen, Yusaku Kodama, if he had practised for the competition. 'Not really,' he replied. 'It is the menu I cook at my restaurant.' He had entered the competition because his boss had told him to, 'But it is much more difficult than I thought working in a different kitchen with limited space. I wish I had thought about how to use my space better. The big problem is the time. Often I let things sit over night, but here I am having to boil them, then put in ice, then boil again, and cool in ice to extract the flavour.'

One of the contestant's bamboo steamers caught fire, setting off the alarms and prompting a flurry of activity from the assistants. Tension was mounting along with the mounds of dirty pots and pans. The chefs were moving more quickly now; the noise was increasing; there were signs of panic.

The chefs had staggered finish times. When each was done, their dish was sent downstairs to a small windowless hall where Hattori and two other judges, both leading chefs, sat at individual tables waiting to taste. The fourth identical dish was placed on a trestle table on the far wall of the hall for the contestants to inspect later.

Downstairs all was deathly quiet but for the occasional chink of chopsticks on porcelain, the scratch of pen on scorecard and gulps of palate-cleansing water.

Hattori was sitting at the centre table. He looked up and raised his eyebrows at me as I tried to sit as quietly as possible in a corner. But as he tasted the different dishes I could tell something was not quite right from the occasional slight shake of his head and heavy sigh every time a new plate was brought forward. After one dish he shot me an exasperated glance. What could be wrong?

After an hour or so the judging was complete, Hattori stood up to leave the room. I followed him into the lift with one of the other judges. As soon as the lift doors closed, his demeanour changed completely.

'Did you see that! Good grief, I don't know what they were thinking of. It was a disgrace!' he said. I was stunned.

'But, the food looked terrific to me,' I said.

'No, no. No one knows how to make dashi any more. They were terrible!' he said. 'It was an amazingly low standard. The same level of my students. Too salty, too strong tastes.'

An hour later we reconvened in the Red Room, the school's flagship demonstration kitchen. The contestants were now in civvies. Some were making small talk, others sat nervously fidgeting with ties and biros. Little did they know they were about to face an execution.

Hattori entered together with his fellow judges and the assistants. One of the process judges spoke first, saying how well the chefs had done considering the time limitations, even though they had obviously been nervous. Hattori rose to address them, stony-faced.

'I have a feeling there are many among you who are just not qualified in the basic skills – things like using salt, making dashi and controlling heat. These are very important things but many of you put too much salt in your food and too few of you seem to know how to make a basic dashi. In some cases the level here was like home cooking. To tell you the truth, I asked myself, "Are these people professionals?" I want you to go back to the basics of Japanese cooking. I want you to master dashi, salt and fire. I want you to master the real tastes of Japan that the world will respect!'

None of the chefs had been expecting a tirade of this kind and I felt sorry for them. It was a national holiday, the Day of the Dead, usually spent visiting cemeteries with family. It was probably their only free day of the week. They had slogged their guts out for three hours to be told their careers had amounted to nothing. They looked shell-shocked, even the winner, who accepted his plastic medal to muted applause.

Afterwards I asked a couple of the contestants what they thought of Hattori's speech: 'He stabbed my heart,' said one pounding his chest. 'Yes, but he was right,' added another.

Chapter 9

The Mother of All Fishmongers

On reflection, if you are travelling through Japan with two fussy children who are refusing point blank to eat a number of foodstuffs, in particular raw fish, a trip to the Parasite Museum is unlikely to assuage their fears. Frankly, coming face to face with an 8.8 metre tapeworm, as we did the next day, almost put me off sushi myself.

I am something of a fascinating paradox in that I am both of a nervous disposition regarding hygiene and the natural world, while at the same time having an infantile scatological nature. I also love a good, freaky medical case history. I had a hunch these opposing base and unedifying instincts would be sated at the Parasite Museum, and they were. I also suspected Asger and Emil would also get a kick out of all the bugs and poo.

There are said to be over fifty different types of parasites that live in fish, some of them, judging by the photographs of swollen, distended and just plain scary body parts on display at the museum, are very nasty indeed. Some boast festering larvae that induce relentless vomiting. Others just kill you. One photograph from the museum, which haunts me to this day, was of a man with testicles each swollen to the size of a duffle bag. How does a parasite do that to a man? And to what end? They don't even get to see the photographs.

Perhaps deliberately, the museum is hidden well away from squeamish eyes on the second and third floors of an anonymous residential block in a humdrum Tokyo suburb. It was founded in 1953 by Dr Satoru Kamegai who, appalled by the number of patients he saw in his clinic suffering from problems caused by parasites, set about trying to educate the Japanese about food hygiene. He collected

45,000 parasite samples during his career and, if you ask me, developed a rather unhealthy fixation with microscopic bugs, effluent and toilets.

Oddly, most of the visitors to the museum the day we visited seemed to be couples – it's a curious date museum – all of whom were studying the various models and diagrams of parasitic cycles in worms, cats, mice and insects with solemn interest. There were gruesome specimens in formaldehyde, as well as three dimensional cutaway models of the parasites themselves: hideous extraterrestrials with multiple limbs and spiny faces.

Other unsettling displays at the Meguro Parasitological Museum, to give it its correct name should you ever want to look it up, included arrestingly lifelike models of dog waste and illustrations of the parasitic chain of invasion from river to fish to man. And then there was the mega tapeworm – removed from the body of a man who had adopted it after eating trout – hanging like a sacred relic in a glass case. 'If I had one of those, I could use it as a rope,' said Emil, channelling MacGyver.

Wild salmon are particularly risky fish to eat raw because they travel between fresh and salt waters picking up the worst of both worlds. They carry tapeworms as well as the larvae of the anisakis parasite which, if eaten, will give you severe stomach cramps and make you very sick (farmed fish are less prone to parasites, not least because most are pumped full of chemicals). They can live in the host human for decades. Of course, either cooking the fish (to 140°C) or deep freezing kills the parasites, but dead parasites aren't a whole lot more appetising, are they? What's more, if you want to minimise the risk of eating fish raw, the chances are your freezer won't reach the required -20°C to kill the larvae anyway, so home freezing isn't going to help. And if you think salmon is iffy, you should run a mile from mackerel which spoils even quicker – the reason why, in the early days of sushi in the eighteenth century, it was typically pickled in vinegar before consumption.

'But how do they live inside your body?' Asger asked, pointing to the giant tapeworm. I'd been dreading this. Scientific-ish museums always put me on my guard because there will inevitably be a number of 'why is the sky blue'-type questions I can't answer, as I don't know anything about anything of any importance. I looked at Lissen. 'They bring packed lunches,' she said.

After stopping off in the museum shop on our way out to stock up on parasite key rings and celebrity tapeworm T-shirts, I felt that we all needed to commune with nature a little, particularly the sea. We couldn't very well continue our travels through Japan with two of our party refusing to eat fish on the grounds that they might themselves be eaten by worms. I had a solution.

The thing that strikes you – but not until *after* you have left the greatest fish market in the world – is that it doesn't smell remotely fishy, despite the fact that two million kilos of seafood pass through its gates every day, and the cobblestones are awash with fish blood, guts and sea water.

If you had told me that all the oceans in all the world had been dredged that day and their contents brought to the Tokyo Metropolitan Government Central Wholesale Market – better known as Tsukiji – I would have believed it, but all of it is so twitchingly fresh – in many cases the creatures are still very much alive – that the only smell is of the sea itself.

We were exceptionally fortunate in that we had the chance to tour the market with a brilliant young sushi chef called Osamu, a friend of my fixer Emi. Osamu runs a local sushi restaurant far out in the eastern Tokyo commuter belt and visits Tsukiji virtually every morning to buy fresh fish and vegetables. He had generously agreed to act as our guide.

Tsukiji is the largest seafood market in the world, feeding twelve million people a day; less well known is its outer market, Jogai Ichiba, which sells everything else apart from fish and is a fertile hunting ground for authentic Japanese ingredients such as whole katsuobushi filets and myriad types of dried seaweed. On our way to the fish we also saw extraordinary open-fronted shops, one of which was selling a stuffed panda as well as crocodiles, leopards and objects recognisable with considerable effort as penises, albeit too dried and wizened to identify the donor species. There was coral, too, just to tick off the final box on the environmental outrage checklist.

Just outside the market we passed the Namiyoke Junja shrine, where some of the 60,000 people who work at or visit the market every day leave offerings of sake to protect against the volatile oceans. Among the Tsukiji regulars are most of the better restaurateurs of Tokyo; Chinese and Korean stevedores; middlemen from companies such as True World, part of the Reverend Sun Myung Moon's organisation and one of the largest wholesalers of tuna in the world; bargain-hunting housewives; shopkeepers; and of course the 1,677 market holders, four of whom can trace their businesses back 400 years to the time, before the Great Kanto Earthquake of 1923, when the original market was based close to the current site of Tokyo Station.

The seafood market is the heart and soul of Tsukiji. You enter at your own risk, which is considerable given that at any moment you could be mown down by one of the hundreds of turret trucks, whose drivers stand upright at their helm to stern to scout a path through the market's narrow alleyways, transporting piles of white polystyrene boxes of fish, slopping about in sea water, at breakneck speed. 'Don't take your kids there,' Toshi had warned me. 'No one ever takes kids there. They'll fillet them and sell them as swordfish!' Pedestrians give way to diesel at all times, Osamu warned us, eyeing the boys nervously. I clasped Asger and Emil's hands and wrists firmly with the extra secure 'little finger lock-over' grip, and we followed him as he dived into the warren of stalls to find his regular contacts.

It was as if we had entered the world's greatest aquarium. Before us was an endless parade of the most extraordinary marine life – in tanks, polystyrene boxes, or laid out on vast mounds of icy scree. Every species was represented and priced by the kilo, from chunks of vampish red whale meat to tiny brown shrimps the size of an eyelash still twitching on delicate beds of soft wood shavings. The market was indoor and artificially lit, the rows of stalls tightly packed making it tricky for two people to pass, let alone turret trucks and stevedores with trolleys. The glistening cobblestones were treacherous.

Tuna is, of course, the star of Tsukiji and much has been written about the early dawn tuna auctions here – the absurd prices paid for the fish (although, actually, pound for pound whale meat is more expensive); the extraordinary lengths wholesalers will take to preserve them (carbon dioxide keeps the flesh raw red); and the precision filleting by master fishmongers. It takes four men to divide up a tuna the size of a man, weighing up to 300kg, using metre-long, thin 'samurai' blades. Osamu explained that of the seven species of tuna, the most sought after is the bluefin, whose most delectable cut is o-Toro, the fattiest part of the belly, closest to the head. But as recently as the 1960s all tuna, and o-Toro in particular, was considered fit only for cat food. The Japanese post-war fondness for fat changed all that, of course, as did the explosion in the popularity of sushi in the West, where tastes also leaned towards rich, fatty meats.

In the summer the best wild bluefin comes from the seas around Hokkaido, in northern Japan, because the tuna here feed almost exclusively on squid. In the winter the best come from the eastern coast of the United States. Mostly though it is ranched from young fish caught in the wild and raised in pens from the Mediterranean, to North America and Mexico – often in breach of quotas and to the great detriment of wild stocks which are perilously low, some say on the brink of extinction. Advances are being made in tuna farming in Japan – that is, breeding from eggs in captivity, once thought impossible for fish that swim so far and fast in the wild – but the process remains controversial and, currently, very expensive.

The record price paid for one bluefin was 20.2m yen (around £100,000) which, though it may well yield 10,000 nigiri toppings, was still ludicrous. The price was paid in January 2001 and the wholesaler subsequently went bankrupt, Osamu said. Six million yen is about the ceiling these days.

We were at the market early enough to catch the end of the auction, which takes place at the rear of the main market in a hall the size of a football field (and has since, sadly, been closed to tourists). Men in blue galoshes and overalls were using hooks and torches to inspect scarlet divots cut in the tails of frozen tuna (in this case from Mexico), lined up on pallets on the floor like frosted, black neutron bombs. The auctioneer was making a bizarre noise: a Muslim call to prayer as read by a steeplechase commentator. Osamu explained that experienced buyers were looking for oiliness, colour and any sign of parasites in the fish, but admitted he had no idea what the auctioneer was saying.

We followed Osamu, stopping to inspect prehistoric-looking barnacles; oysters the size of my hand (from Tsuruga Bay on the Sea of Japan); mussels as big as my forearm from Aichi Prefecture, south of Tokyo; and crabs of all shapes and sizes, foaming disconsolately at the mouth. There were soft-shell turtles, popular as a soup base, and piled hugger-mugger in barrels, their feet sold separately in tubs beside them; gigantic abalone; sea cucumbers resembling freaky sex toys; horseshoe crabs that looked like living fossils; and scallops sneaking a peak at the passing world through tentatively opened shells. Emil stopped dead in his tracks beside some trays of giant fish eyes, each the size of a small saucer. 'Sea monster!' he said, pointing open-mouthed. 'Tuna,' said Osamu.

I spent most of my time simply pointing and raising my eyebrows at Osamu. What were those? Sea pineapple or hoya, gnarled and purple like sub-aquatic dragon fruit. And those? 'Octopus beaks.' What was *he* doing? 'That's an eel, he's filleting it.' The fishmonger had pinned the eel to a wooden chopping board through its eyes, while still alive, with a short, stubby wooden handled knife and was swiftly dividing it into tassels of meat and bone as it breathed its last. And, oh my god, what on earth were *those*? 'Mirugai, sea squirts,' said Osamu, smiling. It was the most extraordinary sea creature

I had ever seen: a clam with, well, a *penis* protruding, writhing, from its shell.

Asger and Emil spent some time bent over a large black bucket filled with wriggling elvers. Asger was goading Emil to stick his finger into the morass and, after a few aborted attempts, he did. 'It tickles!' he squeaked. The fishmonger laughed and gave them two stickers each with fish logos, which made their day. The elvers were not the only live produce, by any means. Everywhere we looked there were bubbling tanks with mournful sea creatures staring out at us – squid all lying in the same direction; octopus, their suckers pressing against the glass of their tanks; and flatfish stacked up one above each other. Asger pointed in horror at a ferociously ugly stonefish, mottled and droopy-mouthed, and, though not so notorious as the poisonous fugu, also carrying a nasty toxin concealed in its dorsal spines.

Emil squealed as a jet of sea water squirted on his arm from some unidentified shellfish. He stepped back, setting off a chain of events that would have been comical had I not been directly related to the protagonist. Emil's sudden movement forced a turret truck to brake, which caused one of its boxes to fall onto a nearby stand scattering large grey-pink prawns on the cobblestones. Lissen hastily bent down to help pick them up, then immediately dropped one as it started to wriggle in her hands.

'Come and see this,' said Osamu calmly, as if he went shopping with the Four Stooges every day. He took us to meet a wholesaler friend, wearing waist-high rubber waders. His stall was surrounded by tanks full of live fish, best described, for lack of more thorough-going marine knowledge on my part, as 'kind of sea bream-ish'. Osamu pointed at one fish in a tank and the wholesaler grabbed it from the water, carried it over to a well-worn, blood-soaked wooden chopping board and brought a cleaver down cleanly to the back of its head only partially severing it from its body. Swiftly, he lifted the fish from the board, took what looked like a straightened wire coat hanger, and thrust it down its spine, right through the heart of the marrow. 'It kind of freezes it,' said Osamu, turning to see four faces looking like something from an Edvard Munch painting. 'It isn't dead, it is suspended.' Asger and Emil didn't know what to make of this. How could a fish still live after having its head half chopped off and its spine kebabed? Naturally, I had no answers.

A little further on I turned my nose up at some small, wooden trays of perfectly arrayed uni, or sea urchin roe (actually these frilly little yellowy-pink morsels aren't roe but gonads – sea urchins are hermaphrodites). 'Tastes like toilet cleaner,' I said to Osamu, wrinkling my nose as I recalled the only other time I had tried sea urchins, in Paris. 'Wait till you try these,' he smiled pointing to some uni, spicy black balls. And he was right.

We ate like kings at Osamu's restaurant that evening and, along with the live shrimp whose flesh moved in a most unnerving manner on our tongues as we ate them, the uni were a highlight. He prepared the sea urchins from whole, while still alive, chipping open their spiny black shells with the square end of his knife as if they were boiled eggs and plucking out their furry 'tongues'. The shell fragments continued to twitch like antennae on his chopping board. The gonads were delicious – not a phrase I ever imagined myself using – rich and creamy and, with no time for the ammonia taste that had put me off in Paris to mature, a transcendently sweet flavour of the sea.

Tsukiji is scheduled to move from its current site to a new, purpose-built, state-of-the-art facility just across the bay within a few years. All I can say is, take out a new mortgage, sell the car or your neighbour's kidneys, just make sure you visit the old one before you die. It contains what is, in my eyes, the greatest man-made wonder of the world, the ultimate symbol of our courage, ingenuity and greed as a species, and there is surely no greater food lover's sight on earth.

Chapter 10

MSG: An Apology

I do my best to give my children pure, healthy food. I use as much organic produce as I can; cook fresh meals every day; check for 'E' numbers, palm oil, maltodextrin, artificial flavours and trans fats on ingredients lists; and know my saturated from my polyunsaturated fats. But there is one ingredient I am more vigilant for than any other: monosodium glutamate, or MSG. You find MSG in the most abhorrent foodstuffs known to man: ready-made sandwiches, ready-made sauces, supermarket pizza, low fat this, diet that; and Pringles, whose manufacturer in 2008 won a petition to have them declassified as crisps, thus avoiding sales tax, on the grounds that they were almost entirely an industrial product that had virtually nothing to do with potatoes.

In other words, MSG is the neon arrow alerting me to foodstuffs I consider toxic for my kids. If I see it, I don't buy it. And that goes for autolyzed yeast and hydrolyzed soy protein, which are MSG in disguise.

We have known about the evils of MSG for decades. In 1968 a doctor called Robert Ho Man Kwok wrote to the *New England Journal of Medicine* to share an observation that Chinese food made his neck go numb, among other troubling symptoms. He coined the term 'Chinese Restaurant Syndrome' to describe it and speculated that MSG was the cause. Others soon wrote in to add palpitations and headaches to the list of symptoms and, since then, MSG has been blamed for everything from Alzheimer's to childhood asthma to Attention Deficit Disorder. And, I read on the Internet recently, according to research by scientists, in large enough doses it can actually make mice's heads explode.

The world's largest producer of MSG is a Japanese company called Ajinomoto, which makes 1.9 million tonnes of the stuff every year and exports it around the world. Ajinomoto – it means, literally, 'essence of taste' – was founded by Professor Kikunae Ikeda who discovered MSG in 1908. He realised that konbu seaweed was a natural source of the particularly delicious amino acid called glutamate, and that if he could manufacture it he would have a powerful flavour enhancer. He patented it in a white crystalline powder form, stabilised with salt, the following year. As frozen foods and canning changed the domestic culinary landscape in the decades that followed, MSG played an important role in adding flavour and mouth feel to processed foods when these were lost during the industrial process – which is why it is particularly prevalent in diet foods.

And that's not all. Back in Paris Toshi had told me, actually looking over his shoulder to make sure we weren't overheard as he said it, that a few years ago Ajinomoto had made the hole in the top of the MSG shaker larger so that people would use more. Now if that's not a scandal right there I don't know what is.

As a serious journalist I could hardly go to Tokyo and not see it as my aim, nay, my duty to infiltrate Ajinomoto and expose their mendacity. But how could I sneak behind the forbidding walls of their Nihonbashi HQ? What cunning ruse could I employ to gain access to the hidden high security world of this sinister cult-like organisation?

I rang their press office and asked if I might pop by and ask them a few questions. They said they would be delighted, when would I like to come? I said: but isn't it supposed to be harder than this, you mean you're just inviting me along? They said yes, see you tomorrow at 11.00 then. I said: all right.

I arrived five minutes early – all the better to catch them off guard – and stood taking in the grand marble entrance hall of the Ajinomoto tower. I took a sneak look at some of the company's products – soups, powdered dashi, pure MSG – while I waited for my contact (although, looking back, maybe it wasn't such a sneak look as they were, like, you know, on display).

My contact turned out to be a friendly young PR lady who welcomed me to the company and showed me to a meeting room on the fifth floor. There, already waiting (damn!) were Shigehiro Yamamoto, the company's PR associate general manager, and Kumiko Ninomiya, the company's scientific affairs spokeswoman, smiling and friendly. AS IF THEY HAD DONE NOTHING WRONG.

I settled into a chair across the table from them, took out my questions, pen and notebook, and commenced the interview, trying to keep thoughts of the Pulitzer from my mind.

Transcript of Interview. 21 September 2007

MB: [Clearing throat and rustling papers] So, MSG. It's really bad stuff isn't it, or what?

YAMAMOTO: [Laughing politely] 'No, it is no more processed than sugar or salt. It originally comes from konbu, seaweed. It is just a basic seasoning.'

MB: [Pauses, looks down at notes] So what about all these headaches and numbness then?

YAMAMOTO: That was disproved years ago. Have you never read the essay by the American food writer Jeffrey Steingarten, 'If MSG is bad for you why doesn't everyone in China have a headache?'? The World Health Organisation, the US Food and Drug Administration and the United Nations have all concluded that it poses no health risks.

MB: Steingart . . . erm . . . it doesn't say anything about that in my notes, wait a minute. [More rustling of papers, the sound of a seat squeaking, nervous coughing.] OK, but what about umami? You say your product enhances the umami in food but no one has actually proved that umami exists, have they?

NINOMIYA: Actually, since the Miami research group discovered the umami receptor in 2000 I don't think there has been any doubt in the scientific community that it exists and that it is one of the basic tastes. It is not really questioned now that umami has a physiological function.

MB: [Long pause, a deep sigh] But isn't it true that Ajinomoto wants to conquer the world with MSG? I have evidence that you deliberately made the hole in the top of the dispenser larger so that people would use more of your product. What do you say to that?

YAMAMOTO: [more polite chuckles round the table] We did make the hole larger about thirty years ago, it's true, but that was simply because when people added MSG to their miso soup the steam from the soup was clogging up the hole. It is true that MSG is our company's original product, but we only want to explain more about umami. We don't want to destroy anyone else's food culture, or get everyone using MSG but we want to spread the word about Japanese food as a whole. We want people to learn more about how to make Japanese food. We want people to know about dashi but even in Japan it is difficult for people to make dashi from scratch with seaweed and katsuobushi. Restaurants can do this but MSG is, in my opinion, a really good product for home use.

MB: Well, if all that is true, how come America has been so hostile to MSG?

YAMAMOTO: Because it is a Japanese discovery, I guess. Perhaps they didn't want to eat something that looked like a chemical and was made abroad.

MB: That's as maybe, but no chefs in the West believe in umami do they? I mean, we've managed without it for centuries. It isn't exactly a hot topic of conversation in Europe and America, is it?

YAMAMOTO: Do you know a chef called Heston Blumenthal of the restaurant the Fat Duck, with three Michelin stars? He wrote to us some years ago, a very simple letter asking for more information about umami and later came to an umami workshop we ran in Kyoto in 2004. He said to me, 'My heart belongs to *umami*.' He uses dashi and konbu in his cooking now, as does Ferran Adrià, who runs the number one restaurant in the world, El Bulli.

Do you know it? Thomas Keller of the French Laundry is coming to our next symposium too.

It seems my research had been found lacking. Before I left that fifth floor conference room, somewhat chastened. I pledged to do a little more research into MSG and umami. Here is what I found out: the truth about MSG.

First of all, a message to Ajinomoto: Please call off your lawyers. I am a man of straw. And neither am I well enough known to be made an example of. To set the record straight, MSG does not make mice's head explode. Nor is it in any way toxic, at least no more than, say, salt. The US Food and Drug Administration has indeed given it the all-clear, as have the UN and European Union. It turns out that the studies carried out in the sixties purporting to show MSG had adverse side effects had involved giving mice absurd quantities of the stuff, equivalent to an adult eating half a kilo. So, while even Ajinomoto concedes some people might have an adverse reaction to MSG, it is no more than are allergic to aubergines, say, or sofas. MSG is merely a man-made glutamic acid made by fermenting carbohydrates and sugars, nothing more, nothing less.

Now, to umami. Umami and MSG are inextricably linked, but are by no means the same thing. Umami is usually referred to as the fifth taste, after salty, sweet, bitter and sour (although some neuro-scientists claim there are fifty or more tastes, but let's not get into that. It has taken long enough for the Japanese to convince the world that umami exists). When Ikeda identified it in konbu he wrote: 'An attentive taster will find out something common in the complicated taste of asparagus, tomatoes, cheese, and meat, which is quite peculiar and cannot be classed under any of the well defined four taste qualities, sweet, sour, salty and bitter.' It is not confined to Japanese foodstuffs. Cheese – parmesan in particular – and tomatoes have a powerful umami flavour, as do air-dried ham, veal stock, consommé, and Worcestershire sauce. Baby milk is rich in umami (far more than

73

cow's milk), as is the crust on grilled or fried meat. In fact, it is often easier to describe what umami is by listing the things that are full of umami flavour, as people do tend to tie themselves up in knots on this subject – 'savoury' and 'meaty' are the words most often employed, but often the Japanese resort to translating it as 'delicious', or 'tasty'.

The other four tastes serve a clear purpose. Salt identifies whether there is salt in a food – obviously – sweet tells you if there is sugar (and that the food is therefore an energy-giver); while bitter and sour are useful as warnings of toxins or unripeness. So why does our body need an umami-detector? Because the flavour of umami indicates the presence of glutamates which indicate protein in food. Protein is essential to our survival, so it makes sense that our tongue has a receptor to identify it in food. Glutamates are one of the key compounds that make food tasty to humans but unlike salt or sugar there are no obvious 'go-to' foods to get your hit. The nature of glutamates and umami is that they support other flavours, add body and enhance them, which is why it has been so difficult to identify. Umami is also an indicator of ripeness, and therefore tells us when vegetables and fruits are at their most nutritious – tomatoes are at their most umami-ish when they are at the peak of ripeness, for instance. What MSG does is artificially replicate the naturally occurring flavour of the amino acid glutamate that makes things taste umami-ey.

Umami has actually been identified in over forty compounds, but is most strongly present in glutamate and certain ribonucleotides, chief among them inosinate and guanylate. No, me neither, but the most important thing to know as far as Japanese food is concerned is that the Japanese are the world masters at maximising the umami in their cooking. This is best exemplified by one dish: miso soup. As Professor Ikeda discovered, konbu has more glutamate than any other foodstuff on earth, while katsuobushi, the other main base ingredient of the dashi, or 'stock' used to make miso soup (along with water), is one of the richest natural sources of inosinates.

Meanwhile, shiitake mushrooms happen to be extremely rich in guanylate, and are often added to miso as well. That's quite an umami triple whammy as it is, but the combination of these three ingredients generates far *more* umami flavour than the mere sum of its parts. When the glutamate of konbu meets the inosinic acid in katsuobushi and the guanylate of shiitake, the umami profile is multiplied by a factor of eight. Apparently it drives one's left lateral orbifrontal cortex quite doolally.

The Italians aren't too bad at generating this so-called 'synergistic' umami effect either, having long ago figured out – albeit intuitively, after all, we are talking about Italians here – that parmesan (which has the second highest amount of glutamate (1,200mg/100g to konbu's 2,240mg/100g) and tomatoes packed a tasty punch when combined. The French, too, have been maximising their umami intake for centuries by reducing veal stock to a meaty, savoury, amino acid-packed essence. The British, meanwhile, found their umami in a more prosaic source: Marmite, or yeast extract.

There is also a clear connection between foodstuffs that are fermented or aged in some way and an increase in umami-ness as these processes tend to break down proteins turning them into tasty amino acids. Katsuobushi is often fermented, for example, as are sake, miso and soy, and all of them have rich umami flavour profiles. To that list we could add bottarga, and other dried or smoked fish roe; those mouldy shark dishes from Iceland and Greenland; the fish sauces of South East Asia, which have much in common with the ancient Roman anchovy sauce garum; and of course aged cheeses. I would guess that Roquefort and Stilton are mightily glutamate-rich.

And a big fat 'So what?' I hear you say. So what if there is a fifth flavour? We've been eating it all this time, now we just have a name for it. Big deal. But it is a big deal because, firstly, if we know what 'tasty' is, then we can learn to make things tastier. Heston Blumenthal makes a dish at the Fat Duck called Sound of the Sea – it is the one where diners sit listening to sounds of the ocean on an iPod – with seaweed, edible sand in the form of tapioca, powdered konbu, miso, abalone foam and wakame stock with oyster juice, along with dashi. Sounds terrific, doesn't it? And what a combination of umami-rich foods. I bet the synergistic effects are off the scale.

But there could also be significant health benefits in learning how to maximise the umami in your cooking. Umami brings extra depth and savoury flavour to dishes which allows the cook to cut back on salt, fat and sugar – all the things that are killing us in the West. Umami gives flavour without the calories or other health risks.

It would also appear that the human body has a kind of automatic umami limiter. Once you've had enough umami, your appetite slows markedly, so you won't want to eat so much umami-rich food as something more bland. The very latest information from the Umami Research Center – which is, admittedly, funded by Ajinomoto who are, quite reasonably, trying to alert people to what umami is so they can sell them MSG to get it into their food quickly and easily – suggests that there are umami receptors in our stomachs as well as our mouths and that they are important for the digestion of proteins. Apparently, these receptors, upon getting wind of some glutamates on the way from the umami receptors on the side of our tongue, prepare the stomach better to digest food, in particular meat. Something similar happens in the pancreas too. And, the simple fact that we enjoy food laden with umami, that we are more content when eating it, makes it easier to digest.

Adding MSG is one way of bringing extra umami tastiness to your cooking. Sure, if you throw great fistfuls of it into the pot there may be some unpleasant side effects and your food will taste awful, but used sparingly it genuinely does make food taste better and give it more 'mouth feel'. That said, as always, if you can generate umami from the primary ingredients in a dish, all the better – after all, neat MSG does taste like bacon-flavoured potato chips which is not the most refined of flavours. A dashi made with dried konbu and fresh-grated katsuobushi will always taste better, deeper, more satisfying than one made from a powder, in the same way that fresh stock tastes better than a Knorr cube.

Chapter 11

The Busiest Fish in the Ocean

There is no way of finessing this: having made your way through a chapter about glutamates, you are now about to read a chapter all about fish processing. I'm sorry, but I was becoming more and more curious about umami and dashi in particular.

I wanted to find out more about the two key, umami-rich ingredients used to make dashi: konbu and katsuobushi. Konbu would have to wait until we headed north to Hokkaido the following week (this was now late September), but I asked Emi if she knew whether it would be possible for me to see how katsuobushi was made while we were still in Tokyo.

Katsuobushi are dried and fermented filets of the bonito fish, as hard as wood and dusty brown in colour. They look like a straight, fossilised banana. They are usually sold already shaved in airtight bags and crop up either as shavings, dancing bewitchingly in the heat atop various dishes, or steeped in dashi to add a deeply satisfying savouriness to soups and sauces. The shavings are fantastically moreish just eaten on their own from the bag too, with an addictive smoky-citric flavour and a mildly fishy aftertaste. Fishiness aside, the closest comparison I can think of is the salty, meatiness of a really good, paper-thin slice of pata negra ham. It really is that delicious.

'No problem,' said Emi. 'My brother works for one of the best katsuobushi fisheries. I'll give him a call.'

Emi filled me in the next day as we rode on the Shinkansen, the bullet train, heading south from Tokyo to Yaizu, a fishing port midway between Tokyo and Nagoya (to my eternal gratitude, Lissen again agreed to entertain the children – this time with a trip to the Mori Tower art museum and aquarium). 'This is great,' Emi said. 'Yaizu is Katsuo Town, it was built on the money from processing bonito. And Yaizu Katsuobushi is famous throughout Japan, it's a brand in its own right. I have even heard that there is a company there that makes it the traditional way by drying the fish in the sun.'

Yaizu is among the top three katsuo ports in Japan and the town was clearly more prosperous than other rural communities I would see in Japan. The price they'd had to pay for that prosperity was apparent as soon we got out of the taxi. The air was heavy with the smell of smoking fish. To me it was deliciously tangy, but I could imagine you might grow immune to its charms if you lived with it on your clothes and in your hair all the time. The smell was accompanied by a cacophony of machinery and diesel engines, forklift trucks and conveyor belts. There was an almighty rubbery clattering noise behind us as a lorry tipped a load of silver-black, glistening torpedoes, together with a large quantity of bloody sea water, into a tank. My first sight of a real, whole bonito.

The Yaizu Fish Manufacturing Park is a town within a town made up of corrugated warehouses housing twenty-four factories. Each is in some way involved with processing every scrap of this dense, oily, red-fleshed fish, making everything from super-fresh sashimi to canned bonito. One company takes the guts and salts, pickles and ferments them to be eaten as a delicacy; another makes calcium supplements for school meals from the dried, powdered bones. Even the essence from the liquid used to cook the bonito is recuperated and used to flavour instant ramen; and of course several make the katsuobushi itself. It is an incredible fish.

'Nothing is wasted here,' a spokesman for Yaizu explained as he showed us into the boardroom. 'Even the guts and hearts are processed for fertiliser. Quantities of bonito are declining and the number of ships catching them are decreasing too. Even though the government [which controls prices] says the number of fish in the ocean is stable, we don't agree. There are fewer fish to go after, oil costs mean it is more expensive to go after them, yet demand is rising, so we have to maximise the yield from every one we catch.'

Yaizu processes around twelve thousand tons of katsuo each year, that's about sixty thousand fish per day, but as recently as 2004 that figure was as high as seventeen thousand tons. I learned all this from what was about the tenth corporate video I had endured since arriving in Japan, all of them opening with the same shaky, synthesised strings, and a portentous voice-over. As well as informing me that they 'make the most of our blessings from the sea', it did explain the bonito's migration pattern: modori is the name given to katsuo returning from the north (specifically the south-east coast of Hokkaido) in the autumn, which are fatter and richer and mostly eaten raw or lightly grilled (bonito is considered a lower grade fish to eat than tuna); while in spring the fish comes from the south on the so-called Black Current, mostly from the Philippines, and is leaner and better for making katsuobushi. The migration is changing, however, with fish travelling further north to spawn while the Black Current itself is changing too.

I asked if they had tried ranching or farming bonito. 'It has not yet become economically viable to farm bonito like tuna; they are too small and are even more active than tuna,' explained the spokesman. Apparently bonito even swim in their sleep: especially industrious Japanese are said to 'work like a katsuo'.

I was curious to see the process that takes the fish we had seen being tipped out of their tanker as we arrived to the dried filets, like glockenspiel keys, that I had seen on sale in the shops in the outer part of Tsukiji.

We headed outside to take a look. The spokesman explained that the fish are defrosted and their heads and internal organs removed. After boiling, an army of local ladies debones every one of those sixty thousand fish by hand – after cooking the fish are fragile and this is the only way of removing the spine and bones while retaining the perfectly shaped filets the aesthetically conscious Japanese demand. We visited one of the processing halls, a dark, strip-lit factory, smelly and steamy, its every surface coated in brown fish grease. Around fifty women in blue hygiene hats, wearing rubber gloves with their sleeves rolled up, stood as the cooked fish passed by on conveyor belts. I watched one as she swiftly picked a fish up, turned it over in her hands a couple of times, dividing the four filets from the skeleton, perfectly, in seconds. The bones disappeared down a hole to be taken off and ground up, while the filets were placed carefully on a wire tray beside her. It was dirty, stinking, spirit crushing work.

Smoking and fermenting comes next. Obviously, different types of wood will affect the final flavour. Some companies use konara oak, others cherry wood, but as well as this the flavour of the finished katsuobushi can also change according to how many times it is smoked: between ten and twenty is the norm to dry the flesh thoroughly until only about twenty per cent of the water remains. We saw the vast smoking kilns, again caked in old fish goo, treacly and brown. The finest bonito of all, however, are cured in the sun for two days. There are records of bonito being mould cured in this way dating back to the Middle Ages and, as Emi said, one company in Yaizu still prepares its bonito this way – weather permitting.

The filets are then placed in a hot, humid storage area, like a huge oven, that has been impregnated with the aspergillus glaucus mould. Some of the storage chambers are decades old and imbue the filets with a unique flavour, each identifiable to a true katsuo connoisseur. It is a kind of fermentation that, as with miso, soy and sake, contributes greatly to the complex flavour and umami power of katsuobushi. The mould creates flavoursome enzymes that turn the fish protein into amino acids, in particular a compound called inosine monophosphate (IMP). The process takes up to six weeks during which the filets will be taken back out into the sun to kill off the mould perhaps several times, each time being returned to the chamber to grow a new layer, which deepens the flavour further. By the end the fish filets are hard as wood, ready for the final stage, shaving.

This is done using a katsuobushi kezuriki, an upside-down

Chapter 12

The Campaign for Real Wasabi

It is rare to find *wasabia japonica* served outside of Japan. I had only ever eaten the Kermit-green, sinus scorching paste served – quite incorrectly, it turns out – as a blob on the side of a sushi plate. But, as I was about to discover, fresh wasabi root has about as much in common with the synthetic kind as aerosol snow and the stuff which falls from the sky.

Not sharing my fascination for rare Japanese produce, Lissen, Asger and Emil had chosen to spend the day at Kidzania, an indoor theme park where children take on proper jobs, such as fireman, dentist or graphic designer, and earn money which they can then exchange for chocolate and fizzy drinks. (From their retelling later it sounded extraordinary, in fact the boys still talk of their shift as Tokyo cops, to the extent that I suspect they genuinely believed they actually *were* police for a couple of hours.)

Meanwhile, I travelled about a hundred kilometres south of Tokyo, again with Emi acting as translator, to the Amagi Mountain area in Izu, Shizuoka, a forested peninsula south of Mount Fuji. This is a popular onsen, or hot spring area but for the Japanese it is also synonymous with wasabi; over sixty per cent of Japanese wasabi is grown here – worth two and a half billion yen a year.

We took a train and hired a car for the final drive up into the hills. Our first stop was for a meeting with Yoshio Ando, head of the local wasabi growers' association, in the small shop and wasabi processing centre which he runs with his wife. Yoshio, in his late fifties and sporting an oversized baseball cap with a cartoon wasabi character on it, explained that he was one of 355 wasabi growers in the region.

Wasabi is one of the most temperamental plants in the world, he said, requiring precise climactic conditions and fresh water, lots of it. 'Wasabi needs very clean, fresh-flowing water to grow,' Yoshio explained. 'The water is the key, it needs to be around 12–13°C [never more than 16°C, never less than 10°C] and flow at 18 litres per second to keep a constant depth of one centimetre. We have wonderful mountain spring water here, but the climate is also crucial. You need a cool summer and water throughout the year.'

He offered me a real wasabi root to inspect. 'This one will sell for more than ¥2,000 (£15) in Tokyo,' he said. 'It is only for the rich. It is very limited quantity.' Although we had passed several giant fibreglass replicas on the roads (the Japanese, like Americans, are fond of promoting their local specialities in oversized roadside model form), I had never seen a whole wasabi root before. It was knobbly, green and unavoidably phallic with floppy leaves at the top end, tapering to a point at the other. This one was roughly the size of a banana. They can grow larger but the ones you see in Japanese supermarkets tend to be more Mars Bar-sized. 'They are harvested throughout the year when the plant has reached between fifteen months and two years, during which time it grows progressively hotter in flavour,' the farmer told me.

The Japanese have been cultivating this enigmatic plant – a rhizome, and distant relative of the horseradish – since 1744. It was originally used as a sterilant to kill bacteria on, among other things, fish, which is how it came to be associated with sushi and sashimi. It is also believed to stimulate the appetite.

I asked about the difference between fresh wasabi and the wasabi you buy in tubes. Yoshio shook his head dismissively. You couldn't compare them, he said. Good, fresh wasabi is hot, but not burning hot, and much sweeter, more fragrant that the industrial stuff. And, needless to say, Japanese is best.

They do grow wasabi in Taiwan and China, but when I asked about this Yoshio shook his head even more vigorously. 'They grow in soil in Taiwan. No running water, lots of chemicals. The same in

China.' But surely there must be other places in the world with similar water supplies and climate, and with a crop so desirable as wasabi others must have tried to cultivate it the correct way? 'Yes, I have heard they grow it in Canada and New Zealand. Maybe that's better.' But the look on his face suggested he thought otherwise.

I was finding it difficult to visualise how wasabi grew. Was there any chance Yoshio could show us? He looked dubious and conferred with his wife in a low murmur for a while. They didn't usually do this, he said finally, and he did like to keep his fields secret for obvious reasons – implying, intriguingly, the existence of wasabi rustlers – but seeing as we had come all this way, he agreed to take us to see his fields, higher up the mountain.

We followed his raggedy Toyota pickup for over an hour up into the forests of pine, cedar and bamboo, far from the tourist onsen towns. It was thrilling to imagine that, somewhere in the trees around us, wild wasabi – as opposed to Yoshio's cultivated variety – was growing in fresh flowing streams.

We came to a deep, dark forested river valley, open at one end with a spectacular view to the landscape below, narrowing at the other end where the river that gave life to the wasabi descended from the summit. As we followed Yoshio along a narrow, overgrown path to the wasabi paddies, dragonflies and butterflies bright as Hermès scarves flapped up from the undergrowth. Lizards scattered every which way and bright green spiders hung from webs in the trees. I had a sense of being shown something secret and precious, for here Yoshio grows what is not just the best wasabi in Japan (and therefore the world – he's won every prize going), but, according to a recent prime ministerial pronouncement, one of the best items of produce in the country.

The entire valley floor had been terraced rather like a rice paddy, but instead of the bright green grass-like rice plants, it was carpeted with the broad, rhubarb-like leaves of wasabi. The sound of running water was deafening, although there was no river in sight. It was all flowing beneath the plants which were packed, Yoshio told us, in a fifteen centimetre-deep bed of sand. The plants themselves were covered with black netting, to keep them from sunlight and falling leaves. 'The angle of the slope is very precise, otherwise the water would flow too fast. The other problem we have is with the local deer. They love the leaves,' Yoshio said. I tried one. It was a little like rocket, but with a sweet burning wasabi aftertaste.

I asked if he had any tips on using wasabi. 'Ooh, you've got to try the stems pickled in sake lees, that's lovely.' When I left Japan I was planning to take some roots home with me. How long would they keep? 'Keep it dry and it will last a month, but if it gets damp it will turn black.'

'You know,' Yoshio said, just as we had said goodbye and were about to leave the fields, 'if you really like wasabi, there is someone you should meet.'

Shirakabeso, or the White Wall Inn, was back down in the onsen region of Shizuoka. It is a traditional onsen guest house, with two communal outdoor baths, run by a husband and wife team, Haruyoshi and Ikuko Uda. Ikuko, Yoshio's contact, is obsessed with wasabi and has spent years studying it at the University of Shizvoka under professor Naohide Kinai, a specialist in the various medicinal properties of this miraculous root.

As we sat on the floor in a simple room with tatami-covered floor in the traditional manner, overlooking an immaculate traditional garden, Ikuko explained the basic principles of using wasabi. 'You grate it on shark skin,' she said. 'Because that is fine and gentle but tough. And you must grate it in a circular motion. When the oxygen mixes with the wasabi, it increases its hotness. The top end is sweeter than the bottom end.' She showed me how to do this, making gentle circles with the root on the shark-skin board.

She could see I was looking a little anxious about consuming the entire wasabi root – it was a large one. 'Don't worry, real wasabi warms the throat, it doesn't burn or go up your nose like the artificial stuff. And you know what, if you eat wasabi and drink you don't get a hangover because it is antibacterial and detoxifying.'

As well as various minerals and vitamins, wasabi contains around twenty different types of isothiocynates (a compound it shares with mustard and broccoli), which have anti-inflammatory properties. This makes wasabi a useful treatment for allergies and eczema. Its anti-microbial qualities also mean it works against tooth decay and, apparently, it can even calm diarrhoea. Most interesting of all, the isothiocynates are thought to stop the spread of cancers at the metastasis stage. Wasabi is, then, a bona fide superfood.

The real thing did indeed taste very different from the paste. The isothiocynates give wasabi a pleasing pungency when grated and, as they evaporate, they release a brief, pleasurable sinus heat. Sometimes chefs will add a little sugar to real wasabi to enliven the pepper flavour.

Ikuko began to present the dishes we would be eating that afternoon: pickled rhododendron, chrysanthemum and jellyfish (surprisingly crunchy), to start. I noticed a beautiful abalone shell on the table and turned it over, inside the creature was still writhing. Ikuko placed it on the hotplate for a minute or so and served it sliced with a small mound of wasabi to accompany. It was sublimely tender. As well as wasabi, this region is famed for its wild boar, which we had a chance to taste next. It had been marinated and tenderised in miso and koji for ten days which helped make the flesh spoon-tender. Its deep, gamey richness went superbly with the sweetness of the wasabi, again neatly placed in a small mound on the plate.

I asked Ikuku how she grew to be so obsessed by wasabi. 'I started seven years ago. I wanted to make the most of our local produce and surprise people.' She had certainly done that, although, in doing so, she had probably ruined my enjoyment of wasabi paste and sushi for ever. How could I ever go back to artificial wasabi? By the end of the afternoon I had consumed half an entire wasabi root by myself, with no ill-effects. In fact, it had been a stunning and nuanced meal. It finished with the juiciest, sweetest melon I had ever eaten, together with wasabi ice cream.

On my way home, I couldn't shake the thought that the world would go crazy for real wasabi if it could only try it. I have had meals based on single ingredients before – I once made a chocolate-themed dinner with chocolate risotto, venison stew with chocolate and a chocolate mousse. I didn't eat chocolate for a while after that. In Paris I have lunched at a soufflé-only restaurant: three courses of soufflé, no matter how good, and again you will not want to see another for some time. But this was in another class. I was addicted.

Herein starts the Campaign for Real Wasabi. Join me.

Chapter 13

Kitchen Street

Clearly, my life would be two mockeries of a sham wrapped up in a disgraceful fallacy without my own wood-backed, shark-skin grater on hand in my kitchen for all my future wasabi grating requirements.

It didn't take too much research to find out the best place to buy one. In fact, Kappabashi-dori had been second only to Tsukiji on my list of 'Must-sees' while we were in Tokyo.

Some people like to shop for shoes or clothes or, if they have given up on life altogether, mobile phone accessories. Others can spend days hunting through record stores, while one friend of mine – not me, you understand – can not pass an old-style gentleman's outfitters without checking out the sock garters and cummerbunds. My biggest retail vice is kitchenware. Give me a good kitchen store and I will browse happily until they kick me out at closing time. I stalk the kitchen stores in Paris – rarely buying anything but tormenting myself with various electric gadgets that I know full well I will use once before abandoning them to the wilderness of the bottom kitchen drawer, along with old washing machine guarantees and freezer bag ties; or expensive, posh versions of things I already have, like walnut chopping boards, or pro-standard food processors; and, best of all, those little steel or chrome thingamabobs for zesting, balling, paring, coring and all those other rarely encountered tasks that can usually just as well be dispatched with a small knife and some concentration.

My real fetish, however, is reserved for the restaurant supply stores, the places the pros go to buy catering-size rolls of plastic wrap and silver foil, or giant tubs of mustard and salt, at a fraction of the price you pay in the supermarket.

London has perhaps a handful of such shops, Paris has even fewer, most of them close to Les Halles or in Chinatown. But for kitchenware addicts like me, the one true Mecca is Kappabashi-dori; a whole street, plus side streets, full of shops selling every conceivable piece of equipment needed to create every conceivable cuisine in the world.

It is not the most attractive of thoroughfares; four lanes of traffic lined with a motley assortment of low-rise shops, none of which pays the slightest heed to contemporary retail convention regarding presentation or promotion. But just as with the city's restaurants, the shops of Kappabashi-dori leave the rest of the world's kitchen stores for dead because each specialises, with an obsessive zeal, in one specific type, or area, of kitchen equipment.

I spent some time and far too much money in a shop that sold only cookie cutters in thousands of shapes, for instance; another had what must be the world's largest range of rice steamers; and in another I stood in silent awe before giant vats of tempura oil and sinks as big as sofas. Next door to that was a shop that sold only menus and menu holders, and another had only tills and order pads. This was just across the way from one of the famous plastic food shops, used for the displays outside restaurants. From a distance it looked like a candy store with its brightly coloured nigiri models. Back in the nineteenth century they used to make the models out of wax, the woman in the shop told me. I wondered how they coped with Tokyo summers without melting.

I was having no luck with the shark-skin wasabi grater, although, admittedly, the mime I employed when asking directions probably caused more alarm than anything. I was happily distracted by a shop devoted entirely to trays and one that sold different sizes of otherwise precisely the same shape and colour of lanterns that hang outside Izakaya restaurants. Asger and Emil were out of their minds with boredom by this point. Reminding them of the hours I had spent patiently following them around various Disney stores like a Muslim bride held no sway.

Time, then, to visit the stars of the kitchen strip, the knife shops:

dark, sombre, dusty places, their walls lined with glass cases displaying an extraordinary array of knives, each with blades like razors, forged from dozens of layers of high-carbon steel. As I explained to my suddenly more interested sons, the oldest knife makers are direct descendants of Samurai sword makers who turned their skills to making kitchen knives when carrying swords was banned in Japan in the late nineteenth century. After weighing up a rectangular *usuba*, for vegetables, and a triangular *deba* for filleting fish, I bought two – one kitchen knife, pretty much a standard Western variety with two bevelled edges, and one *yanagi*, or sashimi knife, ten inches long and with only one bevelled edge to its blade. The two cost less than one Global knife would have back home.

Sashimi knives are made with only one bevelled edge as this causes less damage to the fibres of the fish's flesh, the elderly salesman explained. The flat side doesn't push against the main block of fish in the way that a blade with a double bevel does. Frankly, I don't suppose I could tell the difference between sashimi cut with one or other type of knife, but a Japanese chef could, and that is all that matters. (I did later find mine was also good for cutting slabs of ganache into squares before dipping in tempered chocolate.) They are pernickety fellows, sushi chefs. According to Shizuo Tsuji, the best keep two sets of knives for working with fish: one to use while the other set is 'cooling down' after being sharpened. This isn't quite as ridiculous as it might sound to someone like me who sharpens their kitchen knives roughly once a month. Japanese knives may be the sharpest in the world, but they are very high maintenance, their blades damage easily and require sharpening daily, otherwise – as I was to discover – they go blunt quickly. Yet they heat up under sharpening and, of course, the last thing you want near fresh, raw fish, is a something with even vestigial warmth.

The shopkeeper also recommended that I buy a heavy, brick-sized whetstone, called a *toishi*, for sharpening. He showed me how to use it, telling me to soak it in water for five minutes, then to sharpen the knife by pushing it away against the surface of the stone pressing with some force, then dragging it gently back pouring more water over the stone every few strokes. He threw in a fish scaler for free too, which was nice as I was hardly likely to be a return customer.

But what of the wasabi grater? Eventually, I found a policeman. Not only was this sharp-witted constable able to interpret my humming of the theme from *Jaws* together with a washboard grating action, but he knew where I could buy one and led us there himself.

And there it was, a small, piece of square wood, one surface covered with what felt like extra-coarse sandpaper, for ¥2,000, or just under £15. Later, when I got it home following one of the most protracted and bitter luggage contents selection battles of our marriage (I had to lose both the packaging for my air guitar toy *and* my tubes of sock glue to make room for it and the *toishi*, while Lissen, was somehow allowed to keep *all* her museum catalogues), its purpose and the materials used in its manufacture would prove satisfyingly obscure to all my friends, apart of course from Toshi who pointed out, quite accurately, the folly of buying an implement for grating fresh wasabi and then transporting it halfway around the world to a continent where such a vegetable is unheard of.

Chapter 14

Sushi for Beginners

I doubt whether even the Japanese feel that a shark-skin wasabi grater is an essential element of their kitchen arsenal. There was certainly no evidence of one in the kitchen of Mrs Shinobu, with whom I had a lunch date the next day.

Sixty-year-old Etsuko Shinobu is doing her shopping. 'A small tin of "sea chicken", that's what we call tuna,' she says, dropping one into her basket. 'Some eggs, we prefer brown eggs in Japan; taro root; and some Kyoto sake.' As she shuffles around the aisles in a violet kimono, she is followed by a group of five men, one with a camera, one videoing everything, and another taking notes – all from the H.I.S. travel company – plus a journalist from *Time* magazine (researching an article about the changing food culture in Japan), and me.

I had emailed H.I.S. before we left for Japan. Their website offered some interesting food-themed experiences in Tokyo, and so I signed up for three cooking lessons: one at the home of a 'typical' Japanese housewife, Mrs Shinobu; the second with a top Japanese chef; and finally, a sushi-making class.

After Mrs Shinobu had paid and collected her reward points we all trooped out of the shop to her house nearby: a well-manicured, two-storey, concrete box overlooking a railway line (as most homes seem to do in Tokyo) where she lived with her husband and grown-up daughter. We removed our shoes at the door in exchange for some undersized red vinyl slippers and followed her upstairs to the kitchen-living room. She was going to cook us lunch and we were going to help, Mrs Shinobu announced. The *Time* journalist looked a little anxious on hearing this but dutifully tied on his tenugui, or headscarf, as instructed and set to work chopping daikon into matchsticks.

Meanwhile, Mrs Shinobu set the rice steamer in motion, rehydrated some dried mushrooms and made some dashi with Ajinomoto instant powder. She made a paper thin omelette with egg, salt, sugar and a little mirin in a pan which she first heated, then removed from the heat before adding the egg, letting it cook in the residual heat only. She lined a bowl with strips of the omelette, then filled it with rice and the tinned tuna, which she had heated with some soy sauce.

'They recommend that you eat thirty different ingredients every day,' she said, gently adjusting my knife grip (she had given me a sashimi knife which only works if you slice by pulling towards you in individual strokes). 'So I try to do that. My motto is "a little of everything". The difficult thing is that my husband is rarely home from work before eight and my daughter sometimes doesn't come home until midnight. I learned how to cook from my mother, but my daughter isn't interested. I do worry how the next generation is going to learn this.'

Lunch was ready and we moved through to the tatami living room. As I stepped onto the mat I felt something grabbing me from behind. It was Mrs Shinobu, looking aghast. 'No, no, you must take your slippers off before you go on the tatami mat,' she said.

More etiquette: it is rude to hover with your chopsticks over food; don't use chopsticks to move bowls and dishes around; never lick your chopsticks; never leave your chopsticks sticking down into rice; and never ever pass food from your chopsticks to another person's – that is a funerary tradition.

I did all of these during our lunch. But to their credit, my Japanese hosts didn't bat an eye. Afterwards, we adjourned downstairs to Mrs Shinobu's tea-ceremony room. It takes years to learn how to orchestrate a tea ceremony, and the correct procedure has been the subject of controversial debate for centuries. To give you an idea of the Olympian levels of pedantry involved, the tea ceremony schism starts as you enter the room – one school of thought believes it should be left foot first, the other the right. Both agree that there must be no excess of movement and so each motion is strictly choreographed and laden with meaning, most of which was lost on me and the man from *Time* magazine as we knelt, at a point exactly sixteen ridges of tatami mat from the wall, beside the tokonoma – the display alcove – which held a vase holding a single peony, watching Mrs Shinobu purify, brew, swirl, pour and sip. This went on for a good forty minutes, during which time I initially lost all sensation in my legs, before the numbness was relieved by a million agonising pinpricks.

Finally, after some frothing with a delicate little bamboo whisk, Mrs Shinobu handed us our bowls of perfectly warm tea, instructing us to turn them twice anti-clockwise before drinking from them, then turning them clockwise before replacing them on the mat. The tea itself was thick, frothy, a vivid bright green and awfully bitter with notes of soil. Each of our bowls was different, I noticed. Though beautiful, mine was slightly asymmetrical. Mrs Shinobu spotted me examining it. 'You know,' she said, 'this may be the only time you will ever meet that bowl, you should cherish this moment. The Japanese have a phrase for making the most of fleeting encounters: *ichigo ichie*, it means 'one encounter, one chance'.

I cherished my tea ceremony encounter, and my morning with Mrs Shinobu. How many visitors get a chance to see inside the home of a Japanese person, let alone make and eat lunch with someone as wise and dignified as our gentle, smiling host?

Next stop on the H.I.S. food experience tour was Hifumi, a traditional restaurant in Kagurazaka, a former geisha neighbourhood in eastern Tokyo, now renowned for its top-quality, but elusive restaurants. Our chef for the afternoon was, Takamitsu Aihara, a, welcoming but stern man with twenty-four years experience and a recently earned Michelin star. It was his mission to impart to us the techniques and etiquette of traditional dining.

'The colour of food is very important to the Japanese,' the chef began. 'It reflects the seasons – spring is green, then dark green for summer, autumn is orange and brown, winter is white. It is all reflected on the plate.'

We took some cold mashed potato, which we patted out into discs on plastic wrap. On top of this we placed a minced chicken filling, then pulled up the dough to form something the size of a tennis ball. Next, the chef gave us a dashi master class.

After showing us how to make Ichiban dashi – in much the way the chefs had at the cooking competition at Hattori's school in Tokyo, though with less katsuobushi – the chef went on to explain how you can use the same katsuobushi and konbu to make a Number Two, or Niban, dashi by boiling them gently for another ten minutes. 'Ninety-nine per cent of Japanese stock is water,' Aihara said, adding just a dash of sake, some light soy sauce and, finally, arrowroot flour to thicken it as a sauce for the potato-chicken bun.

Next came a sashimi lesson. 'You cut the fish as if you are drawing a line on the board towards you with your index finger,' the chef said, carving up a fresh bonito filet, black-skinned with dark red flesh. He set a torch to the bonito to char the flesh slightly, then placed the slices on top of a bowl of rice, sprinkled a fine julienne of Japanese ginger around, and placed an egg yolk that had been marinated in soy sauce until it had firmed up, in the middle. We all had a go, and ended up with a meal which was, for me, utterly original and pretty.

The final part of my cooking lesson trilogy was the sushi class, which took place in a rather down-at-heel local sushi restaurant in south-west Tokyo, our session squeezed in between the end of lunch service and the start of the dinner rush.

Chef Eiji Hayashi had the face of a boxer and the physique to match. He was a tough, no-nonsense sushi chef, with over two decades' experience on the front line serving the most discerning sushi eaters in the world, in the city where nigiri was invented.

'There are no female sushi chefs,' he announced gruffly, eyeing a couple of female students. 'Their make-up and perfume taint the fish and rice. Also they have a higher body temperature, which warms the fish.' (This is not actually true, but I wasn't about to contradict him.)

He showed us how to mould the rice for nigiri, using two bowls of cold water, one for washing our hands after each moulding, the other for wetting them to stop the rice from sticking. He formed his hands into a 'ninjitsu' – so-named because it resembles the secret ninja hand signal – by placing the index and middle fingers of the right hand across the palm of the left hand, where they press a bite-sized block of rice into a small rectangular box.

The rice had been steamed with a small piece of konbu and some sake, the chef explained, then tipped out into a hangiri, a traditional, round, shallow cedarwood tub. 'It doesn't have to be cedarwood, but metal bowls might react with the rice,' the chef said. 'The tub must be wet, though, otherwise it will soak the moisture from the rice.' In the tub, the chef cut through the rice – now slightly cooler, but not too cold – with a wooden paddle, cooling it further and mixing in the vinegar, salt and sugar. This rice seasoning – typically seven parts rice vinegar to five parts sugar with a half teaspoon of salt – is the real reason, I suspect, that sushi has caught on to such a degree in the West: it consists, after all, of essentially the same flavours that keep us coming back for Big Macs – sugar, salt and vinegar. The rice for making sushi should be neither too hot nor cold – according to Eiji-san around 25°C is optimum, although others say it should be body temperature. The main thing is it should act as a contrast to the chilled fish.

The better restaurants use expensive, short-grain rice, the best being koshihikari which is dried naturally in the sun, but most use medium grain japonica, often grown in the States (domestic rice production can't meet demand). Many also add an MSG-laced flavouring to their rice called *miora*. 'When I was training to be a sushi chef I had to spend a year just making rice before I was allowed near a fish,' Eiji-san said – adding that the total period of his training had been six years, average for a sushi chef in Japan.

He invited us to try and make our own nigiri as he had shown us. We each held the lumps of unformed rice in the palm of our upturned hand, curled the fingers of the same hand up to form a coffin-shaped hollow, closed the thumb over one end of the 'coffin' and then pressed the rice into shape with the index and middle fingers of our right hand. Then the chef did something odd. He showed us how, once he had made what looked like a perfect oblong-shaped block of rice, he took his index finger and pressed down in the centre, spreading the rice out once more, before reforming it again. He did this 'To air out the rice,' before adding with the care-free chauvinism common to chefs the world over, 'Like treating a woman. You don't want the rice packed too tightly, you want it to just hold together long enough to get into the mouth, where it should fall apart easily. And the top of the rice should be slightly pointed so that the fish stays on better.'

But this 'airing' just made my blocks of rice look even more ragged and shapeless, like lumps of clay randomly squeezed by a five-year-old child, prompting open laughter from the chef and the six other students most of whom were Japanese. I tried again, this time with more success.

I asked the chef if it was true that the best sushi chefs can get all the grains of rice in a nigiri pointing the right way. He rubbished the idea. No, that wasn't possible, he said, you should try instead to be 'natural', a word he repeated several times during our demonstration.

Next we made gunkan maki (gunkan means battleship, which they vaguely resemble), in which the block of rice is wrapped with a sheet of nori seaweed and topped with, say, sea urchin or crab. Nori is an algae or laver, as used by the Welsh to make laver bread. In its natural state nori starts off reddish brown and turns green when it is dried. In the better restaurants the chef will briefly wave the sheets over the grill to get them really crisp before using. Shizuo Tsuji points out that one side is rough, the other smooth and that you should make sure to make your maki rolls with the smooth side pointing outward. The trick with gunkan maki is to anchor the nori with a single grain of rice.

That was quite straightforward, but I made an almighty hash of my ura-maki, or inside-out rolls. The trick here seemed to be to spread the rice evenly and thinly over the large sheets of nori, summon all the courage you have, and then lift the whole thing up, turning it over on your maki mat, or makisu. When I lifted mine, the rice avalanched inelegantly onto the table.

The best sushi chefs don't provide soy sauce for dipping, the chef continued, but make their own milder blend of dip, called nikiri, with dashi, mirin, sake and soy, (200ml soy; 40ml dashi; 20ml sake; 20ml mirin, briefly heated). And they don't provide extra wasabi either – the wasabi they add within the nigiri or maki should be enough. Anyone spotted mixing wasabi in with their soy will immediately be marked down as an ingénue – after all, how can you expect to have any sensitivity left to your taste buds if you blitz them with artificial wasabi? I had already noticed that most Japanese don't use chopsticks to eat sushi, they just pick it up with their hands, and so Japanese chefs will generally pack their nigiri more densely for foreign diners who insist on using chopsticks believing it to be 'correct'. Sashimi, on the other hand, should always be eaten with chopsticks.

One of the other students asked the chef which was his favourite nigiri topping. Was it Toro? she wondered. No, he said he preferred uni, or *engawa*, the frilly bit from the edge of flatfish (which I was taught at cooking school to throw away).

The chef gave us some other useful tips: if you really want great service from a Japanese sushi chef it requires just one word: *Omakase*, which means 'I'll let you decide'. And if you want to really piss a sushi chef off, just keep ordering tuna, which many restaurants sell as a loss leader. If they bring you miso soup to start, the place is probably run by Koreans or Chinese. Miso soup should come at the end of a sushi meal as it is thought to aid digestion of the fish. Meanwhile, if you are picking from a conveyor, choose white fish or lighter fish to start before working your way to the salmon and tuna. Ignore spiced-up maki rolls, often employed to disguise the taste of aged fish.

In the foreword to *A Simple Art*, M. F. K. Fisher recalled how 'fish leapt from glass tanks to the cleavers and pans and then into our mouths, in a ballet of accumulated motions and flavours,' but in truth, fresh fish is not always desirable for sushi and sashimi. As with meat, fish needs to be left for some time – days even – after being caught in order to reach its peak flavour. There are some exceptions, of course: eel, shellfish and squid are worth keeping alive until the point of preparation and shouldn't be left too long after, and mackerel is notoriously perishable, but with most fish the enzymes in the flesh need time to break down the proteins and connective tissue and produce the all-important, and very tasty inosinic acid that goes so well with the glutamate in dashi or soy. The bluefin tuna, for example, is better a week after it has been defrosted – kept well chilled, of course; sea bream needs a day; fugu, or blowfish, apparently is best aged between half a day and a day. The world's greatest sushi chef, Jiro Ono, eighty-two, who still works every day in his Ginza restaurant, will wrap tuna in ice for ten days until it reaches the ultimate flavour, with white fish he might leave it for three days.

If you enter a restaurant to see fish with what Tsuji describes as, 'the flaccid look of hospital patients,' turn and flee, pausing only to make a quick call to your local health authority.

Instead he offers this useful advice: 'When I enter a sushi restaurant I can tell at a glance by the texture of their skins – like the bloom of youth on a young girl – whether the fish is really fresh.'

Chapter 15

The 'Special Stuff'

Tsuji offers no advice on evaluating whale meat. Ordinarily this wouldn't have been a great loss as far as I was concerned. As an especially self-righteous teenager growing up in the UK in the seventies and eighties there were two indisputable certainties in my world. The first was that Mrs Thatcher was evil incarnate, the second was that killing whales was as bad as, if not worse than, killing a human being.

Star Trek IV: The Voyage Home, in which, you'll recall, Kirk and his crew kidnap a humpback whale to communicate with aliens, merely bolstered my argument with hard facts. I can remember marching on Downing Street at some point in the early eighties to protest at some unspecified Nordic people who were either harpooning whales or clubbing seals and working myself up into a right old lather. So I hesitated for a brief moment when Emi, who had popped by our apartment to plan the next week's activities (it was now late September and we were about to leave for Hokkaido), asked if we would all be interested in popping out to grab a bite of whale for lunch. Admittedly it was only a brief pause. Like all foodies, I like to boast about the obscure and unpalatable dishes I have eaten ('Kangaroo? Pah! Of course I've tried it. But have you tried crocodile? Oh, but you must; it is rather like chicken you know.'). I am always looking for the next food thrill, and the more it makes girls squeal the better. Nevertheless, I still had qualms about eating a creature that makes soft mournful clicking noises and could outthink me in a plankton-herding contest.

In the end, I said yes but Lissen wrinkled her nose. Asger and

Emil looked at me as if I had taken leave of my senses and, I have to admit, their horror did make me hesitate once more. But who was I to judge the Japanese? In my time I'd eaten a fair few battery chickens, drugged-up cows and plenty of cute bunnies, ickle quails and frogs whose legs had most likely been rendered from their bodies without anaesthetic. I know whales are meant to be really smart, but pigs are no fools either.

Of course there are rather more chickens, cows, frogs and quails in the world than there are whales. Japan, Iceland, Greenland and Norway stand alone as whale-eating nations these days, circumventing or simply ignoring the recommendations of the International Whaling Committee. Of the three, the Japanese are by far the most rapacious in their consumption of all kinds of fish, eating around a tenth of the world's catch overall. On average, a Japanese person will consume almost 70kg of seafood, compared to a global average of 16kg. Much of the whale meat harvested by Norwegians and Icelanders goes straight to Japanese tables.

Wherever fish are being caught in the world, there will be Japanese middlemen waiting with their wallets open and a large box of ice. In remote parts of the southern Philippines I have seen huge Japanese fishing harbours supporting entire local economies with their demand for tuna and bonito, while over half of the tuna ranched in the southern Mediterranean ends up at the end of Japanese chopsticks. Wild Mediterranean and Atlantic tuna stocks are at perilously low levels, perhaps as low as ten per cent of the levels they were at in the sixties, a state of affairs for which the Japanese must take a good portion of the blame.

But if you ask ordinary Japanese either about the threat of tuna extinction or whales they will regard you quizzically. This is genuinely news to them, and certainly not a pressing issue in the media. What is, from time to time, is foreign interference in what they see as the essential traditions of Japanese cuisine. The Japanese usually claim that they only really started eating meat as a nation in 1872 after the Emperor casually announced he had eaten beef for dinner – signalling a Liberty Hall for Japanese carnivores. Until that point it was technically illegal and, although the law was widely ignored, it is true that the Japanese historically ate far more fish than meat – they still obtain more than a third of the protein in their diet from fish. It is one of the reasons too, of course, for their general good health.

Today, the Japanese still kill around 700 whales a year 'for scientific research', a figure surpassed only by the Icelanders who kill around a thousand, many of them, as I've said, ending up in Japan anyway. The Japanese have recently started calling for increased quotas following reported gains in the populations of some species, such as Southern Right whales and humpbacks, which have now been removed from the endangered list. Every year at the annual assembly of the International Whaling Commission, Japan presses to be allowed to commence unrestricted hunting again. 'We've been eating whale since 300BC,' they complain. 'This is culinary imperialism.'

Despite the national conversion to Buddhism in the eighth century, consumption of whale was always permitted because whales were categorised as fish not mammals (this pragmatic approach to food classification saw wild boar re-named 'mountain whales'). By the 1820s whale cuisine had become so refined that there were recipes for up to seventy different cuts – they even cooked with whale faeces. Mmm, no? With the food shortages following WWII whale became a vital source of nourishment for the Japanese, providing an important protein and omega-3 oil source. Indeed, today most adult Japanese remember whale meat with nostalgia from the time it was a regular on school lunch menus. The Japanese continue to eat whale, albeit in smaller quantities, as a delicacy as we might eat venison. They claim – and to be fair, I don't think this is the disputed point – that its meat is extremely healthy with proven anti-ageing properties.

So I accepted Emi's invitation, and met her outside Shinjuku station. From there she led me deep into the shimmering maze of girly bars and karaoke joints of Kabuki-cho to a doorway at the side of a shop. Up some flights of stairs we climbed until we came to the entrance to Taruichi, famed for its whale meat dishes and top-notch sakes.

The room was packed with people. Countless paper menus hanging from the ceiling, each decorated with large kanji characters, some with delicate pen and ink drawings of fish, lent it a festive air. Aside from the beautiful illustrations of frolicking whales on the screens and doors it could have been any normal Japanese restaurant, assuming one could ignore the giant, dried whale penis hanging from the ceiling like some obscure Alpine wind instrument. Which I couldn't.

We set about the menu with Emi translating. There was whale bacon, whale tongue, ovary, brain, skin, testicles, penis, internal organs and various cuts of meat, but sadly no droppings. You could have it raw as sashimi, on sushi, deep fried, or as a steak. We ordered a little of everything and soon the plates began to arrive from the dark, hole-in-the-wall kitchen behind us. First was a bowl of glistening, chewy, beige blubber, not unlike tripe. Not nice, although Emi, who had grown up on whale meat at school, tucked in happily. A tinfoil-covered plate came next. Underneath the foil was a large, stiff brown leaf, as big as half the table, covered with thin cuts of whale bacon and sashimi, all slightly different, with a smudge of mustard and yellow chrysanthemums for decoration. Some were edged with pink, others looked like air-dried ham, some were grey and quite unappetising looking (this was skin, Emi said). The sashimi looked similar to Japanese beef, with rampant marbling and purple-red flesh. Some was challenging to chew, most of it had a fatty mouth feel with a not unpleasant faint, beefy flavour. I wouldn't rush to sample any of it again, particularly the deep fried cubes of whale meat which I struggled to break down into digestible chunks, but neither did I gag, and some of it, like the sashimi, was very good indeed. The whale ice cream was green with small chunks of whale where you might ordinarily hope to find chocolate chips. I wouldn't care to revisit that.

On our way out we met the chef, Hiroyoshi Gota. I asked what breed of whale we had been eating. He pointed to a wall chart depicting all the different types of whale, singling out the minke, caught mostly in the Antarctic. Which was the best eating? This one: he pointed with a sigh at the picture of the Blue whale not, I suspect out of pity for its plight, but because he had no ready supplier. As we made to leave, he gave me a whale's tooth, like a giant, brown, frilly fingernail, to take with me as a souvenir.

Whale might be the largest sea creature eaten by the Japanese, but fortunately it was by no means the tastiest. This we would encounter at our next destination, the northern island of Hokkaido, famed for its abundant fish and shellfish.

Chapter 16

Crabs

We flew from Haneda airport, Tokyo's domestic terminal. Though I am not exactly phobic of flying, I have now reached the 'bored' stage of what experienced fliers tell me are the three acts of air travel: at first it's exciting, then it becomes tedious, and then comes the Fear. I find the whole getting to the airport, checking in, going through security, getting to the gate, queuing to get into the gate lounge, then queuing again to get on the plane – at each stage being asked to present your boarding pass, remove your belt, 'No not your boarding pass, your passport, stupid,' and so on, deeply harrowing, like being a part-time refugee, but with worse catering: the Exodus sponsored by Tie Rack. But Haneda Airport was a revelation: clean, quiet, efficient and full of excellent shops and restaurants representing virtually every main category of Japanese food. If I had been told our trip would end there and that I had to make do with the facilities at Haneda for the next two months, I could have survived quite happily.

But we were leaving Tokyo, and wouldn't return for over two months. I have to say I was a little reluctant to go – so many restaurants, so little time – and Lissen felt the same, but the capital had hardly provided us with the gentle acclimatisation to Japan we might have hoped for. It is true, the Western influence is stronger here than anywhere else in Japan, but by no means can the city be described as Westernised. Of course, we hadn't come to Japan to experience a Japanese take on Western culture, so this was all well and good, but after three weeks the time did feel right for a break, particularly where the children were concerned.

We had had a few food battles with Emil and, in particular, Asger, but they were gradually becoming more open to new things, and we had successfully adhered to our strict, 'no pizza or burgers' principle. They had enjoyed tempura, and loved the ninja restaurant in Shinjuku which we had had to enter through a hidden door and over a glass drawbridge, and where the waiters performed magic tricks. They were also now genuine sushi enthusiasts to the extent where, left unsupervised, they could easily amass a sizeable tower of plates at a conveyor belt sushi joint. That said, we did have to remember to ask the chefs to go easy on the wasabi after one slightly traumatic incident involving a heavy-handed chef and some nigiri during which Emil turned quite red and had to drink three cups of water in a row.

But, though thrilling for us all, I did sense that the ceaseless clamour of the Japanese capital had been quite difficult for Asger and Emil to adjust to. Though Tokyoites are friendly and helpful, and showed great interest in our boys, their's is not an especially child-friendly city, even compared to Paris. There were no real play parks to speak of, nowhere for them to run wild and let off steam, and the sheer number of people was, I sensed, a little unsettling from time to time. Unsettled build-ups of steam are never good in young boys.

So, after Tokyo, Sapporo's space and pace came as a breath of fresh air. As did the breath of fresh air that greeted us as we disembarked from the plane. Hokkaido's climate is markedly different from Japan's central island, Honshu. At its northernmost tip Japan comes within two kilometres of Russian territory and even in the south-west of Hokkaido the winters are harsh and invariably snowbound. Even at summer's wane, when we arrived, the temperature was pleasantly cool, yet still warm enough for short sleeves.

Hokkaido is vast, accounting for roughly a fifth of Japan's land area – equivalent to the size of Austria. You would have thought that with twice as many people as the UK but only a quarter of the habitable land, the Japanese would have swarmed over Hokkaido centuries ago. Yet it has historically been thought of as remote and inhospitable. It was only colonised 150 years ago, and then only following government inducements to business and industry and countless, 'Gosh, Look at all this Space!' billboard campaigns. Until that point, it had been the home of the Ainu, Japan's indigenous people who had arrived there many hundreds of thousands of years ago, most likely from Siberia. Despite continued government prodding, still only around one twentieth of the population lives here – just under six million people – and it boasts large tracts of wilderness, and virgin forest, neither of which are the first things that spring to mind when one thinks of Japan.

But Hokkaido's geography is not its only USP. The food is quite different here too.

The island is the centre of Japan's dairy farming industry, producing excellent butter, cream and milk, and not so excellent cheeses (a vaguely artificial, flavourless brie sold in most supermarkets springs to mind). They also grow potatoes and corn and, ironically, given that this is one of the poorest parts of the country, Hokkaido is also where those £100 melons are grown. Hokkaido is also renowned for its varieties of crabs and its wild salmon. Japan as a whole only manages to produce forty per cent of the food it needs (compared to, say, the US, which produces almost one hundred per cent), and a large proportion of that comes from Hokkaido. It is, then, the nation's larder.

Sapporo, its capital, seemed like a cool, relaxed city. No one was rushing, there was plenty of space on the vast, American-sized pavements and the traffic was sparse. Our hotel was an eighties throwback, but pleasant enough. (If you've ever read the Murakami novel, *Dance, Dance, Dance*, it reminded me of the Sapporo hotel the protagonist checks into only to discover a mysterious extra floor: a dark, dank portal into a parallel mind-zone inhabited by a strange man dressed as a sheep. Ours didn't have this.) From our room on the sixteenth floor we could see mountains; the ski jump built for the 1972 Winter Olympics and, right across the street, a Ferris wheel.

The air was thick with dragonflies, many of them mating as they flew.

From the moment they clapped eyes on the Ferris wheel, Asger and Emil petitioned without pause for a turn. I had my own petition going for a visit to Ramen Yokocho (Ramen Alley), filled with nationally renowned ramen noodle shops. It was a toss up as to which of us was the most whiny and irritating, so we split into two groups, with Lissen's requests to visit the city's art museum being sadly drowned out entirely.

Ramen Yokocho is the best place to eat Hokkaido's famed Batakon ramen – or 'Butter Corn' – made with two local ingredients. It was only when a local shopkeeper eventually led me there – leaving his shop to do so – that I realised I had walked past the anonymous entrance several times. From the street, Ramen Yokocho looked like the back entrance to an office basement, an impression that was hardly altered by how it looked inside: a dingy corridor, lined on one side by small counter-style ramen restaurants. Unusually for Japan, the owners of the half dozen or so restaurants called out to me as I walked down the corridor, gesturing to their laminated picture menus. I chose one at random, and settled down at the counter for a nuclear-hot bowl of butter-corn ramen, piled high with sliced roast pork, cubes of chilled butter, tinned sweetcorn, shredded spring onion, sheets of nori and half a boiled egg, all atop a tangle of frantic, curly noodles.

It was sensational. The best ramen I had eaten so far. The oil globules on the surface of the soup had given me cause for concern as I dipped my ceramic spoon in for the first taste, but after that, well, I was in ramen heaven. It was porky; mildly greasy in a satisfying way; incredibly salty and garlicky; with the chilled butter and corn a shock to the palate amid the piping hot soup. The spring onion gave it a welcome acidity and the chilli oil a lingering masochistic pleasure. I tell you, that soup had it all.

I had planned to taste the ramen in at least three different places, but my compulsion to finish every last morsel of this first one, combined with its monstrous scale, meant that any thoughts of eating further were ruled out by the disconcerting sloshing of my stomach as I rose to pay.

Ten minutes later I was sitting down to eat again. Sapporo is famous for its crabs which grow to an enormous size in the cold waters here and are exported throughout Japan. As I had left Ramen Yokocho nursing my balloon belly, my eye was caught by a giant fibreglass crab waving its claws, beckoning to me from the front of a restaurant across the street. Inside, I crossed a small crab-filled moat, removed my shoes and settled on the tatami floor at a window to taste of one of Japan's most revered delicacies.

The menu listed a royal flush of crabs: king, queen, snow, spiny and hairy, each, judging from the picture menu, like some deep-sea H. R. Geiger nightmare. Japanese music played as, around me, families and couples went to work diligently dismantling these fearsome crustaceans. Mine arrived: various cuts and species arranged beautifully in pieces in a bowl made from ice, with leaves, twigs and purple and green seaweed for decoration. The taste of the raw crab was indescribably delicate; initially my taste buds struggled to find any flavour, then slowly a faint sweetness of the sea and traces of iodine emerged from the pleasantly slimy texture. The green part of the crabmeat had more flavour, and the king crab the most resistant texture but I really couldn't see what all the fuss was about. Sitting there on the floor watching a pair of giant mechanical crab claws slowly waving back and forth outside my window, I felt quite underwhelmed.

Which made what happened over the coming weeks all the more peculiar. As we travelled on south through Japan I began to pine for those Hokkaido crabs; in quiet moments on trains and planes, my thoughts would return to its elusive flavour, but mostly it was the texture – that intriguing half liquid, half solid state of raw crab meat that gave it just enough resistance to remain on one's tongue for long enough to tease with its taste. It was another example of the Japanese's ultra-refined sense of texture. They value the feel of food in the mouth almost as highly as its flavour, and certainly employ it with greater nuance than they do temperature (scorching hot is the default setting for most hot dishes), whether it be in the unsettling chewy-crunch of jellyfish; the soft rubber of mochi (rice-flour sweets); or the sharp spikes of fried Panko breadcrumbs. More challengingly, the Japanese also value a mealy texture in some foods – like adzuki bean paste, which features as a filling for various sweets and desserts, and also cooked yam. Texture variation and contrast was one of the most revelatory aspects of my eating odyssey through Japan. There is, I am sure, a tremendous amount we can learn from the Japanese about combining textures in a dish, or throughout a meal, to heighten the physical sensuality of food.

The Sapporo crab was sensuous to the point of perversion. I still pine for it, indeed it is one of the abiding regrets of my eating career – and unusual for me when I find something I like – that I didn't take the opportunity to stuff myself silly with Hokkaido crab every day we were in Sapporo until I never wanted to eat it again. I have, in my life, done just this with a whole range of foodstuffs, from Milky Ways to pickled onions: yet here was something really worth getting sick of and I let it go after one tasting. A lesson for the future there, I feel.

But it was the ramen I raved about when I met up with Lissen, Asger and Emil half an hour later. Despite my distended belly and indigestion-induced grimaces they insisted I take them back to Ramen Yokocho. I was glad they did as Lissen's map-reading lead us to the second, more inviting, part of the alley, which I hadn't realised continued across the street from the inhospitable corridor I had dined in. Ramen Yokocho II was much more atmospheric, with tightly packed diners and a bustling Friday evening mood with crowds of locals wandering, like us, bewildered by the choice and the siren smells from the various kitchens.

We chose a shop run by an elderly husband and wife who were initially alarmed to see an entire gaijin family enter their restaurant. They soon softened and the wife – whose only English was 'I'm sorry, OK?' – caught a dragonfly by the wings and handed it to Asger with a big smile, saying something that sounded roughly like, '*Hey chow shey wa chey ma shay!*' Asger took the insect gently with his thumb and forefinger. He and Emil examined it in wonder for a while, Emil not feeling quite bold enough to hold it himself but impressed by his brother's courage.

I was served some shochu, a potent domestic spirit distilled from wheat, sweet potato, buckwheat or black sugar depending on where in Japan it comes from. I can't understand why schochu is not more popular in the West; it is extremely strong but has a light, mild taste, and is a friendly spirit to guzzle. Normally served in a tumbler with a gigantic spherical ice cube, here it came in a glass jar with a removable ring-pull top. Lissen had a beer, and soon our ramen arrived, not quite as epochal as my first, with more chilli and oil, but still good enough for me to drain the bowl. By now I felt as if I was undergoing some kind of arcane Japanese torture, my stomach and bladder pushed to bursting point. 'I'm sorry, OK?' the wife asked, meaning, 'Would you like something else?' I pointed to some gyoza on the menu. Well, you never know when you're going to eat again, do you?

Our introduction to Sapporo had been revelatory. What else could you ask of a city but a Ferris wheel, randy dragonflies and great ramen? But the next day cemented its place in our hearts for ever.

We began with an uninspiring morning visit to the one-room Ainu museum. Today there are thought to be less than 200 pure-bred Ainu left – that is people with two Ainu parents – and their language and culture is on the brink of extinction. As with the Moari, the Native American, the Aborigine and Indian's low cast Dalits, the Ainu suffer from varying degrees of persecution and prejudice in Japanese society. Unemployment is disproportionately high among them; educational standards low. This being Japan, the establishment does a very good job of keeping quiet about the Ainu, although recent legislation has helped their cause slightly. And it has to be said there are other minorities as badly off, if not worse, in Japan – the

Burakumin, for example, who are genuine outcasts, ghettoised descendants of butchers or tanners and thus thought of as unclean, or the Korean and Chinese communities in Osaka and elsewhere.

The official Ainu population including those of mixed heritage is said to be around twenty-five thousand although Ainu pressure groups claim there are twice as many – they simply choose not to admit to it. Alcoholism is a major problem for the Ainu as, prior to the arrival of the modern Japanese, they drank only occasionally during rituals, and have a low tolerance even today (this is not unusual, around half the population of Japan suffer from Aldehyde Dehydrogenase Deficiency which means their blood pressure drops when they drink).

Now, I don't want to sound even shallower than a man who drags his family to the other side of the world for some dinners may already sound, but although I was of course touched by the Ainu's plight, I was more interested in what they eat. Back in Tokyo we had visited an Ainu restaurant, Rera Cise, or House of Wind, which opened in 1994 as a focal point for the Ainu cause and to promote awareness of their culture.

An Ainu spokesman we met there had told us a little about his people: 'Our religion is quite similar to Shinto, but the bear plays a very special role,' he said. 'Do you know any bears?' asked Asger (once, to impress him, I told Asger I was friends with Winnie-the-Pooh – I was born quite close to Hundred Acre Wood – and he is still pushing for an introduction). The spokesman looked puzzled. 'No, but we do have a ritual where we kill a bear.' Asger went quiet.

In fact, they don't just kill the animal they revere, they eat it too. Nineteenth century British anthropologist John Batchelor – who founded the Ainu museum in Sapporo – recorded that the Ainu ate bear cooked in horse fat, concluding drily that, 'In no sense are the Ainu epicures.'

The spokesman had a present for Asger and Emil, he said, and pulled from a woven wool bag what looked like two fancy chopsticks. He placed one end of the chopstick over his open mouth and began to twang the other end. It was a mukkur, a kind of wooden Jew's Harp, which he was obviously skilled at playing.

The food began to arrive: pickled cucumber and seaweed, and what the Japanese call mountain vegetables, edible wild ferns and bulbs, although these were special Ainu mountain vegetables, called kito piro. 'They have lots of vitamin E, D, iron and minerals, good for colds and constipation, high blood pressure, contagious diseases and getting rid of evil spirits,' our Ainu friend said. This was followed by rather less appealing, deep-fried potato and pumpkin cakes, and venison, cheese and onion wrapped in filo pastry, which was delicious but rather greasy and, it turned out, not all that authentic.

As I tried some slightly bitter greens I asked why so many Ainu left Hokkaido for Tokyo: 'The discrimination is much worse for us in Hokkaido. We stand out because we have thicker hair, thicker eyebrows, darker skin – people say we are stinky or dirty. There are many more foreigners in Tokyo so we aren't so obvious. The government says there are 2,700 of us in Tokyo, but I think there is double that. Many Ainu keep their heritage a secret. You know, if you are Ainu you can not join the police force, for instance, and there are many other areas where there is prejudice against us. We don't have much money, so it is difficult to get a good education. The Japanese are still in denial that there were people on these islands before they arrived from Japan. They say we were only in Hokkaido, but there were Ainu people all the way to Okinawa.'

Back in Sapporo, after visiting the Ainu museum, our spirits were raised by some deliciously nutty black sesame ice cream, and a sighting of a Daihatsu Naked. Across town, in the small but thriving indoor Nijo market, we saw vast sacks of salmon roe, taut and bursting with luminous orange eggs; herring being smoked on the pavement; and a gigantic boiled octopus, its deep red tentacles curled like the ends of a Victorian villain's moustache.

A visit from two blond-haired European boys was clearly a rare occurrence at Nijo market and the stallholders were friendly, offering tastings eagerly.

We entered a shop entirely filled with open tanks of crabs. The owner, a young woman, approached us. The hairy crab was the best to eat she said, but also the most expensive at ¥5,000 each (around £24). She was from the south-west of Hokkaido, konbu, or sea kelp, territory. I mentioned that Asger and I were taking a trip there the next day and she enthused about the people and the beauty of the coast. Suddenly, before we could protest, she had removed the largest king crab, with a span of almost a metre and a body as large as Asger's head, from one of the tanks and was offering it to him to hold.

Lissen, Emil and I took a step backwards, and made encouraging faces. Asger offered his arms outstretched, and was soon holding an eight-legged, pinky-red, prehistoric monster, easily big enough to overpower a small dog. Asger stood rigid, proud and exhilarated but with a beseeching look best described as, 'Will you just take the damn photograph?' To Emil, who had already seen his elder brother defeat a sumo ten times his size, Asger now attained the stature of a hero of Greek mythology. What neither of us knew was that the next day we would encounter a far more dangerous natural predator.

Chapter 17

Seaweed

There are bears in Hokkaido. Not just cuddly koala types either, but proper, big, scream-for-your-mummy grizzlies. It's hard to imagine where the *higuma* hide themselves in a nation of a hundred and thirty-five million people sardined onto useable land the size of two football fields. Perhaps a number are passing themselves off as hairy geishas, who knows, but there are, it is claimed, thousands of them roaming free as the breeze on Japan's northernmost island.

I know for sure there are bears in Japan because I saw one. Vicariously, but that still counts, doesn't it? It was the day Asger and I drove with Emi (who had flown up for a couple of days to see friends), to visit the konbu kelp farms that lie south-west of Sapporo, along a coast road that sticks in my memory for two reasons, the first being its majestic, volcanic splendour with giant birds of prey wheeling in the deep blue sky above, the second, as I said, because I *didn't* happen to look up into a forested hill above the motorway and see a large dark, bear-shaped shadow moving through the undergrowth.

Emi did.

'I just saw a bear,' she said matter of factly, before looking back down at the map on her lap.

'What do you mean, you saw a bear?' I said, frantically craning my neck as I drove, the car veering towards the central reservation.

'A bear. Up there,' she pointed to a fast-receding point behind us.

I repeated the question a few times during which, to her credit, Emi remained patient.

'Emi just saw a bear, Asger!' I shouted above the strained din of

119

the Daihatsu's electric toothbrush engine, but he was as under-awed as Emi. Of course she'd just seen a bear. What was the big deal? Hadn't he just the other day watched a ninja make five red sponge balls appear in his hands from nowhere at the ninja-themed restaurant in Shibuya?

We continued along the coast road besides Uchiura Bay heading south to Hakodate passing through shabby, desolate towns of low rise, corrugated iron houses and shops. Great mounds of buoys littered the empty lots between buildings, while twenty or so metres out at sea the surface of the water was covered with hundreds more, like a giant, unfinished game of solitaire – the telltale signs of a konbu 'field'.

I was still glancing around nervously on the lookout for nine-foot, hairy carnivores when we finally arrived in Minamikayabe-cho on the Pacific coast, an area famed throughout Japan for producing some of the finest konbu (sometimes spelled 'kombu'), or kelp, in the land. Over fifteen per cent of all Japan's konbu – worth ten billion yen a year – comes from this part of Hokkaido; they even supply the Emperor.

It is hard to overestimate the importance of this great, green, leathery sea plant to the diet of the Japanese. They eat around fifty different types of seaweed, but konbu is king. It is the one constant ingredient in dashi. In traditional Buddhist cuisine they even have a dashi that is made simply by letting a piece of konbu sit in cold water for a few hours – it is delicious, with a delicate, Zen-fresh taste of the sea.

Konbu isn't just used to make dashi – although given the myriad uses for dashi in soups, sauces, marinades, batters and dips, that would be enough to warrant it podium position in Japanese cuisine. They also soak it in vinegar, dry it and then shave it to make tororo konbu, which is often used in miso soup instead of nori; or cook it slowly with water, soy, mirin and sugar then sprinkle it with salt to make shio konbu (salt konbu), a popular snack. It is also used as a wrapping for saba-sushi (pressed mackerel sushi). And, as I learned from my chastening visit to Ajinomoto, konbu of course has the highest levels of glutamate of any natural substance and was the inspiration for the invention of MSG.

There is every reason to believe konbu is one of the most significant foodstuffs in terms of the Japanese's famed good health and longevity. It has more minerals than anything else they eat, including potassium, iron, iodine, magnesium and calcium, as well as vitamins B and C, and is thought to aid the removal of toxins from the body. Seaweed also contains lignans, believed to prevent cancer. Plus, of course, it is fat- and calorie-free. As I would discover a couple of months later, the Okinawans eat more konbu per capita than any of their compatriots. And guess who lives not only the longest in Japan, but in the world? The Okinawans (although, there are considerably fewer bears on Okinawa, which I can't help feel must be a factor).

It is difficult to get a sense of how konbu looks in the wild from the small, dried black-green strips the Japanese buy pre-packed in their supermarkets. I really wanted to see where konbu grew and talk to the people who farmed it. Hence the five-hour drive from Sapporo (Lissen stayed in town with Emil who was threatening to hold his breath unless he got to go on the Ferris wheel again). But konbu farmers are a secretive and suspicious bunch, wary of outsiders, perhaps because they are rumoured to earn upwards of $100,000 a year for tending their small plots of ocean. It had taken weeks of emails and phone calls from Emi to set up a meeting, and even then I eventually had to send a copy of my passport to assure them I wasn't involved in some kind of seaweed espionage.

'It's been the worst year ever for konbu,' Takahiko Sasaki, head of the Minami Kayabe Fishery, explained to us when we finally arrived. 'We usually produce around 3,500 tons a year, but this year it's been less than half that.'

'Ah yes,' I nodded sagely. 'Global warming.'

'No, not really. Last year was a bonanza year. There is no major downward trend. The problem is storms. The konbu is very exposed and is damaged easily by rough tides.'

We were standing in a warehouse beside the harbour watching a team of robust looking middle-aged women tying together 7kg bundles of whole, dried seaweed leaves, which looked not unlike tobacco, each bundle roughly the size of a bale of hay. They quite overwhelmed the tiny pickup truck sent to transport them.

One of the women handed two pieces of dried konbu to Asger, who pretended they were giant chopsticks. The ladies all laughed. Another disappeared into an office and returned with a handful of sweets, which she offered him, cooing over his blond hair.

Sasaki-san, wearing a polo shirt embroidered with a small cartoon of a bear playing golf, explained that the konbu is grown just beyond the harbour walls, a few metres out at sea. Konbu leaves, which are narrow and tongue-like with frilly edges, can grow up to six metres long (twenty metres has been known). They are a translucent, browny-green and are harvested at either one or two years of age by men with bamboo poles with hooks on the end who use them to rake the leaves aboard boats. Drying has to be done within a day or the seaweed starts to turn white and the quality suffers. When it is finished, the seaweed is very dark green, stiff and brittle, like sheets of dried spinach lasagne. They traditionally begin to harvest natural konbu on 20 July and continue until late August, with folk flocking from all over the region to help pick the leaves. It is tough work, starting at two in the morning and working through to eight in the evening.

They still dry some of the konbu the natural way in these parts, first brushing it clean on a machine that looks like a giant shoe polisher, then hanging it out in the sun in large, wooden-framed open sheds. But most is dried in small warehouses by machine at around 70°C for twelve hours or so. Should you ever need to, you can tell the difference between sun-dried and machine-dried konbu as the former is greeny-brown, while machine-dried is darker, almost black. Real konbu connoisseurs can also tell where on Hokkaido a piece comes from. For instance, in the area around Mihami Kayabe, cut a piece of konbu and it will be white inside, hence its name – White Mouth Beach – elsewhere the konbu will be black inside – which comes from, you guessed it, Black Mouth Beach, near Hakodate. There are over ten species of konbu and it comes in a variety of quality grades, depending on colour, gloss and thickness. The thicker the better (an 8kg bundle of prime konbu will contain eighty-four pieces, a bundle of lower grade leaves will contain more), but of course, this being Japan, appearance is the most important factor in grading – the straight, uniformly shaped konbu is most prized of all. The ultimate piece of konbu would, then, be wild grown, naturally dried, thick as a passport, glossy and symmetrical.

The variety of konbu can have a radical effect on the flavour of dashi, ranging from delicate and light to rich and dark depending on the beach where it grew and even the year – as with wine, climate has a large effect on the flavour of each year's konbu. The very best rishiri konbu is laid down for two years in a temperature- and humidity-controlled process known as kura-gakoi which deepens the glutamate flavour. It is much appreciated by so-called konbuliers, the konbu equivalent of a sommelier.

Drying makes the konbu leaves crinkle up at the edges so they look like ventagli pasta, so the higher grades of leaves are steam softened at a 100°C to enable them to be rolled flat. This is done by hand using a machine rather like a mangle. We followed Sasaki-san in his truck further west along the coast to watch this being done by a husband and wife team in a ramshackle shed on the beach. The husband gently fed each piece of konbu through the machine before passing it to his wife who would trim it by hand with a pair of shears and fold each metre piece into three for packing. She'd been doing this job for thirty years, she told me.

They also harvest 'wild' konbu in these parts, which both tastes better and has more minerals than the farmed variety because it grows on the ocean floor, unlike the farmed variety which they cultivate close to the surface. It is far harder to harvest, of course, which means it costs twice as much. It is also even more vulnerable to the weather.

'This year there has been practically no natural konbu,' Sasaki-san told us. 'Maybe 50 or 60kg in all. Usually we harvest a thousand. Low pressure in October meant that the sea bed was damaged by rough water.'

So, forget about the polar bears and Holland, the decimation of the konbu crop through climate change would really be something to worry about, especially for the Japanese. Perhaps it will prompt them to rethink their carbon footprint and switch off all those electric toilets.

We wished Sasaki-san and his ladies well and thanked them for their time. Asger departed with yet another handful of sweets, Emi and I received a gift pack of konbu, I gave Sasaki-san a box of English tea, and we set off for home in our Daihatsu buzz-box.

Incidentally, as we were driving back to Sapporo along the highway through a dusky sunset, up in the forests just above the road, wouldn't you know it but I really did see a large, brown shadow. A bear! At least, that's what I reckon it was. Asger says it was a wheelie bin.

Chapter 18

Kyoto Stories

We flew from Sapporo to Osaka the next day passing over Mount Fuji along the way. Fuji is the perfect mountain; not even the tangle of golf links encroaching on its base can spoil the quasi-spiritual effect of seeing it for the first time from the air.

From Osaka airport, a striking example of Japanese futurescope engineering on reclaimed land in the Inland Sea, we took the train to Kyoto. It was clear from the ceaseless sprawl of urban development that the two cities are, essentially, one gigantic conurbation with precious little countryside to provide breathing space between them. And the concrete sprawl continues west, too, merging into the third major city of the region, Kobe.

The three cities and their inhabitants could not be more different. Kyoto, 370km west of Tokyo, is the cradle of Japanese culture and religion. It was the imperial capital of the country from 794 to 1868, home to the royal household, as well as the country's spiritual and cultural heart. The legacy of Kyoto's royal history has, it is said, bred a people who are refined and aloof, not a little stand-offish and secretive. Kyotoites are famed for their obfuscation in matters of diplomacy and pride in their local cuisine. The best families in Japan still keep houses here, although they might live in Tokyo.

Kyoto is located well inland and surrounded on three sides by mountains. Because of this it remained relatively sheltered from the otherwise pervasive cultural influence of China during the Middle Ages, allowing a distinctive Japanese culture to foment in the arts of calligraphy, poetry, theatre, painting, ceramics and, of course, food.

Kyotoites consider themselves to be the most discerning diners in Japan, if not the world. The city was the birthplace of the tea ceremony and has its own highly cultivated cuisine, kyo ryori (meaning Kyoto cuisine), from which evolved kaiseki ryori, the extravagant and costly multi-course feast usually served in private rooms in ryotei, or inns, overlooking Japanese gardens. It still has almost two thousand temples and gardens, famously saved from atomic attack during WWII by Henry L. Stimson, the then US secretary of War, who had visited Kyoto in the 1920s. He realised its cultural importance, and the eternal bitterness there would be towards America were it to be destroyed.

The more everyday Kyoto cuisine is known as obanzai ryori and is centred on tofu and its by-product yuba, the skin that forms on the surface of simmering soy milk which is either dried or sold as it is and has the highest protein content of any foodstuff on earth. Kyoto is also known for another intriguing substance called fu, a kind of dough made from wheat gluten. And as Kyotoites have never tended to eat out as much as Tokyoites, the city also has a strong market culture, centred on the famous Nishiki Ichiba which still exists in the city centre.

Obanzai ryori is remarkably healthy, largely vegetarian, very low in fat and sugar and heavy on vegetables. Recent years have seen a revival of traditional strains of local vegetables – radish, aubergine, burdock root, pumpkin and cucumber – known collectively as kyo yasai (Kyoto vegetables). These previously rare strains have been rediscovered by Tokyo food lovers too – partly out of sheer fad value, partly because they are full of flavour, but also as a symptom of the Japanese's inherent xenophobia, exacerbated by recent health scares regarding Chinese produce. The senshu mizu (Kyoto aubergine) is the height of chic on the dining tables of Tokyo.

In contrast, Osaka is a massive modern metropolis with giant office towers and endless malls, great swooping fly-overs and an industrious and fluid populace, quick to react to trends and demands. It has always been a trading city, dependent on constant reinvention. Its people are supposedly down to earth, somewhat impatient and hungry for innovation – there is virtually nothing in the city older than thirty years. I was perhaps more excited about eating in Osaka than any other city in Japan, having been told by François Simon, esteemed restaurant critic of *Le Figaro* (and the inspiration for Anton Ego, the coffin-faced critic in the film *Ratatouille*), that Osaka was, in his opinion, the greatest food city in the world.

Osakan cuisine is usually characterised by one word, kuidaore, which literally translates as 'eat 'till you go bust' – both physically and financially. Osakans have big appetites, they love fried fast food and, unusually in Japan, they cook with wheat flour – most famously in the form of tako yaki (small doughnuts filled with chunks of octopus); okonomiyaki (a kind of thick pancake with various fillings); kitsune udon (soft, squidgy udon noodles served in a slightly sweet dashi with deep-fried tofu skin); and kushikatsu (deep-fried, breaded skewers).

Kobe-ites, meanwhile, have a more international outlook. There are said to be a hundred different nationalities living in the city, squeezed on a slender strip of land between the mountains and the sea, including some of the country's most influential expat communities. Kobe has always had stronger links with the outside world than the rest of Japan; from 1868–1911 it was, in theory, the only port open to the outside world and ships would stop off there to stock up on the city's excellent fresh water from springs beneath the mountains. Today its residents drink more wine than other Japanese and have more European-style patisseries per capita than any other city in the country (I ticked off about twenty in one afternoon with Asger and Emil – for once eagerly – in tow). Above all, though, its great culinary gift to the world has been Kobe beef – a much misunderstood name, of which more later.

We arrived at Kyoto Station late in the morning. It was warmer here. Autumn in Kyoto is characterised by an oppressive, humid heat caused by its location, surrounded by hills and mountains, quite unlike the refreshing weather we'd experienced in Sapporo.

The station is a splendid cathedral-like place, whose ten-storey atrium makes those old European steam-era stations, like St Pancras or Leipzig, look like parish churches. As usual, even for the most densely populated parts of Japan, all was calm, quiet and ordered and I can't express the joyous sense of ease I felt as a neurotic father, expert at fantasising nightmare scenarios wherever I travel, to be in a country where no one will steal your bags or try to cheat you. I know there is crime in Japan, but I suspect you'd really have to go looking for trouble to find it.

We had arranged to pick up the keys to a house Lissen had found for rent on the Internet from a woman called Junko, a friend of the owners, who worked as a lecturer at the International Centre on the north-eastern outskirts of the city. We took a taxi across town, passing mammoth 'bird perch' gateways to temples and dark, shadowy machiya – Kyoto's historic wooden townhouses. We found Junko in the middle of a class showing a group of foreign students how to make tako yaki.

Tako yaki, or 'octopus balls' are a kind of savoury doughnut with a chewy nugget of octopus tentacle hidden within. In Osaka they are usually served freshly made from street stalls in a cardboard 'boat', eight at a time, and come slathered in a dark, gloopy sauce made from mirin, Worcestershire sauce, ginger, garlic, sugar, sake, and perhaps dashi. They are sometimes also topped with katsuobushi shavings, which do their customary shimmy in the heat blast from the dough beneath.

To make tako yaki, you need a special, cast-iron tako yaki griddle, with ten or so, three centimetre-wide, semi-spherical cups (by chance at home we have a very similar Danish griddle used for making *æbleskiver*, traditional Scandinavian doughnuts). Heat it up over a hob, oil the cups with sunflower oil or something similar (not olive oil) and pour in your batter until it fills the cups to around the ¾ mark. This is a runny batter made from cold dashi and flour, plus eggs (a ratio of 2:1, say, 400ml dashi, 200g flour, with two beaten eggs). You don't need to mix it too thoroughly, but a little more than with a tempura batter. Then add a chunk of octopus tentacle – or if you prefer, king prawn – and perhaps some chopped benishoga (pickled ginger), spring onions or something with a bit of tang to cut through the batter and complement the seafood. As the batter sets (timing is everything here), use a toothpick to turn it over so that the central, uncooked batter falls down into the cup creating the other half of the sphere.

We tried some of Junko's tako yaki. They were pretty good, a tasty, almost liquid dough with the rubbery crunch of cooked octopus inside. We all soon learned, however, that you have to treat fresh-cooked tako yaki with great caution. You need to break them open with a toothpick to let out some of the raging steam before you gingerly nibble a little dough.

After Junko's demonstration she introduced us to some of her students, from Canada, Australia and South America. A Serbian man, called Sasha, introduced himself and explained that he was working at a restaurant in Kyoto. We must drop by, he said.

Another taxi took us together with Junko across Kyoto. We skirted the grounds of the Imperial Palace, obscured by trees, before the taxi dived into a warren of residential backstreets in an area called Kamigyo-ku.

Our house was located deep among tightly packed houses, some modern and functional, others, like ours, wooden and ancient. The streets had no pavements, only tiny front yards crammed with bicycles and pot plants – or occasionally one of those boxy little Japanese cars designed like carry-on luggage to fit an exact space – divided the front doors from the street.

The house was built in the traditional Japanese style and over a century old, Junko told us. The sliding windows had mesh covers and heavy wooden shutters. They opened onto the neighbour's windows which were almost close enough to touch. It was as close to authentic Kyoto as we could have hoped for, not least as the doors had no locks.

Inside, it was cool and dark and smelled of dust and jasmine. The first floor consisted of one large room, empty apart from a pretty vase in the tokonoma. The futons, Junko explained, were folded away in the cupboards, so we began to unpack them to see if we would have enough. 'There's something funny in my pillow,' said Asger. It turned out to be stuffed with buckwheat husks, a traditional pillow filling. There was a small kitchen with a two-ring hob but no oven – Japanese domestic kitchens rarely have ovens, but do usually have a small grill – and a tatami floor with a low slung futon sofa. Emil had followed a trail of tiny brown pellets that led underneath the sofa to several large cockroaches which Lissen dispatched with the heel of her shoe as I supervised from halfway up the stairs. 'They look like Transformers!' said Asger, as the last came to an end in a crunchy squelch.

Also in the cupboards were several lightweight patterned dressing gowns. These were yukata. We all decided they were the coolest thing we had ever seen and put them on, only later learning that to tie them right over left is a serious breach of yukata etiquette as this is how they dress the dead (but it at least explained the look on the face of one of our neighbours one day when I went down to take the trash out while still wearing mine). Emil in particular hadn't been so attached to an item of clothing since his Spiderman costume.

We ventured out into our new neighbourhood for the first time shortly after Junko had left, and soon found ourselves lost in a maze of houses.

We knew the royal palace and its park were nearby but our map was useless as there were no street signs and no obvious landmarks. It didn't matter. I could have wandered for hours peering in through front windows and savouring the details of Japanese everyday life – the unlocked bicycles, the miniature shrines on every street, and the smell of incense in the air. In one parade of shops an elderly woman sat in the middle of an open shop-front mending clothes. There was a pretty good supermarket, small but still with superb fresh fish, perfect fruit and vegetables and astonishing cuts of heavily marbled, deep pink beef. Just around the corner from our house was a traditional soy sauce brewery. We peered in through the doorway to see three giant, dark wood barrels, each around three or four metres high with ladders up the side. I asked the man behind the counter if I could take a look, and climbed up and peered into a bottomless, black hole of soy: the smell deliriously rich and yeasty. Nearby was a unicycle shop; a French patisserie, run by Japanese students of my cooking alma mater, Le Cordon Bleu, serving perfect croissants and tarts just like back home; while outside on the street we passed a woman leading a dog with two wheels where his back legs had once been. 'Transformer dog!' said Emil. It seems the kind of neighbourhood where anything could happen.

A short walk away we came to a wooden workshop clearly of great age, where they made fu, the Kyoto wheat-gluten cake. Fuka, as we discovered, is the supplier to the royal household and numerous top restaurants and was founded over a century and a half ago. Inside I met Shuichiro Kobori, the son of the owner who very generously – considering we had no appointment – showed us round and explained how this curious foodstuff is made by mixing flour with the beautifully soft water from their centuries old well in the back yard. The resulting dough is kneaded under constantly flowing water so that the starch sinks to the bottom leaving pure wheat gluten which is formed into a sticky, rubbery brick-like block. The technique originated in China and came to Japan with the Zen monks as a kind of meat substitute used to bulk out hotpot dishes. You can fry fu as well as boil it, and Fuka sold theirs in a variety of colours and flavours. Kobori-san was especially proud of their new bacon and basil flavours.

On our way home we were drenched by a thunderous downpour. We had no choice but to brave the rain as we had no umbrellas and were, again, slightly lost. The wind was whipping up too. Tree tops were bending. A rubbish bin bounded across the road, narrowly missing us. As an old typhoon hand, I recognised the signs.

We huddled in the doorway of a private home in the vain hope that the storm would blow over, but after five minutes it had if anything, grown worse. A shadow appeared behind the glass panel of the door. It flitted past a couple of times, then lingered for a few seconds and went away again. A little later the figure pressed itself right up against the textured glass and, suddenly, the door opened. A young man, in his early twenties, stood smiling nervously. He looked down at Asger and Emil and beckoned us in, chatting rapidly in Japanese.

He showed us into what was a conventional Western-style home, apart from the fact that virtually every surface, wall, shelf, table and some of the floor was covered in Beatles memorabilia.

'Beatles!' He exclaimed. 'Yes,' I said. 'Wow. I love the Beatles.' I gave him a Macca-esque thumbs up. He invited us to sit down, clearing away a pile of CDs from one chair, and some probably quite valuable ceramic figures of the Fab Four from another. Over the next hour or so, as the typhoon raged outside, the man, whose name was Yuzo, respectfully presented just about every item of memorabilia he owned along with some green tea and mochi cakes for the children.

Luckily, the Beatles would probably be my chosen specialist subject on *Mastermind* so Yuzo and I bonded immediately. I was taken aback that he had an actual lock of George Harrison's actual hair, stuck with brittle yellow Sellotape to the back of a Kellogg's Cornflakes package.

The typhoon, which we later learned was a force eleven – far stronger than the one in Tokyo – showed no signs of abating but we had to make a move. We thanked Yuzo for his kindness, exchanged business cards, and made a dash for it back to our house which fortunately turned out to be only a few seconds away.

I don't know how he found out where we lived, although I suspect we had become a hot topic of neighbourhood gossip, but a few days later we came home one afternoon to find a small envelope on our doorstep. It was from Yuzo and contained George's hair on the corn-flakes packet and a small card that read – I later learned – 'From Me, to You.'

Less welcome was the wasp nest that had appeared just above the front door which I first became aware of the next morning when I was dive-bombed by insects the size of Coke cans. Something had to be done. Preferably by someone else.

I made a dash for it, engulfed by loud buzzing, and grabbed a passing neighbour, a mother out with her two sons. She looked aghast and hurried off, returning a few minutes later with a large can of insecticide. She said something in rapid-fire Japanese and hurried off again, this time leaving her two sons standing looking at me with shy curiosity. She returned, spoke at length again then just stood, waiting. I smiled awkwardly. Did she expect me to do something? Surely not to go and spray those monstrous zeppelins? I could see Asger and Emil peering out of the first-floor window at the two Japanese boys who were around their age. Knowing they were play-mate-hungry, I beckoned them out, somehow in that moment stupidly forgetting all about the wasps.

Emil exploded from the front door, in his customary, excitable pre-play manner and, almost immediately, as if they had been waiting for just such an opportunity, one of the wasps stung him slap bang in the middle of the forehead. He screamed, which only made the other wasps even more agitated. I rushed him indoors where Lissen applied some mum magic (from the same knowledge bank that knows exactly what to do with red wine stains on white carpets and bubblegum on a woollen sweater,) in the form of a hastily assembled unguent.

By the time Emil's screaming had subsided there was a knock at the door. A young man in a grey suit was outside with a bicycle and a clipboard. He didn't look like a pest controller but I assumed that's what he was and followed him outside where, from a safe distance, I watched him liberally douse the wasps with the neighbour's insect repellent.

This really annoyed them. They swarmed from their nest and flew off on various seemingly random trajectories. They didn't get far. Within about ten seconds they began dropping from the sky like a biblical plague, landing on the ground where they twitched and fizzed before finally conking out.

The man made a few ticks on his clipboard. I tried to offer him some money, but he looked horrified, bowed, got on his bike and cycled off. I thanked the neighbour and she beckoned us into her house for tea and mochi and awkward smiling silences.

That night on television we watched Baruto, our Latvian sumo friend, win seven bouts out of seven at a tournament in Osaka, which meant that he stood a good chance of ascending to the next division. There was an unforgettable moment during the third bout. 'Look,' said Asger.' His nappy's coming off!' The two wrestlers had literally frozen in mid-grapple while the referee helped Baruto's opponent re-tie his gusset. Once he was neatly trussed once more, they resumed the bout exactly as they were, as if nothing had happened. Asger and Emil were so taken with this spectacle they spent the rest of the evening re-enacting it for us.

I know I promised not to mention anything about Japanese toilets. I am sure you have heard plenty before about how they have bracing jets of water and steam, play music or fake flushing noises and generally make going to the bog a thoroughly twenty-first century experience. But such things were all very new to Asger. Our house may have been traditional in virtually every respect, but there was one room that had more micro processing power than Apollo 13: the water closet. It contained the most sophisticated lavatory I have ever seen – it did everything short of reading the newspaper aloud for you – and it didn't take Asger, renowned in our family for his ceaselessly inquisitive fingers, long to start exploring the control panel for its blue sky/clean bottom capabilities. He grew rather obsessed to the extent that, throughout our three weeks in Kyoto, whenever Asger had gone missing for more than a few minutes, we always knew where he would be: sitting on the loo with a faraway, almost transcendental smile on his face.

In the evening of the wasp attack, with Emil now sporting a bindi on his forehead, we walked beside the Kamogawa River, which runs through the eastern side of Kyoto. Cranes and bats caught the moonlight as they skimmed the water. Courting couples sat with their legs dangling over the sloping embankments. There were distant sounds of traffic, clamourous pachinko parlours and a rushing weir. The western bank of the river is overlooked, high above on stilted platforms bedecked with lanterns, by the restaurants of Pontocho, the nightlife area frequented by the 'practitioners of the arts' or geisha, of which there are still said to be around five to ten thousand in Japan.

A few minutes later we were sitting down to eat on one of the restaurant terraces ourselves, tucking into deliciously tender beef cheek cooked in soy sauce. Emil chomped happily on crunchy chicken cartilage yakitori, which was becoming one of his favourite Japanese dishes. Through the bamboo fencing that divided our restaurant from a more expensive neighbour we saw occasional flashes of butterfly-like kimonos and glossy black hair. It was, sadly, as close as we would get to the world of the geisha.

Chapter 19

The Kyoto Cooking Circle

Kyoto is a small, rather insular city in which it is impossible to pass unnoticed for too long, particularly if you are a temporarily resident foreigner with an entourage of two small children who have no qualms about going out dressed as their favourite superheroes. It is a city of whispers, rumour, secrets and gossip, so it didn't take long for word to get out of our arrival. But Japanese whispers clearly have much in common with the Chinese kind as, a week after arriving, I received an email from something called the Kyoto Cooking Circle, the city's leading cooking club, run by a woman called Natsumi. How she got my name and email address, I never really found out, but her sources were clearly a little 'out of the loop'.

She wrote:

Dear Mr Michael,
Welcome to Kyoto! We are here at the Kyoto Cooking Circle, welcome you. You are French chef? Yes. Please to come to show us French cuisine? We meet on Wednesday. Please telephone.
Thank for kindly intercourse,
Natsumi.

I rang the number.

'Ah, Mr Michael, please to talk to you!' said Natsumi.

I explained that I wasn't really a chef, but had written a book about training to become a chef and worked in a couple of Michelin-starred restaurants in Paris.

'Yes! Good! So you make, erm, de-mon-stra-tion?'

'What, you mean, come and show you how to cook? I don't thi . . .'

'Yes, yes, that's good, thank you. We looking forward.'

'Well, I suppose so, I mean what kind of . . . ?'

'Good! Good! You come Wednesday, eleven. Hello!'

And she hung up.

'I think I've just been press-ganged into giving a cooking demonstration,' I announced to the rest of the family.

'That's great,' said Lissen, who had often let it be known she didn't think I got out enough. 'It'll be good for you to get out a bit. Think of it as "giving something back".'

I replied that, personally, I would have thought travelling halfway across the world might count in some quarters as 'getting out a bit', but had to agree that, having spent the last month making often unreasonable demands upon Japanese hospitality, it would be good to offer something in exchange. But what was I going to show them? What ingredients were available to work with? It was time for a trip to Nishiki koji, Kyoto's famous food market.

If you are looking for ingredients for a classic French cooking demonstration, you could hardly choose a less fertile hunting ground than Nishiki market. Aside from the fresh fish, virtually nothing is recognisable from the European larder. Come to think of it, even some of the fish looked like they had come from other planets, not least the dried, flattened octopuses hanging on a line like Neptune's washing. That, of course, is part of the thrill and, to me, Nishiki is as thrilling a market as they come, its 123 vendors, lined up on either side of a coloured glass-roofed corridor, sell the kind of produce you simply will not find anywhere else in the world. There were freaky things to see at every turn; even Asger and Emil were captivated.

The smells were captivating too – dried seaweed; roasted chestnuts; funky, fruity miso, and tangy pickles all mingled in the muggy, crowded alley. The market was packed the afternoon we visited with housewives, chefs and tourists pouring over ¥50,000 matsutake

mushrooms; inspecting the local kyo yasai – the rare Kyoto vegetables that even other Japanese would be hard pushed to identify;
the knives at Aritsugu, knife makers to the imperial family; and vast
tubs of pickles. Kyoto is the pickle capital of Japan and there were
entire shops dedicated to vegetables preserved, mostly in glistening,
wet rice bran.

Emil's eye was caught by a packet of dried scallops that looked
like Queen Elizabeth I's wooden false teeth. He had mistaken them
for boiled sweets. Though usually well behaved when shopping, Emil
can sometimes become intensely covetous of improbable items. He
once had a screaming meltdown in a hardware store over a bulk
pack of red clothes pegs, for instance. From experience, I could tell
from the way his body had gone rigid like a pointer on a scent, that
we were in for a torrid battle. He wanted those scallops, and he
wanted them bad.

EMIL: I'm hungry. [Translation: I am not remotely hungry, but I want
    those.]
ME: Well, you will have to wait for dinner now, Emil. We've had
    lunch. [Translation: We both know where this is going, but we
    have to follow the usual procedure.]
EMIL: [Pulling hard on my arm.] Can I have some of those? [You
    know what's coming if you say 'no'.]
ME: No. You won't like them. [We both know I will say 'yes' even-
    tually, but after that you are on your own.]
EMIL: [Makes noise like a car alarm.]
ME: How much are these please?

Emil immediately spat his scallop out onto the floor and started
licking his brother's T-shirt to eradicate the taste, something I don't
think the shopkeeper had ever seen before. I apologised and started
to clear up the mess, making a big deal out of tasting the scallops
myself and showing my approval. Dried scallops are one of a range
of unique Japanese drinking snacks, most of them challenging

(dried fugu fins are another, as are fermented sea cucumber entrails). The scallops are supposedly excellent with sake, but I never want to see one again as long as I live. Emil made it clear that he felt the same way. 'Dad, why did you give that to me?' he asked, bewildered by his father's cruelty.

This did little to calm my mounting sense of panic that I wasn't going to find any ingredients that I could use in my demo. The lack of ovens ruled out half my repertoire; there was no pork to be seen, nor any whole chickens; the beef was all Japanese, and so suitable really only for Japanese dishes; the only flour was rice flour; and there was no dairy produce. There was plenty of kamaboko (ground white fish, steamed and formed into cakes), tofu, yuba, and fu, but nothing I had the faintest idea how to cook.

In the end I decided on a simple fish dish – sea bream with a sauce made from a reduced fish *fumet* that I would make from its bones, with a *brunoise* of tomatoes and fine-chopped chives for a little colour. I found some fennel bulbs, which, sliced fine and wilted in white wine and butter, would make a bed for the filets. I also picked up some Valhrona chocolate – at a quite shocking price – and, after much searching, some tiny cartons of cream, both from a posh supermarket food hall. I figured that, if things went badly, I could also show them how to make truffles. After all, everyone likes truffles, right?'

The Kyoto Cooking Circle met in a light, airy kitchen on the third floor of a large educational building in the centre of town, just a couple of minutes' walk from Nishiki market. Two dozen expectant faces – all but one of them female – greeted me as I entered the next morning with my produce, confident that, as I would be making a dish I had made many times, and I had the session planned, things should go well.

Kyotoites are possibly the most inscrutable, some would say snobbish, of all the Japanese – a legacy of the city's time as a royal seat during Japan's most highfalutin cultural era. So, I don't know for sure what the lunching ladies really thought of my demonstration, but I do know this: halfway through, as I was frying the bream filets in a cast iron pan to get their skins nice and crispy, I looked up and saw just the slightest flickers of consternation on the faces of my audience.

This unsettled me slightly but it took a few more moments, as the smell of frying fish began to fill the air, before I realised the gravity of my error: the Japanese don't really do fried fish. Judging by their faces, they found the whole notion not a little repellent. How could I be such a tool? They might charcoal grill a whole ayu (a river fish) or eel, or at a push steam a whole fish, but the Kyoto Cooking Circle was not impressed by this self-proclaimed French chef frying up what the Japanese consider to be their 'king of fish'.

Finally, one of the class sheepishly raised her hand to ask a question. 'Yes,' I said, thankful for the interruption. 'Why you cook the fish?' she said. 'In Japan, we not do this.' I thanked her and tried to explain how the protein in fish changes its texture and enhances the flavour if you heat it, how nice the crispy skin is and so on, but my heart wasn't really in it. Cooking a fish as beautiful and fresh as that sea bream was like spraying a wild orchid magnolia to match your furnishings.

I did redeem myself slightly with my fine dicing of the tomato which prompted appreciative cooing sounds, but things soon took a turn for the worse again when I moved on to the chocolate truffles, which melted almost instantaneously in the heat.

As I stood there, soft chocolate oozing through my hands, smudged on my white shirt, and dripping on the floor, I had one of life's great 'What the fuck am I doing here?' moments. Not for the last time in Japan a thought struck me: Everything I know is wrong. Everything I have been taught about food, is overblown, over-complicated, fussy and wasteful. What am I doing showing these people what to do with bream and some tomatoes? I should be watching them cook.

So that is what I did.

Luckily, I wasn't the only act on the bill that day and soon we had all gathered round a new teacher, Mrs Oka, who was going to show us how to make proper Japanese food. At least, that's what I had hoped. However, in honour of their Western visitor, the Kyoto Cooking Circle had decided to demonstrate a yoshoku dish, one of a range of Japanese-Western hybrid dishes, like 'rice and curry' and tonkatsu (pork schnitzel), that the Japanese have adapted and made their own – in this case it was 'omurice', or rice-filled omelette covered with ketchup.

Mrs Oka began by making a stock from carrot, onion and celery, to which she added two chicken tenderloins. After they had cooked a while, she sweated some onion while adding the stock to a roux, made from flour and butter. She cooked with the quick efficiency of an accomplished chef, no movement was extraneous, there was no stress. To the stock she added some mirin, red wine, and Worcestershire sauce – a favourite with the Japanese since the late nineteenth century, when it was introduced by the British via India. Reduced, this stock made for a lovely, dark brown demi-glace sauce.

Into the steamed rice went the tenderloins and carrots, now chopped, along with the onion she had sweated earlier, some boiled peas and ketchup. For the omelette she gently beat milk and eggs together with chopsticks, poured the mixture into a hot pan and, when cooked, used it as the wrapping for a mound of the rice mixture, moulding it into the shape of a rugby ball with some grease-proof paper. An elegant drizzle of the sauce and some ketchup finished off the dish.

Mrs Oka and the rest of the Kyoto ladies looked at me expectantly as I tasted the omurice. It was my turn to be inscrutable. 'Mmm, it's really good, yum,' I said.

As I was finishing off my mouthful the lone male of the group approached. It was Sasha the Serbian whom we had met briefly at Junko's tako yaki demonstration a week earlier (I did say it was a small city).

'Good demonstration, but I don't think cooking the fish was such a great idea,' he said, smiling warmly.

Sasha, it turned out, was training to be a chef, working by night in a restaurant in the city and attending cooking classes during the day. It takes six years to train to be a chef in Japan, and he had already completed three years of his improvised education, working in the kitchens of various Kyoto restaurants and learning Japanese. He looked washed out, pale and exhausted. 'It is very, very tough,' he said. 'They shout at you a lot, and the hours are endless. The food in Kyoto is very, very beautiful. The Kyoto style is small and expensive, but the most beautiful in Japan.' He paused, picking at his portion of omurice, and looking at it doubtfully. 'But I am not sure it is the best tasting . . .'

We talked about the Kyoto food scene. Sasha insisted that I come and eat at the restaurant he was currently working at, called, for reasons I never fully understood, the New Sapper. 'The chef is old, but he is a master. He is amazing. He changes the food every night. Once a month the richest man in Japan eats there, and he cooks something very special for him.'

What kind of a restaurant was it? 'It is karaoke restaurant,' he said. I wrinkled my nose. 'No, I know they are usually bad, but this one is very sophisticated. There are no separate rooms, you sing on a stage in front of the other guests. Very elegant.'

I thanked him for the invitation (and we did later eat a memorable meal at the New Sapper. I shan't easily forget Asger's karaoke version of Aqua's 'Barbie Girl' – the slow-dawning realisation of just how explicit the lyrics actually are, and the open distress on the faces of the other diners at having to endure a heavily amplified six-year-old singing his heart out). But I had a proposition of my own for Sasha the Serbian. It involved hard alcohol, massage and farm animals . . .

Chapter 20

Gardening

Haiku inspired by a whoopee cushion.

> A perfect garden
> Grey stones raked in smooth Zen waves
> Whoopee Frisbee chaos!

The gardens of Kyoto are tranquil oases of peace and contemplation. Meticulously pruned, coppiced, raked and sewn, these are spaces made for looking at but, under no circumstances, touching.

Try explaining that to a four-year-old.

I did, of course. As we made our way to the eastern part of the city, which has the highest density of temples and gardens in the country, I tried to describe the importance and sanctity of these gardens, how they were saved at the very last minute from being the target of the second atomic bomb, and so on.

'Will there be ice cream?' asked Asger.

We entered the stone archway that led to the garden and began to follow a stepping-stone path around the ancient wooden house in its centre. The garden was empty. The pond gently steamed in the fresh morning sun. It was silent. We could hear our own breath. The stepping stones led to an open veranda, the *engawa*, that ran around the rear of the house and overlooked a meticulous gravel garden, its small, grey stones gently raked into swooping, swirling furrows around mossy boulders, and piled occasionally into cone-shaped effigies of Mount Fuji. Lissen and I stood in silent, awed contemplation of this masterpiece of aesthetic precision, trying our best to commune with the Zen spirit of simplicity and natural harmony that had inspired it.

Emil chose a different form of communion. He flung the deflated whoopee cushion he had bought at a toy shop the previous day out across the gravel. Before I had a chance to stop him, he had climbed down from the wooden platform and was hastening across the stones to retrieve it.

'Oh my God! Emil!' hissed Lissen. 'Come here right now!' We both leaned as far as we dared over the gravel, stretching our hands out as if trying to save a drowning man, but Emil, using that sixth sadistic sense that all children seem to possess, saw our desperation. He stood still and shook his head insolently.

I tried a more authoritative approach. 'Emil rrrrright now. Or, or . . . no more Pokémon.'

Emil pursed his lips tightly, glared at me, picked up the whoopee cushion, and stomped stroppily back over the gravel adding another track of footprints, deeper and closer together than the first.

I made a doomed attempt to try to rearrange some of the stones as they had been before Emil's encroachment, but lacking a rake I had no chance. I am ashamed to say that we hurried from the garden as quickly as we could, avoiding the gaze of the guards at the gate as we bustled into a waiting taxi, never to return to the gardens of Kyoto.

Chapter 21

The Most Beautiful Meal in the World

The most exquisite recipe book I have ever seen is called *Kaiseki*, a lavishly photographed journey through a year in the Kyoto restaurant, Kikunoi, written by its head chef and owner Yoshihiro Murata with forewords by Ferran Adrià and Matsuhisa Nobu. The recipes are, for the most part, dauntingly complex – some have up to fourteen separately prepared elements – staggeringly beautiful, and all founded upon a devout appreciation of seasonal ingredients.

The recipe for chilled tomato soup is one of the simple ones: 'Push some tomatoes through a sieve. Simmer half the juice until it thickens, then add the other half, some salt, light soy sauce and lemon juice.' That's it. Of course, it relies upon the very finest fruit plucked straight from the vine at the point of optimum ripeness, but for elegant simplicity it can not be surpassed.

Kaiseki is named after the traditional meal that is, for many, the pinnacle of Japanese cuisine: an ultra-refined, multi-course piece of culinary performance art which, in its modern incarnation, has developed from the twin, paradoxical principles of Zen-like restraint with no expense spared. Many chefs in the West are coming to appreciate that kaiseki may well represent the ultimate expression of the culinary art.

Kyoto is the home of kaiseki. It evolved there from the fourteenth century onwards, initially as an accompaniment to the tea ceremonies so beloved of the city's noblemen and royal court. From the early seventeenth century until well into the nineteenth when Japan was virtually closed to the world during the *sakoku*, or National Seclusion, the tea ceremony and all those other intimidatingly rarefied, pastimes like kabuki, flower arranging, calligraphy, pottery and bunraku, began to mutate into their uniquely Japanese forms.

Kaiseki began rather more simply as just miso soup with three side dishes (in fact 'soup and three' remains the basis of any Japanese meal, like 'meat and two veg' in the West), intended to soak up all the undesirable elements – the tannins, the caffeine – in the vast quantities of tea participants had to drink. This chaiseki, as it was called, then developed under the influence of the vegetarian cuisines of shojin ryori and the local Kyoto cuisine, kyo-kaiseki, into the nine-course kaiseki meal for which, today, Japanese captains of industry pay tens of thousands of yen to eat in a handful of what are, essentially, private members' restaurants.

This ritualistic repast didn't get the name kaiseki – meaning 'bosom' and 'stone', referring to the practice of monks holding warm stones to their chests to stave off hunger during winter – until the 1850s. I read about this in an interesting book, *Modern Japanese Cuisine*, by Katarzyna Cwiertka, who argues that though the Japanese revere it as an ancient art, the kaiseki we know today was created by two twentieth-century chefs, Kitaoji Rosanjin and Yuki Teiichi, and given economic and social impetus by the post-war economic boom and food television. Modern kaiseki's roots could, then, be said to be about as deep and meaningful as Trick or Treat, but never mind.

Today Kyoto's finest kaiseki restaurants are housed in ancient wooden villas, mostly in the eastern temple district, and surrounded by some of the most extraordinary gardens in the world. Their tatami rooms are graced with priceless wall hangings and ceramics, and meals are served on porcelain and lacquer ware that can be hundreds of years old, and valued at millions of yen. The ingredients used are no less rarefied. As Shizuo Tsuji writes in *A Simple Art*, when the Japanese talk about seasonal ingredients, this can sometimes refer to a type of produce that is available for just a couple of weeks – sea-cucumber roe, for instance: the sea cucumber spawns only once a year and its roe has to be eaten at the peak of freshness. These are some of the ingredients kaiseki chefs value most highly of all.

The plates and bowls will change with, and evoke, the season too, often obliquely. To give you some idea of what the outsider is up against in trying to decode a kaiseki meal, the bowl the soup is served in might be a copy of another more famous bowl, the reference being the season the *original* bowl references.

To experience a kaiseki meal was one of my abiding ambitions. But not only are most Kyoto kaiseki restaurants fearfully expensive, many have an unwritten 'no foreigners' policy, and others are closed even to most Japanese, apart from invited guests. But Murata is unusual among the world of kaiseki masters in that he has, over the years, built a public profile in Japan and beyond, appearing on television and publishing books. He had, I also knew, trained in France in his early years, before taking over Kikunoi from his father (who had inherited it from his father), and had a more relaxed attitude to kaiseki traditions. He was the first kaiseki chef to use a food processor, for example, which even today is felt by some to be sacrilegious – part of the essence of kaiseki being the effort that goes into its preparation. The more hard-core kaiseki chefs only serve raw or cold food, but Murata serves hot dishes and meat, including duck and foie gras. He calls his restaurant 'a culinary amusement park for adults'.

There are some Japanese who say that kaiseki can never be properly understood by outsiders, that the symbolism, the references within references, the 'humour', the intricate appreciation of the seasons and the tiny portions are beyond our ken, but if I wanted to learn more about kaiseki, Murata was my best chance.

Lissen and I agreed that it would be testing Asger and Emil's patience beyond reasonable endurance to expect them to sit through a contemplative dinner lasting several hours, plus they probably wouldn't do much for the restaurant's serenity levels so, as we had no babysitter I would dine alone (believe me, of all my self-indulgent dinners during our time in Japan, this was the one I had to barter most heavily with Lissen for; the starting point for negotiations being that she and I would return together some day). It was a misty, steamy evening as I made my way to Higashiyama, the temple district in the eastern part of Kyoto, my taxi passing the famous twelve-hundred-year-old To-ji temple, featured in many a Kurosawa film, on the way. The low clouds touched the rooftops, hugging the base of the hills that enclose the city and, with the tourist hoards gone for the day, the only sound as I walked through the flagstoned alley-ways was the calling of crows and the chirruping cicadas.

As I arrived at the large, ornate wooden building, an Australian woman, clearly overawed by the occasion, had misunderstood the doorman's invitation to remove her shoes, and was attempting to enter the restaurant on her knees. The restaurant staff rushed, embarrassed, to help the poor woman to her feet. There but for the grace of God go I, I thought to myself. Kaiseki has an intimidating reputation for elaborate ritual and etiquette, which I was almost certain to fall foul of during the course of the evening.

I was shown into a large tatami room with wooden beams, an elaborately woven wooden ceiling and beige clay walls. There was just one low, red lacquer table at the far end of the room and a floor seat – just a back and base, no legs. I was to be the sole diner. I creaked down into place and sat, imbibing the stillness, looking out through the large plate-glass window over the moonlit courtyard, the air conditioning humming gently in the background.

I was already feeling pleasantly relaxed as a young waitress in a kimono poured me a sake. It was Kikunoi's own, delicate yet full of nuanced floral flavours, the best I had ever tasted. She returned moments later carrying a woven basket. She lifted the lid, inside was an ayu fish, a small river fish at the height of its season. It flapped around, glistening, fresh and alive. The waitress indicated the ayu and I would meet again during the course of the evening, put the lid back on, and left.

My next visitor was an older woman, immaculately coiffed. She introduced herself in English as Mrs Murata, the chef's wife. 'This is a special room,' she said, smiling calmly. 'We call it the bridge, just like the bridge of a ship. You can see everything coming and going from here. In the spring the front garden is full of cherry blossom. You must come back then.'

I would love to, I said. We chatted about children, and the seasons, which she said were the beginning and end of Kikunoi's cuisine. We talked too about her husband, who she clearly adored, then she bowed and left me to enjoy my meal.

The first course of a kaiseki meal, the sakizuke, is, according to Murata, the most important. 'It must be something to put the diner at ease,' he writes in his book. Mine was a walnut tofu with Delaware grapes, tiny shiso flowers and a dashi en gelée – thickened with some kuzu root to a light paste. The walnuts brought a welcome crunch to the cool, fresh tofu, while a touch of raw wasabi added a playful zing. It was soothing and stimulating, and gone all too quickly.

The hassan, or second course, is 'an overture to establish the seasonal theme' – in this case a dashi with chrysanthemum leaves floating on the surface. As I write this some weeks later, I can still conjure the aroma of the clear dashi, lightened by yuzu juice, with its spongy piece of hamo (pike conger, technically a fish though closely resembling an eel, which must be sliced twenty times per inch with a special knife to cut its many bones into edible sizes), a slice of the rare and expensive matsutake mushroom – sometimes called Japanese truffle, rich and woody – and a golden crescent of solid egg custard within. It was autumn in a bowl, and at the bottom were pieces of toasted rice that must have been added literally as the bowl went out of the kitchen door to retain their crispness. Sashimi; lightly grilled barracuda sushi; consommé; duck breast marinated in koji (the fermenting agent added to sake); chestnut rice; and pickles all followed in leisurely succession, slowly stretching my belt like the ring around a bulging barrel. Each course – and these were just some that I ate that evening – was rigorously constructed, immaculately plated, pretty and full of compelling flavours and textures.

One course was yet more entrancing still. It came contained within a bamboo cricket cage. I lifted the cage to find a cube of hamo, alongside another cube of eel-roe cake (looking like a chunk of omelette but with a mealy texture and mildly fishy flavour), with chewy, bittersweet sake-glazed gingko nuts and a grilled chestnut the size of a golf ball. Placed on top were a couple of what looked at first glance like pine needles, but were in fact delicate, thin green tea noodles. Salted ayu entrails were stuffed into a hollowed out sudachi (a type of citrus) alongside. In his book Murata-san writes of this dish that he wanted to 'evoke a little of the sad and sentimental feeling we have for departing friends,' in this case the crickets leaving as autumn arrives. This kind of sentiment, inspired by the passing of the seasons, is characteristic of kaiseki and can equally apply to a new ingredient. Of another dish he writes, 'I hope to evoke a feeling of picnicking under cherry trees on a regal crimson carpet, while watching the delicate pink petals fluttering elegantly to earth.' Hard to imagine Gordon Ramsay writing something like that, isn't it?

The ayu fish turned up later, incidentally, salted, grilled whole and threaded through a skewer in an 'S' shape, as if leaping across the waves.

The next day I had arranged for a precious hour with Murata-san himself, back at Kikunoi. I was shown into a large meeting room overlooking the front yard and decorated, somewhat incongruously, with mid-nineteenth century French antiques. Murata entered, a stocky man with short, wavy black hair and a lived-in, walnutty face. I had been expecting a severe, humourless Zen master type but Murata-san was relaxed and informal. He smiled warmly and invited me to sit opposite him.

I thanked him for the meal the previous evening, and we talked a little about some of the dishes I had eaten and their ingredients. I wanted to know if he thought Kyoto was still the pre-eminent food city in Japan. I knew he had opened a restaurant in Tokyo, so I wondered if Kyoto wasn't perhaps rather too stuck in its past to be relevant today?

'Yes, Kyoto is still the best,' he said, as if there were no question. 'The level of quality is actually low in Tokyo. It is too easy to have a success there, there are too many people. We only opened there to be able to serve authentic Japanese cuisine there because they didn't have it and it is the gateway to the world, like Paris is for France.'

I knew that as a young man in the early seventies Murata had served an apprenticeship in Paris. What was that like? His smile vanished. 'I soon learned that the French knew nothing about Japanese food. They laughed at me. They said Japanese food was never a proper meal, just food. Even today I sometimes can't like the French. I think they are a little crazy, but in a way everything started for me there.'

I thought of my friend Toshi, who had experienced similar chauvinism some decades later. Having trained in France and Japan, how did Murata compare the two nation's cuisines? 'For me, the difference between Japanese and French cooking comes down to this: in Japanese cooking we think the ingredients are a gift from God and we try not to change them too much; we think a daikon is in its ultimate form as it is. It seems to me that often French chefs want to change the things they cook with, to put their own mark on them.' In other words, in Japan the chefs work with what God provides, in France the chefs think they are God. Murata echoes this in his book: 'When I was young I thought it was my job to always add another taste dimension to every ingredient. But these days I find that approach a little arrogant. The real work of the chef is to coax out the fundamental taste that is innate to any ingredient.'

Murata put it another way which, for me, distilled the essential difference between Japanese and Western cooking: 'In haute cuisine you cook by adding or layering flavours of different ingredients in complex ways; in Japan, and particularly in Kyoto where we cook mostly with vegetables, the aim is to extract the essential flavour of each ingredient by removing those we don't particularly want, like bitterness. Japanese cuisine is a cuisine of subtraction.'

153

It must be gratifying that the world is starting to take notice of kaiseki, I said. 'Yes, indeed, very, because I hadn't expected to reach the point where the world is watching with deep interest. They are starting to realise that Japanese cooking fits well into a civilised era, it uses many ingredients in small volume, just a thousand calories for an entire meal. This has been my life's work.' He sat back in his chair with a broad smile.

Right now kaiseki is the hottest restaurant trend in New York, but can it conquer the world? 'I see some possibilities but kaiseki doesn't use oil or grease and the food is extremely lean. It will be rather complicated to bring it to a wider audience. You need to eat a certain quantity of a food to understand, to appreciate it, for your senses to adjust. As when you eat truffle for the first time, you don't really understand the flavours. The first time people eat kaiseki food they do not notice the tastiness. It took some years for uncooked fish to be eaten in the West, for you to discover how tasty it can be. Right now kaiseki is too subtle, I think, for Western palates. Think about wasabi. That was a taste that you had to acquire. In Japan we had to learn to like bread. At the start we used to sweeten it with bean paste, we thought French bread was too crispy, so we made it softer to suit our palates.

'And then there are the cultural differences,' Murata continued. 'Once in America I was invited to a Japanese meal. I was served yakitori, sushi, teriyaki, and they said that was kaiseki! NO, I said, that is not kaiseki. For kaiseki you must have two elements: nourishment for body and mind, and the seasonal element.'

At times the meal I had enjoyed the night before had veered close to the transformative theatricality of 'molecular' cuisine. I knew that kaiseki had directly influenced the multi-course style of meal pioneered in the West by French chefs like Joël Robuchon, which the molecular chefs have in turn taken to an extreme, but I wondered if Murata-san saw any parallels.

'Ferran Adrià is a good friend, he has been here of course. He is a genius. But for me food is either delicious or not, interesting or not. My philosophy is to do anything I can to bring pleasure to my guests, regardless of whatever category of cooking other people call it, and I think Adrià is the same. If he thinks it will delight his guests to use liquid nitrogen, then I can not argue. If I have to stand upside down, then so be it. Although, obviously I can't,' he laughed. 'I have to say, he makes tempura at -270°C but I still think authentic tempura tastes better and for me taste comes before surprise. Saying that, in order to pass down traditions you need to protect some things but to break from traditions too. I am cooking for my guests not for me, or for posterity. I am not interested in acclaim.'

As we talked, behind him, in the courtyard below, I could see his many chefs scampering to and fro carrying pots and plates. No one walked, everyone trotted. Later, after proudly showing me his new, state-of-the-art kitchen ('All Japanese') Murata-san introduced me to Derek Wilcox, a young American intern who had been working at Kikunoi for six months. 'It has been tougher than I ever imagined,' he told me, looking a little shell-shocked. 'I work from six in the morning to midnight every day without a break.' I half expected him to slip me a note saying, 'Please help me, they are holding me hostage.' What kept him going? 'Sometimes I really don't know. I think it's about how deep the education is – you learn everything here from simple home cooking to the most sophisticated exotic ingredients. Murata-san is so open to young chefs. It can take decades to learn this stuff. For the first year, all I do is clean up, wash dishes, wash towels, scrub the bathroom in the dorm, prepare vegetables, gut and scale fish – some days I do over a hundred fish. But I decided Kyoto was the best place to come to learn to cook.'

The night before, I had left Kikunoi in the late evening. The air was humid. I took a deep draft of the smell of fresh rainfall and damp pine. The alleys of Higashiyama were deserted and dark. If it hadn't been for the glow of the soft yellow street lights I might have been walking through the city in the fifteenth century on my way to an assignation with an obliging geisha or to be ritually disembowelled by a samurai for some or other breach of chopstick etiquette.

I turned a corner and arrived at a great, four-storey pagoda lit only by lanterns and candles. I stood still. It took my breath away and I think, perhaps only fleetingly, I glimpsed something of the spirit of Kyoto that night.

Chapter 22

First take your crystal clear, free-flowing mountain stream . . .

If nagashi-somen didn't exist, then a visiting food writer prone to romantic flights of fancy would be forced to invent it. It is a unique and improbable dish that few people even in Japan have tried, though most have heard of it; a near-mythical meal that is symbolic of the purity, simplicity and natural harmony that Japanese cuisine so often strives to achieve.

Here is how it works (because nagashi-somen is very much a 'how it works' dish, as opposed to a 'how to make' dish): The chef boils some somen noodles, ultra-thin (around 1.3mm uncooked) wheat noodles made with a little sesame oil and dried in long, thin bunches like rope, the Japanese equivalent of vermicelli or spaghettini. When they are ready he drops them, in small servings, into a nearby, fast-flowing mountain river. The noodles travel downstream becoming chilled by the glacial water along the way and, as they pass by, diners, sitting on wooden platforms called yuka over the water, pluck them from the stream with their chopsticks, dip them in a sauce and eat. It sounded like an unlikely fast-food delivery system, and not without its health and safety issues.

I told Asger and Emil about nagashi-somen and they did a 'Yeah, so?' shrug and continued playing with their new eternal bubble-wrap toys (the kind of playfully nihilistic gizmo only the Japanese could invent). A month and a half had left them blasé about such oddball culinary practices. What was so weird about picking your dinner out of a river?

The fresh, clear, clean, soft water that flows from the mountains that surround Kyoto is an essential ingredient for its renowned and mineral-rich tofu, as well as its excellent sake, the tea ceremonies and the dashi that is the foundation of kaiseki. I knew that there was a nagashi-somen restaurant close to the city from one of the dozens of guide books I had read before our journey, but I had left that particular one back in Europe. I spent some fruitless days asking everyone who ought to know where it might be until, in the end, I did begin to wonder if the whole concept wasn't just a myth propagated by the city's tourist and water boards. But then came a chance meeting with an elderly kimono dealer in one of the city's atmospheric old machiya, wooden houses built narrow but deep to circumvent the sixteenth-century shop frontage tax. We'd gone to browse for vintage kimonos, a project which I naively thought might take an hour or so, but which ended up lasting the best part of a morning. As you can imagine, there are an awful lot of vintage kimonos in Kyoto, and I think I must have offered my considered opinion on a good number of them, while Asger and Emil slowly imploded with boredom.

But there was one silver lining: one of the kimono vendors managed to interpret my drawings of how I imagined a nagashi-somen restaurant might look. It turned out that one of only two nagashi-somen restaurants that she knew of in Japan was in a small onsen town called Kurama Kibune, in the hills outside of Kyoto. She wrote the restaurant's name – Hirobun – in both kanji characters and English and gave me detailed directions. We had to catch a train from the north-eastern part of the city, get off at a station close to the end of the line and walk uphill. There was only one road, which ran alongside a river towards the Kibune Shrine (dedicated to the god of water), she said. It wasn't far from the station.

This was late September, the very end of the nagashi-somen season, she warned. She gave Hirobun a call just to check they would be open and discovered that it was due to close for the winter the next day. This was our last chance to taste nagashi-somen.

We hurried to the nearest metro for the ride across Kyoto to take the local train up into the deep green, pine-covered mountains to the north. After an hour or so, we got off where the kimono seller had told us, at the station by the Kibune-Gawa River. The station master there told us it was just a five-minute walk to the nagashi-somen restaurant. 'Keep to the road beside the river,' he said, somewhat unnecessarily as there was only one road, lined on the other side with impenetrable jungle.

This is where things started to go awry. 'Five minutes! We can walk that, no problem,' I said gamely. 'Are you sure, Michael? It is quite a steep hill, and there's no pavement,' said Lissen. Asger and Emil were too preoccupied with a large, now dead, hairy caterpillar they had found on the road to argue, and so we started walking, me a few metres ahead whistling a cheery hiking tune.

What was supposed to be a recreational family lunch outing soon turned into something rather more challenging, up a one in three incline on a forest road strewn with the corpses of poisonous snakes and overhung with branches woven with the webs of spiders of a size I had never previously seen beyond the confines of a zoo.

We walked for over an hour – the shallow, sparkling river taunting our thirst – pausing every few minutes initially to let Emil and Asger catch up, but then, after a while, to let me catch up. It had been some years since I'd tried to walk up a hill, particularly in humidity such as this. From time to time we were forced to jump into the undergrowth by rampaging buses whose timetables and stops remained a taunting enigma. I started to whimper, and I could sense Lissen's mounting irritation at yet another arduous lunch pilgrimage, but Asger and Emil were happy enough poking the dead snakes.

We spotted civilisation amid the pine trees ahead. We climbed further until we eventually came to an onsen hotel and restaurant complex. But it was not our restaurant. Naturally, Hirobun would turn out to be the very last in the village, a further twenty minutes hike uphill. Along the way we passed about a dozen seductive, wooden restaurants and hotels many with wooden platforms over the river, decorated with soft glowing red lanterns and peopled by happy, relaxed diners and waitresses in lavish kimonos.

Finally we came to Hirobun. I looked down to the platform over the river in the valley below. It was empty but the waitress still sucked her teeth doubtfully as they are taught to do at waitress school. She wasn't sure whether she could fit us in. She disappeared into the kitchen to ask the owner, reappearing a while after to show us, grudgingly, to our table. At last, we were going to try nagashi-somen – to commune with the mighty spirit of the mountain river.

We descended a steep flight of wooden steps down the river bank, passing a small bamboo hut, like an outhouse. We sat on the tatami platform suspended a foot or so over the shallow riverbed, beside the mossy rocks of the bank. In front of us was an open zinc gutter. It led from the wooden outhouse, down to the platform where it continued along a narrow counter in a loop in front the diners' seats.

As it turned out, rather than being dropped by the chef directly into the river for us to pluck as they flowed by, as if we were blessed visitors in some sylvan Arcadia, our noodles would be dumped into the gutter by the waitress just a couple of metres away, hiding out of sight in the hut.

It was something of an anticlimax. The waitress stuck her head round the corner of the hut to tell us to prepare for noodle launch. It was at that point, just as the first noodles rushed down-gutter towards us, catching us all by surprise, that I realised that I was sitting furthest downstream from the source of the noodles, with three other very hungry people, none of them renowned for their restraint at mealtimes, ahead of me. Needless to say, I spent most of lunch scrambling for leftovers. It soon became apparent that nagashi-somen has another flaw: the more wet noodles come your way, the more you dip into your sauce, and the more the sauce becomes diluted, so that, after a few mouthfuls, you ended up dipping watery noodles in even more watery sauce. But by that stage we all just wanted to fill our groaning stomachs, and it was at least a quick and efficient delivery system.

The last bundle of noodles was pink and ume-, or pickled plum-flavoured, which our waitress had said would indicate our meal was over. 'That was great!' said Asger. 'Every dinner should be like that. They should do burgers like that, and everything.'

Chapter 23

The Sake Crisis

The Japanese sake industry is in crisis. Consumption of what was for centuries the country's most popular alcoholic drink, so integral to the economy that it was used as a tax substitute and its industry run by the government, is in decline, and has been for years. The Japanese now drink just over a third the amount of sake they did thirty years ago – 700,000 kilolitres compared to 1.7m in 1975. Instead, beer has been the drink of choice for the majority of Japanese since 1965, with wine rapidly on the ascendant too – both are now produced with varying degrees of success domestically (Japanese beer: terrific. Japanese wine: I've tasted it, so you don't have to).

Sake breweries are closing up and down the land (down from 30,000 a century ago to just 1,450 today), with many more facing bankruptcy. Making sake is a tough, labour intensive, low profit business and young members of the Japanese workforce would rather work in offices and shops than slave in uncomfortable conditions making a drink no one wants any more. The skills of the master sake brewer are in danger of disappearing for ever. The world of the sake brewery is one of the most traditional, hierarchical and chauvinistic in this most traditional, hierarchical and chauvinistic country. Until very recently – and still to this day in some cases – sake breweries were run more along the lines of a monastery than a business, closed to the outside world and suspicious of innovation.

Which makes it all the more improbable that my two sake contacts turned out to be an Englishman and a woman. We'll meet the Englishman first, because he gave me my first real introduction to the intriguing world of sake, a baptism of firewater.

Philip Harper and I had arranged to meet in a vast sports hall an hour or so outside of Hiroshima. I could already smell the sake in the car park, the sweet, yeasty aromas of rice wine wafting gently on the breeze. Inside the fumes were almost overpowering as Japan's best sake producers displayed their wares and tasted each others. The hall was filled with ten rows of trestle tables sporting serried ranks of green sake bottles; each table had a long winding queue of patient sake enthusiasts – around five hundred in all – brandishing plastic tasting cups. This was the largest and most prestigious sake tasting event of the year, the National Assessment for New Sake, founded by the Sake Research Institute, itself founded by the tax department of the Ministry of Treasury in 1904.

It was clearly a serious-minded occasion. The hall was virtually silent but for the odd chink of glass and porcelain, and a symphony of staccato slurps and exaggerated sniffs. The floor, covered with plastic sheeting, was sticky with spilt sake. I joined a queue with my own plastic beaker, having spotted the only other Westerner – presumably Philip – in the room, a little ahead.

I began tasting my way up the table. Each bottle had a small dish in front of it, like an ashtray, decorated with a blue spiral and traditionally used to judge the clarity of a sake. Tasters used small plastic pipettes to pipe sake into the dish and their cups.

I tasted my first, from a bottle with a promising gold medal hanging round its neck. It was flowery and fruity with a milk-like viscosity. The second was a little sour and yeasty, not so nice. By the third sake, and from that point onwards, my only real tasting note was 'petroleum'. Apparently my palate was not all that well-equipped to appreciate the nuances of sake.

'There's no cheap stuff here!' said Philip, finally spotting me. 'We're all checking up on each other, the competition. Everyone wants to win a medal here, it is about the only acknowledgement you can get in the sake world. I have had a silver medal in the past, but nothing this year.'

I asked Philip, 42, with curly ginger hair and a plump, expressive fàce, to explain a little what was going on. 'This is the higher echelon of sakes. The rice used to make them will have been polished to thirty-five per cent.' I must have looked a little befuddled at this point, as Philip stopped suddenly.

'Do you know anything about sake?'

'I erm, uh . . .'

'OK,' he said, metaphorically rolling up his sleeves. 'Sake is graded according to how much of the rice used to make it has been polished away before fermentation. They take the rice, put it in large revolving tanks, and spin them until the outer husk of the grains is worn away. It is the single most important element of sake making. The rice used to make the sakes here will have been polished to thirty-five per cent, which is used to make the most refined type of sake. The less they polish the rice, the less refined the sake will be.'

Why was sake in such decline in Japan? I asked. 'Consumers in Japan perceive it as old-fashioned. Also there is a lovely convention with sake that you never pour for yourself, the person you are dining with should pour, but I think part of the problem is that in the corporate world this has been abused so that the new guy always has to drink until he pukes because the bosses keep pouring. It has that association for some.' Apparently, a few years ago rumours also spread – I'd guess from the beer industry – that sake gave you bad breath and was acidic on the stomach, which can't have helped.

We were tasting as we talked and, though we were spitting into aluminium bins, I was beginning to feel a little 'swimmy'. My mouth had gone slightly numb too. Philip was encouraging me to note the 'melon, honey and yeast' flavours of the sakes, but all I was getting was 'white spirit'.

'Luckily it is picking up in the States. Sake has kind of followed in the wake of sushi over there and they take it very seriously,' he said. 'Wine people are discovering sake and realising you can do things with it that you can't with wine because it isn't as acidic as wine, it doesn't mess with your stomach so much.'

As well as the degree to which the rice used to make it is polished, sake is graded on a sweetness-to-dry scale, ranging from +15 for the most dry, to -15 for the sweetest. It is slightly stronger than wine (typically fourteen to sixteen per cent alcohol, although genshu sake which isn't diluted prior to sale as other types are, boasts an alcohol content of twenty per cent). I assumed that, as with wine, there are sake snobs, and that they would prefer the dry stuff. Philip shook his head: 'There are good sakes throughout the range. Actually, I don't think there is enough snobbery about sake. It is really under appreciated in Japan.' The Japanese are famous for paying massively over the odds for French wines and Scottish whiskies, but when it comes to sake they will rarely spend more than ¥10,000 on a bottle, and even the most expensive bottle of high-grade dai gingo sake, the types being tasted here, won't cost more than ¥30,000 (£150). 'The gold medal winners here won't sell for more than ¥10,000,' Philip added. That said, true sake obsessives take their passion to extraordinary lengths: there are sake fans who devote themselves, not just to one type of sake or rice, but to one type of yeast, for example. And they are not averse to using the wine snob's florid similes; comparing one sake to 'the smell of slate when it's split,' is one of Philip's for instance.

Philip first came to Japan as an English teacher twenty years ago. There was no revelatory moment on his road to sake obsession, but he gradually grew to appreciate Japan's national drink. 'When I first came I would often drink the cheap stuff but then met some friends who were into good sake.' There was no looking back from that point; the drink became his life as he went to work at a brewery in 1991, after almost a decade becoming a toji, the master brewer – the first foreigner ever to achieve this ranking. It wasn't an easy journey: 'They all pretty much ignored me to start with, it was like joining a monastery. Early on I had one Japanese person tell me that I would never be able to taste things the way a Japanese person could. There's no point in talking to those people.'

By now my mouth was in a state of near-paralysis. 'Here, taste this. It's from Tokyo. Tokyo's known for its rather rough sake,' he said. I tasted. It was sickening – aggressively floral, cloying, acidic with more petrol aftertaste. 'Now try this one.' 'Ugh, that's not much better,' I said. 'Oh,' said Philip. 'That's mine.' I blustered about no longer being able to taste anything, but Philip was very understanding. 'Don't worry, it's not one of my best. And, you should know, this event is designed to show the sakes at their very worst – room temperature really shows their faults. If a sake tastes good at this temperature then it is really good.' That explained a lot.

I asked Philip, who has written an excellent guide to sake called *The Book of Sake*, about the myths surrounding sake. What were the most misleading? 'Some people still think it is a spirit [sake is brewed and has more in common with beer]. Then there are some that say only the best ones should be drunk cold and otherwise it should be drunk warm. Actually that's complete bollocks. There are good sakes at every temperature but even the Japanese are quite ignorant about sake. Another is that they shouldn't be aged, at least, not beyond two years, but some can be and I think aged sake will be the next big thing. Aged sake tastes a little like sherry, it's great. Unpasteurised sakes are also getting more popular – although they have to be kept refrigerated and drunk young.'

The Japanese have never really paired sakes with food in the same way that we do with wine in the West. With wine it is often the case that local food goes well with local wine, or the wine becomes an ingredient in a dish, but in Japan, though you can sometimes note regional consistencies in sake, sakes from the same town are just as likely to be different from one another depending on the type of rice used and, of course, the degree to which the rice has been polished. Shizuo Tsuji writes, firmly, that sake should never be drunk with any dishes containing rice, basing this on the flimsy logic that, as it is also made with rice, these two like poles will repel. Philip disagrees. 'Most sake goes with most food because of its umami content [it has high levels of amino acids]. People also say sake doesn't go well with Western food, but it does. Sake is packed with umami flavours – it goes particularly well with Italian food, for instance. And, you know, all those people you see drinking beer with sushi are making such a mistake. Beer goes horribly with the vinegar and sugar in sushi, but sake is brilliant with all fish. It is also nonsense that sake gives you bad hangovers.'

That was good news as, by now, having tasted over forty different sakes, I was well and truly in my cups. I bade a slurred farewell to Philip who, as we parted, gave me a contact for a brewery in Kyoto which he said might be of interest.

Sake brewing has much in common with soy and miso production – you take a crop, in this case rice, steam it, add a bacterial fermenting agent, or koji, and leave it for between a fortnight and a couple of months. Thus, you can make sake wherever there is a good supply of water (you need up to 10,000 litres in a day during the busy season; preferably with a low iron content). But the Fushimi quarter of Kyoto, on the banks of the Uji Gawa, is especially renowned for producing quality, refined sakes, largely because of its good supply of soft spring water. We happened to be staying in the city just as the brewing season started (sake is brewed in winter because it is easier to control fermentation and discourage bacteria in cool weather), so I went along to the Tama no Hikari brewery, one of seventeen breweries in this part of town, where I was met by Akira Toko, Philip's contact.

Tama no Hikari is a small, high-quality producer of a junmai ginjo sake (made with rice polished down to sixty per cent or less), founded in 1673 by the Ukita family, who still run it to this day. Akira-san, a petite, friendly woman in her early thirties, took me on a tour of the brewing plant. The rice harvest had recently finished and they had begun the polishing, the first stage of sake production. All rice starts off brown, of course (and, unfortunately for the Japanese who prefer the appearance of white rice, nearly all the vitamins and nutrients are contained in the brown husk). To make sake this brown husk is removed, layer by layer, depending, as Philip had said, on the quality of the sake that will result: the best sake is made with rice stripped down to a small, pearl-like nugget.

The noise from the five polishing machines was deafening as they churned the rice to remove, in this particular case today, forty per cent of each grain. After it is polished the rice takes a month to cool down naturally.

'Good fermentation means slow fermentation,' Akira-san shouted. 'No sugar or alcohol added. But the real secret is really good rice. We use omachi rice, which is an old type of rice which our company revived. It is difficult to grow because it grows very high and that makes it vulnerable, and the yield is low. You know, even some sake experts don't know that omachi rice was the original sake rice.'

I asked Akira-san if she agreed with Philip that there was a crisis in the sake industry. 'It's true, it is very bad economically. It's since we started getting so many more different wines to choose from about twenty years ago. Chinese sake has given it a bad name as well and sake is not cool among the young. But they are starting to appreciate it in America. If we could just get a small portion of the premium wine market over there . . .' With this in mind, the company president was leaving for the States the next day, where they hold the world's second largest sake tasting.

We passed through the bottling plant run by a man with a T-shirt with a slogan that said: 'I am getting in touch with my inner bitch.' Next we washed our hands and donned white hats to enter the brewing house and temperature-controlled seed mash rooms with walls 20cm thick.

The smell inside was wonderful: heavily sweet, sweaty and yeasty. It was the smell of fecund decay, noble rot Japanese style – in this case prompted by the addition to the steamed rice of a yellow powder, a koji, or aspergillus oryzae. This produces enzymes which turn the starch into sugar and kicks off the fermentation. 'I think making sake in the traditional way like this makes for very different flavours,' Akira-san said. 'High-quality sake needs human senses, touch, taste, smell.'

Akira-san introduced me to the toji, the man responsible for the fermentation of the rice, Masuo Kobayashi, a short, squat, stern man with forty years experience of tending mouldy rice. I asked him the secret of good sake. 'Lactic acid is the key to good flavour,' he said enigmatically (Akira-san translating), then walked off to attend to his rice. He showed me a rice mash that had been fermenting for just one day – it looked like rice that had been boiled then left to dry. But the two-day mash was already liquefying thanks to those powerful enzymes and it was beginning to smell a little more funky too. He told me that over the next two weeks it would warm to almost 40°C. Apparently, after a while, the mash begins to move in waves, all by itself, caused by the fermentation; it looks as if a sea snake were hunting beneath its surface. It produces a good deal of carbon dioxide too.

I left Tama no Hikari with a generous gift of a large bottle of their finest grade sake. It was a revelation after my tasting trauma in Hiroshima. Philip was right, it was full bodied with a satisfyingly rich umami depth and a lovely, fresh fruitiness. Perhaps I could become a sake fan after all.

Chapter 24

Beyond Sushi

It is virtually unheard of for a Japanese taxi driver to give up on a destination, but that day mine, (after twenty minutes' fruitless circling,) finally had to admit defeat, his sense of honour in tatters. He let me out and waved away the fare with a dejected shake of his head. I was on foot from here, with not much to go on.

We had been in Kyoto for over a week and I was on the trail of a culinary missing link which I had heard could be found in Higashiyama, the eastern quarter of Old Kyoto. The trouble was, no one seemed to know where, or for that matter what, Izuu was.

I'd been reading about the history of sushi. Some believe it came to Japan from Thailand, from the Mekong Delta, where locals have, for more centuries than anyone knows, used cooked rice to pack and preserve fish. The alcohol and acids created when the rice started to go mouldy killed off any bacteria in the fish, which meant it could be kept for months. The fish itself was rendered a stinking mush, but at least it wouldn't kill you and, besides, decomposing fish is not to be sniffed at: from the Roman sauce, garum, made from rotting anchovies, to modern day Vietnamese *muoc mam* and other related fish sauces from South East Asia, fermented fish create what we now recognise as powerfully umami-packed flavours. From Thailand the practice of preserving fish in rice spread to China, where it appears ultimately not to have caught on, and then, in the eighth century – along with so much from its western neighbour – it travelled to Japan.

Here, possibly around Lake Biwa, close to Kyoto, locals discovered that the lactic fermentation of the rice added a pleasantly acidic

171

touch to their muddy-flavoured freshwater fish. The dish was called nare-zushi (the 'z' and 's' in sushi seem to be interchangeable), and can still be enjoyed in the villages close to the lake, where these days it is called funa-zushi. Funa are carp, which in this case are pickled with rice during spawning time, their eggs still *in situ*, and left for six months before the rice is discarded. The dish is sometimes referred to as 'Japanese fish cheese' and, I'd guess, is one of those acquired tastes few rush to acquire.

As historian Naomichi Ishige put it, when recounting sushi's evolution, 'Impatience is often counted a Japanese trait.' After some years enjoying nare-zushi, the Japanese decided that they couldn't wait for the lactic process to run its course and at some point in the fifteenth century they started to eat the fish earlier, discovering that the rice – previously too rotten to eat – was edible too and tasted rather good.

The next step in sushi's development came with the discovery of rice vinegar in the seventeenth century. Rice vinegar allowed cooks to add tanginess to the rice without having to wait for it to ferment. This they called haya-zushi, or 'quick sushi', which they made using stones to press the fish on top of rice in a large box, before cutting the resulting 'cake' into smaller rectangular pieces.

By the late eighteenth and early nineteenth centuries Tokyo, then called Edo, had usurped Kyoto as the capital of Japan, becoming the largest, most populous city on earth in the process. A series of fires, however, threatened the future of the world's first conurbation, and so open flames were banned in restaurants and the city's burgeoning fast food industry was virtually wiped out overnight. To the rescue came sushi, which could be assembled without need of a flame. Of course, the fish served with sushi in those days was unlikely to have been raw – there being no refrigeration – but it was a simple matter for sushi chefs to lightly poach, pickle or grill their fish before bringing it into the city to add to the vinegared rice.

Tokyo's nineteenth-century workers, much like their descendants today, were time poor. Noren, the curtains that traditionally hang at the entrance to sushi restaurants, date from this time, for example, and were originally there for customers to wipe their hands on as they hurried in and out, an especially filthy noren being a sign of a good restaurant. Once in, customers needed to be fed in double-quick time and so, in the late nineteenth century, a local Edo chef called Yohei Hanaya came up with the idea of squeezing the rice into blocks by hand and topping them with fish as the orders came in. Nigiri means 'to squeeze', sushi refers to the vinegared rice – it is, as I'm sure you know nothing to do with raw fish – and thus nigiri sushi, sometimes still referred to as Edomae sushi after its home city, was born.

Meanwhile, back in Kyoto one of the great schisms of Japanese cuisine was unfolding. As well as deciding to put more sugar in the sushi rice than Tokyo chefs do – as we also tend to do in the west – Kyotoites had developed their own type of 'pressed' sushi, not unlike the original haya-zushi. When making this so called saba-zushi – or pressed mackerel sushi – they took this usually highly perishable fish and first briefly salt-cured it, then lightly pickled it in sugared vinegar, placed it on top of some rice, and wrapped the lot in simmered konbu and then packed it in foot-long bamboo logs. As with a ceviche, the acid in the vinegar slightly 'cooked' the mackerel, which was useful in a landlocked city half a day's journey from the sea.

But while nigiri and maki conquered the world, saba-zushi, and its Osakan cousin, oshi-zushi – a similar kind of pressed sushi made in cedar boxes – remained local delicacies only, slowly declining in popularity even in their home cities as the invention of refrigeration negated the need to pickle fish to preserve it.

It was this pressed, heavily vinegared saba-zushi I was in search of – the historic, hard core, über sushi, if you like. The most famous saba-zushi restaurant in Kyoto is Izuu, which opened in 1781. How anyone ever finds the less famous saba-zushi restaurants is beyond me, as no one seemed to know where Izuu was. In the end, one of the legion of helpful pathfinding strangers I was to encounter during our months in Japan came to my rescue. A skinny young man in a dark, shiny suit carrying a Hello Kitty manbag kindly led me to a small wooden-beamed building, both windowless and nameless. There, he parted the clean, white noren, and smiled expectantly.

I felt obliged to invite him to join me, not for a moment expecting him to agree, but he eagerly accepted. Inside, the restaurant looked like something from feudal era Kyoto with rough wooden furniture, paper screens and a slate floor. A heavily made-up lady in a kimono sat in a booth on the left, and gestured that we should take a table. The only other diners were an aged Japanese couple, who stopped eating and eyed us suspiciously as I bowed and smiled my way to our table.

My dining companion told me his name was Haruki.

'Ah, like the writer!' I said. He looked perplexed.

'Marukami! You know, *Norwegian Wood*?'

'No,' said Haruki, thinking for a moment.

I let it go. 'Nice umbrella,' I said. He beamed.

'Herro Kitty! You know? I rub it!'

'You *rub* it . . . ? Ah, you *love* it!'

'Yes, rub it!'

I didn't like to mention that where I come from Hello Kitty was particularly popular with ten-year-old girls and a certain type of gay ma . . .

Oh.

In my excitement at having finally found Izuu I had, it seemed, been a little naive. At the risk of sounding like one of those racists who protests that he has a friend whose neighbour is black, I really do have many gay friends, but I have to admit that at this point I did shuffle slightly away from Haruki, who had eschewed the chair opposite and sat close enough beside me that I could smell his Calvin Klein aftershave.

He asked where I was from, whether I liked Japan and Japanese food, how long I had been in Japan – the usual questionnaire. And then . . .

'I rike you!' said Haruki, gripping my thigh and flashing a smile.

I laughed nervously. 'Shall we order?' I said.

After a short wait, our saba-zushi arrived on a blue-patterned porcelain plate. It was a sizeable cross-sliced log, almost a foot long, of densely packed rice topped with mackerel and wrapped in glistening, dark green konbu.

'Is there no soy or wasabi?' I asked.

'No, no,' Haruki shook his head. 'Saba-zushi no soy, no wasabi.'

Saba-zushi is eaten unadorned, he explained, picking imaginary lint from my shoulder. All the better to appreciate the acidic rice and delicate, oily fish. It made sense. Soy would be too heavy a flavour to compete; wasabi too much of a challenge to a palate already coping with the vinegar.

I asked what Haruki did for a living and he explained that he was a host in a bar close by. For women, he added, raising his eyebrows conspiratorially. It is quite common in Japanese cities for young professional women to pay to go to bars where pretty young men like Haruki flatter them, ask them about their lives and make them laugh.

'We not do sex,' he said, suddenly serious. 'It just fun.'

I asked the name of the bar. 'Explessions.' And did he like his work? It must be frustrating meeting all those girls but not being allowed to date them. 'I rub it!' he said, one of his feet brushing mine under the table.

I turned my attention to the saba-zushi. The rice was the star of the dish – it was the finest-quality short-grain rice, each grain as wide as it was long, probably koshihikari, soft on the outside with a slightly resistant core to give bite, glinting and lucent. The fish was excellent too, a muted rainbow ranging from pale rose to deep purple to light brown.

I had a misunderstanding with the elderly waitress/cashier at this point. At first I thought she was gesturing at me from her kiosk *not* to eat the soft konbu the sushi was wrapped in. Then, when she saw I was leaving it on the side of my plate, she seemed to be encouraging me to eat it. I looked over to the elderly couple who instantly averted what had until that moment been a fixed gaze in our direction. By now their were sipping their tea and I noticed all their konbu had gone. I ate some of mine. It was leathery and sticky, a bit like eating fly paper, but almost certainly very healthy. Haruki left his to one side, gently nibbling at tiny morsels of rice as I shovelled whole lumps of fish, rice and konbu down.

I have to say, saba-zushi was pretty fantastic – that bit sweeter, more vinegary and fishy-in-a-nice-way than conventional nigiri. Izuu sells it to go in the form of one giant, foot-long log for ¥4,400 a piece. If I lived nearby it would be my Saturday treat of choice, at home, by the TV, as opposed to snuggled up with Haruki in Explessions.

I made a motion to pay, but Haruki took the bill. 'I like practise Engrish,' he said. Then, shuffling closer, 'I like you.'

'No, no,' I said. 'Please let me pay.' But he had already unfurled some notes, around ¥5,000, or £25.

As we left Izuu it became quite clear that Haruki had no intention of letting me walk off into the sunset. I had mentioned my wife and children, and toyed meaningfully with my wedding ring, but I can only imagine that my mesmeric sexual allure had entranced him as it has so many unfortunate lost souls – he certainly hadn't taken the hint.

'Well, now, I have to be going I'm afraid. I have an appointment um, over there.' I pointed vaguely up the road.

'OK,' said Haruki, and started to walk with me.

'Where are you going?'

'I come with you, it's OK.'

'Oh no, don't worry, I can find my way.'

'No, no. I come with.'

The truth was I was still hungry and, not for the first time in Japan (or elsewhere, come to that), alone and without Lissen to reign in my gluttony, I had thought I might try to squeeze in a second lunch that day. I had something in mind, just a little snack really, but it required that I shake off Haruki, if only to conceal my shame at my own greed. How could I ever explain to a Japanese person the notion that someone might be capable of consuming two lunches? I would have hated to spoil his impression of me. He would have been crushed. But how to escape?

I suddenly stopped walking and, pretending I had seen someone a couple of hundred yards ahead, I started to wave and shout.

'Hey, Lissen!' I shouted. Then to Haruki: 'That's my wife, I just saw my wife up there, I must run and catch her.' Haruki looked confused. 'My wife, I just saw her disappear around that corner. You wait here, I'll run and get her. I'd love you two to meet. Wait there,' I said, my hands firmly placed on each of his shoulders. 'I'll be back in just a second. You wait there,' I shouted over my shoulder as I ran. I turned the corner and didn't stop running until I got to the metro station, where I ran down the steps and boarded the first train north.

I did feel terribly guilty, but you must understand that I really, really wanted that second lunch. Kyoto is the undisputed tofu capital of Japan, and Toshi had warned me that I would regret it for the rest of my life if I didn't eat in a local tofu restaurant.

Until the seventeenth century tofu was a luxury dish enjoyed mainly by noblemen, which is odd as it is a relatively simple food, made from cheap ingredients. It is made by soaking soya beans, then boiling them and squeezing their milk out. To the milk a coagulant of some kind is added – be it magnesium chloride, which the Japanese call nigari; magnesium sulfate, better known as Epsom Salts; or calcium sulphate, also known as gypsum and particularly rich in calcium. The liquid is then poured into cheese cloth-lined moulds to set.

Tofu is rich, not just in protein from the soybeans (pound for pound it has more protein than meat, in fact), but also iron, vitamins B1 and E, zinc, potassium, magnesium and calcium. It is said to lower blood pressure, slow the ageing process and be good for one's bones. It also contains oligosaccharides, a type of 'simple sugar' which is excellent for promoting healthy bacteria in the gut, preventing constipation and lowering blood pressure.

Depending on how finely the tofu is strained, whether or not it is pressed, the result is either momen-dofu, or 'cotton tofu' which is firm and stands up better to cooking, or the finer, lighter kinu-goshi-dofu, or 'silk tofu' – a slight misnomer as it isn't actually strained through silk. According to Shizuo Tsuji, if you can't get hold of tofu then 'calves brains are remarkably similar'. He's right, in a way, at least in terms of texture; good-quality sweetbreads also have something of the same, loose jelly density and melt-in-the-mouth texture, but the flavours are hardly comparable.

As with the sake, the tofu is especially good in Kyoto, because of the city's endless supply of fresh, soft mountain water – the quality of the water used in its making being the most important determinant of good tofu. Close to the famous Nanzen-ji shrine, on the very eastern edge of the city where majestic, swoopy-roofed temples emerge from the forested hills, is one of the city's most famous tofu restaurants, Okutan, housed in a large, wooden thatched hall, dating back over three and a half centuries and surrounded by customarily serene gardens. I left my shoes in the rack outside and was shown to a place on the tatami floor by a low table. The restaurant, which was full even late in the lunch service, serves only tofu dishes, so I ordered their classic tofu hotpot and some dengaku. The hotpot arrived within a couple of minutes, piping hot and featuring luscious cubes of tofu, the texture of crème caramel and served with small side dishes of spring onion, ginger and soy. Picking ectoplasmic tofu from a cauldron of hot water is surely the ultimate test of chopstick technique and, I must say, as I glanced in embarrassment around the room, I could see a number of Japanese people were struggling too.

The dengaku was easier to handle. In this dish tofu is skewered on double pronged wooden skewers – the name comes from the Japanese for stilt-walker, whose legs the skewers evoke – coated with white miso and grilled. The fresh, clean tofu is the perfect foil for the fruity, nutty, salty miso. Actually tofu is the perfect foil for all sorts of assertive flavours, although a little fine grated ginger, spring onion or katsuobushi is all the dressing you need for really good, fresh tofu, served chilled in summer.

The golden rule with tofu is that it must be eaten the day it is made, like a baguette, otherwise the flavour turns stale. This, I think, explains the bad rap tofu has in the West, where it has become synonymous with flavourless piety food for sanctimonious vegans. It perhaps also explains tofu's declining popularity in Japan where small, local tofu makers have been going out of business over the last few years. Tofu used to be delivered to households daily, as milk once was in the UK, but that tradition has been lost in most cities.

As I left Okutan, my hunger sated, at least for now, something really rather terrible happened. I turned left onto the street, planning to head towards the nearby shrine, and walked straight into Haruki. Of all people. I did say this was a small town, but what were the odds of bumping into the same person, at random, during the same day and why do I never beat those kinds of odds when I play lotteries? (Then again, I can actually better this: back in Tokyo, some hours after we had shared lunch at Mrs Shinobu's, I had passed the journalist from *Time* magazine on the zebra crossing outside Shibuya Station – it's the one in *Lost in Translation*, the busiest crossing in the world.) Haruki looked as surprised to meet me as I was inwardly dismayed to meet him.

'Where you go, Michael?' He asked in a hurt tone.

'I . . . I . . . I tried to find you, but you had disappeared. Where did you go?' Attack, I felt instinctively, being the best form of defence.

'I waited for you. Where you wife? I look for you. I went Izuu.'

'Oh, I am so sorry, Haruki. I don't understand . . .'

'You were eat Okutan?' he looked more confused than ever.

'Wha . . . oh, you mean that restaurant? Oh, no, no, ha, ha, eat?

179

No, I was just . . . I was looking. Is that the time? I really have to go. So sorry about earlier, thank you again for lunch.' And with that, I spotted an open taxi door and dived in headfirst, deeply ashamed of myself, but at least now full.

Chapter 25

The fastest food in the world

Which of these useful Osakan-defining trivia facts are true, and which are false?

i   In Osaka the conveyor belts in sushi restaurants move fourteen
    per cent faster than they do in Tokyo.
ii Osakans walk faster than anyone else in the world at 1.6 metres
    per second, compared to 1.56 m/sec in Tokyo.
iii The coin slots on public transport ticket machines are wider than
    anywhere else in Japan, so that they can get the coins in faster.
iv A customary greeting is, 'Are you making any money?'
v   It is the convention to stand on the right while riding on escala-
    tors; everywhere else in Japan, you stand on the left.
vi The fastest fast food in the world was invented in Osaka.
v   Osaka has a GDP equivalent to Switzerland's.

Answer: all of the above are true. (Even the escalator thing: which
means, presumably, that there is some point between Osaka and
Kyoto where people switch sides, which in turn begs the question,
how do they know where it is? Is there an official dividing line? Or
is there some kind of razor-wired escalator no-man's-land?)

Osakans are the most frenetic, impatient, contrary, mercantile
people in Japan. They make Tokyoites look like slackers and, perhaps
as a result, their city rarely features on tourists' itineraries – the city
has virtually no historic sights, few museums, and consists almost
entirely of featureless high-rises, endless arcades and densely packed
side streets. Nevertheless, I had been looking forward to coming to

Osaka perhaps more than any other city in Japan, and could hardly contain my excitement as we took the short train ride there after our three weeks in Kyoto.

Asger, Lissen and Emil were ready for something a little more twentieth century too. Though we had finally found the Emperor's palace and gardens, which had afforded some space for Asger and Emil to hare about burning off excess energy, and though we had all fallen in love with the city's atmosphere and 'otherness', Kyoto is even less child friendly than Tokyo. It's the kind of city where you can often feel metaphorically 'Ssshhhed'.

Meanwhile, I felt guilty about the amount of time I had left Lissen and the children alone to amuse themselves during our three weeks in Kyoto. It's not that I am at all intrinsic to my family's ability to find enjoyment or satisfaction in life, more that I was keen to spend more time with them – seeing Japan through their eyes was turning out to be the most enjoyable element of the trip. I also sensed that Lissen could do with some time on her own, as any sane adult who had spent almost every other day alone with her kids while her slightly demented husband went off on mad food investigations would.

But, of course, man can never entirely suppress his baser instincts and frailties, and I was already drooling at the prospect of Osaka's culinary smorgasbord.

Osaka has a growing reputation as culinary capital; as I have mentioned earlier, the respected French restaurant critic François Simon told me it was his favourite food city in the world, and I have seen it name-checked in several interviews with top European and US chefs as a place they visit for inspiration.

Osaka has several unique dishes; is home to the world's largest cooking school; and is famed throughout Japan for its open-minded, progressive approach to contemporary haute cuisine. The Osakans' insatiable hunger for the new, combined with their general irreverence towards convention and a traditionally cosmopolitan outlook bred over centuries of international trade, seems to have provided the optimum conditions for a culinary Mecca. I couldn't wait to get eating.

But, still, it was a genuine shock arriving there after several weeks in well-mannered, tourist-paced Kyoto, looking out from the taxi as we drove past the numerous mega-malls and skyscrapers between Osaka Station and our hotel, the – for us – unprecedentedly lavish Dojima.

Shortly after checking in, Lissen announced, 'Right. Shopping!' while rubbing her hands together briskly, and left. Which left the day free for me, Asger and Emil to explore the city. I knew exactly where we would head first: Dotombori, the fast food heartland of Japan's fast food capital. I wanted to show them that there was more to life than pizzas and whoppers.

Dotombori is a brash Vegas-style food street – about the only place in the country where it is acceptable to walk and eat. It is famous throughout Japan as the spiritual home of two Osakan fast food specialities, tako yaki – the octopus dumplings we first encountered in Kyoto – and okonomiyaki.

I've heard okonomiyaki described as everything from 'Japanese pizza' to 'Osakan omelette', but its only real resemblance to either is that it is round. It's more a pancake-tortilla hybrid made with a flour and egg batter with cabbage mixed in, and can come with a variety of fillings/toppings. As one would expect from a dish whose name translates as 'cooked to taste' or 'as you like it', finding an exact recipe is like asking a Frenchman to make the definitive cassoulet (or asking a Frenchman to do anything, I suppose). Some use wheat flour, others insist it must be made with fresh puréed or ground yam as well – flour-only okonomiyaki can be a little dry and rubbery – and others add dashi to the batter instead of water. The typical topping/filling (there's another disagreement right there – some say the other ingredients go *into* the batter, but in Hiroshima, where I ate a sensational oyster okonomiyaki, they layer the ingredients individually) is pork and kimchi, the pungent pickled cabbage from Korea; but seafood or chicken okonomiyaki are just as common, and others add yakisoba (fried ramen noodles) and tenkasu, crispy, fried tempura batter. Techniques for making okonomiyaki also differ. Usually you are given a bowl of batter and ingredients which you mix yourself, then pour onto a hotplate built into your table, flipping the resulting inch-thick disc with a metal spatula when one side is cooked and serving it divided into pizza-style slices with the same spatula. But there are other restaurants where they compress and steam the okonomiyaki before serving; and in Tokyo they serve it as monjayaki, using a more sloppy batter that never really sets (which was frankly just annoying). The sweet, brown teppanyaki-style savoury sauce (the familiar mix of ketchup, soy, Worcestershire sauce, perhaps dashi, mustard, sugar, mirin and sake) that is slathered on the top with a shaving-type brush is an essential ingredient too, although, of course, pinning down a chef's secret recipe for this sauce is impossible, and most buy ready-made sauces when they make okonomiyaki at home. Oh yes, and some add mayonnaise, aonori (dried seaweed flakes) and katsuo shavings too.

I knew it was too late to convince Asger and Emil of the pleasures of tako yaki – they were already wise to the lurking octopus body parts – but I felt I had a chance with okonomiyaki, as long as I could shield from them the fact that it contained vegetables and seafood. But which restaurant should we try first? There are said to be over four thousand okonomiyaki joints in Osaka, a good number of them located on Dotombori. The first we came to had over ten different types of plastic okonomiyaki models in the window, and we agreed we simply couldn't deal with that level of choice at this early stage in our okonomiyaki education.

We walked on a little further, hand in hand and open mouthed at the cartoonish extravagance of Dotombori's restaurant fronts – a chaotic jumble of animatronic clowns and giant crabs, lanterns, liquid crystal and inflatable fugu fish. Yet amid this visual cacophony, Asger and Emil zoned in with Exocet intensity on one establishment in particular.

They were initially drawn to the 'Bow Wow Relaxation of Dogs

Gallery' by the two small dogs tethered outside, and tended by a uniformed member of staff. 'Wow, look Daddy!' said Emil. 'He's licking my hand!' 'Yes, but, we were looking for okonomiyaki, remember?' I said. Asger, meanwhile, had his face pressed against the glass window behind which were more small dogs, lounging listlessly. They were for sale, for telephone number prices, but this wasn't a pet shop. The staff member beckoned us inside. I tried to resist, politely, but Asger and Emil were already halfway up the stairs to the first floor before I could grab their hands. I followed them to what turned out to be a dog showroom-cum-café, a kind of canine harem where guests came to enjoy the company of small dogs while sipping coffee. There was no way I was going to persuade Asger and Emil to leave without risking a conniption fit on an enormous scale from one or both of them, so I paid the entrance fee, we removed our shoes, and entered through a small gate to the dog-frolicking zone.

The admission included a drink each and a bag of doggy treats. The dogs, of which there were about twenty, none larger than a handbag, roamed freely among the tables. They were clearly familiar with the drill and we were soon engulfed by the pack. One stuck its wet snout into my crotch, another began to forage between my buttocks until one of the waiters came to my rescue, shooing them away with a menu.

Meanwhile Asger and Emil had disappeared into the pack and were roaming the tables on all fours begging for snacks along with the rest of the dogs, something I don't believe the waiting staff had ever seen before. It was remarkable how quickly they assimilated into dog society, although I had always suspected they had it in them. As I often do when my kids turn feral, I pretended they were nothing to do with me and sat back with my Coke to take in the scene around me.

The guests ranged from mothers with their daughters, to lone middle-aged females and even businessmen, which was weird. I guessed that Bow Wow catered to residents of high-rise apartment blocks with no room for pets, or people who worked standard Japanese hours and so had to make do with these prostitute Pekinese. It was all a bit tragic really. Lonely people seeking the company of greedy animals. The smell was appalling, too. Several of the dogs were wearing nappies. One of the dogs stopped its scrounging for treats for a good old scratch, another became engrossed in its own genitals for a while, before jumping up onto the lap of a morose young girl and giving her a good slurp in the face.

Finally, I managed to isolate Asger and Emil from the pack by scattering some doggie snacks in the opposite direction, and attempted to bundle them out of the shop. But their new gang were having none of it and soon our ankles were engulfed by furballs again. Asger and Emil could quite happily have made their home here indefinitely, but my stomach was rumbling and the knowledge that some of the world's greatest fast food was still within my grasp spurred me on through the canine melee. I grabbed Asger's wrist and scooped Emil up under my arm, to barks and yelps from both. The dogs, sensing their new leaders were under attack, lunged properly for my ankles. It took three waiters to hold them off as I forced my way through the gate to where our shoes were waiting.

(Needless to say, the pressure to return to Bow Wow was ceaseless for the rest of our stay in Osaka, and we did return twice. Asger and Emil still talk about it as their undisputed highlight of the entire trip to Japan, ahead of lunch with sumos, meeting ninja warriors at Himeji castle, and even finding a real, live dead turtle on the beach in Okinawa.)

Clearly, as a money-making idea, a dog café was right up there with phone companies charging for their complaint lines: people pay to play with your dogs and are either emotionally blackmailed into buying them by their children, or at the very least foot their food bill. I made a mental note to add it to the list of brilliant Japanese business ideas that were going to make my fortune once we returned, along with the soft-closing loo seat.

We wandered on for about half an hour, inadvertently straying into the love hotel quarter, where sheepish couples loitered hesitantly beneath signs for the Hyper Sexy Club and Happy Love Make Joy Hotel. We ended up back in the centre of Dotomburi outside Sammy Ebisu Plaza, an intriguing restaurant complex which inside turned out to be an exact recreation of 1950s Osaka with authentic-looking restaurants and shops from the period. It was one of the several food theme parks that have sprung up in various cities in Japan in recent years which typically contain groups of restaurants arranged in indoor malls decorated to a particular theme, usually jazzed up with vintage shops fronts and period advertising (and all set in the immediate post-war era for some reason).

In the first restaurant we came to I ordered one okonomiyaki and one modanyaki – an okonomiyaki with yakisoba mixed into the batter. Both were slathered in the sweet brown sauce which I felt sure would guarantee their appeal to a six- and four-year-old, but Asger and Emil toyed with them briefly before rejecting them on the grounds that they had 'too much stuff inside'.

I gave up. We had a Mos Burger from the national chain of the same name, which was organic and actually not bad.

Later on during our stay in Osaka I ate – alone this time – at a very different style of okonomiyaki restaurant, the President Chibo, also on Dotomburi. It opened in 1967 with the aim of taking okonomiyaki upmarket – hence the low lighting, marble counters and chefs dressed in the French style. The okonomiyaki I ate (let's say I had 'more than one, less than five') were superlative but it didn't feel quite right somehow. Okonomiyaki is best in cook-it-yourself form I think. It seemed odd having the chef cook it for me with tinkly music and attentive waiters, like having an *haute* hot dog.

Oddly, given his book generally takes an Osakan or Kansai-orientated slant on Japanese cuisine, Shizuo Tsuji makes reference neither to tako yaki or okonomiyaki in *A Simple Art*. Perhaps he felt street food was beneath his remit, I don't know. I do still think, though, that okonomiyaki could be the next global Japanese food trend: it's quick, cheap, simple, relatively healthy (it is around fifty per cent cabbage, after all), theatrical, and utterly, compulsively delicious. If I were younger, more foolish, and had some venture capital behind me, I'd be looking to roll out a chain before Christmas.

As it is, the world has instead embraced two other Osakan fast food innovations: kaiten sushi (conveyor belt sushi), and instant noodles, both invented in the same year: 1958.

The idea for kaiten sushi came to restaurateur Yoshiaki Shiraishi during a visit to a bottling plant, but took him a while to perfect. The speed of the conveyor was the trickiest part: too fast and people grew anxious (I call this 'uni angst', and suffer from it terribly when I eat at conveyor belt places: *what if someone takes the sea urchin before it reaches me?*), too slow and they were bored. Eventually he found eight centimetres per second to be the optimum rate. His Genroku chain was wildly successful as the so-called 'dwell time' of diners was reduced to around twelve minutes, which meant he could pack as many as four sittings in one hour, instead of three over an entire evening. The original restaurant is still going in the east of the city, but Shiraishi died in relative poverty after he tried to take the staffless restaurant concept too far, and ploughed all his money into developing robot waiters.

Instant ramen noodles were the invention of Momofuku Ando, who died in 2007 a revered Japanese national hero and multi-billionaire. Inspired by seeing how air and water instantly evaporated from tempura leaving tiny holes in their wake, he reasoned that the same could be done with noodles, which could then be rehydrated via the holes with hot water. Over eighty-five *billion* servings of instant ramen are consumed in the world each year. That's an awful lot of Pot Noodles, although, naturally, the instant ramen on sale in Japan is of a different order altogether.

That afternoon, with Lissen maintaining radio silence somewhere in a distant changing room, we took a quick trip to the north of the city to the Momofuku Ando Museum. In a swish, modern building that looked more like a contemporary art museum than a memorial to a noodle magnate, we learned of the early days of Ando's invention, which he refined in his garden shed, and marvelled at a vast wall covered with different plastic noodle pots through the ages. Upstairs we could create our own recipe, and then sit down to eat it, but none of us quite had the appetite by that stage.

We finished the day at Osaka's one, true, original tourist attraction, the aquarium. It is the world's largest, its main tank several stories high. The star is a captive whale shark, the largest fish in the world, and a staggering sight to see behind glass.

Big fish, dog cafés, and fat pancakes: we couldn't have asked anything more of a day's sightseeing.

Chapter 26

Miraculous Miso

This is what US food writer Harold McGee has to say about miso soup in his seminal work on kitchen science, history and culture, *On Food and Cooking*:

> ... miso soup is a delight to the eye as well as the palate. When the soup is made and poured into the bowl, the miso particles disperse throughout in an even haze. But left undisturbed for a few minutes, the particles gather around the centre of the bowl in discrete little clouds that slowly change shape. The clouds mark convection cells, columns in the broth where hot liquid from the bowl bottom rises, is made cooler and so more dense by evaporation at the surface, falls again; is reheated and becomes less dense, rises, and so on. Miso soup enacts at the table the same process that produces towering thunderhead clouds in the summer sky.

Isn't that fantastic?

Shizuo Tsuji writes that: 'In many ways miso is to Japanese cooking what butter is to French cooking and olive oil to the Italian way.' From what I already knew about miso, this didn't sound quite right. Miso isn't used for frying, for instance, or to add gloss to sauces, but he was right about its ubiquity. Over half of Japanese still wake up to the smell of miso soup for breakfast – to them it is like fresh-made toast and coffee.

I was still a little suspicious of miso paste itself. I had tasted it in miso soup, of course, and in that ubiquitous modern fusion dish, cod with miso, as well as in the Kyoto tofu restaurant, grilled on tofu as dengaku. It had been wonderful each time with a meaty, peanut flavour and a complex acidity. But there was also whiff of the sewer, a fermented, farty undercurrent that – as so many of the tastiest foodstuffs do (truffles, well-hung game, Roquefort, Ginsters meat pies and so on) – repelled and intrigued in equal measure.

All of this and worse was confirmed before I had even entered Tony Flenley's miso factory in the shadow of the spaceship-style Osaka Dome stadium. What *was* that appalling smell of backed-up toilets?

'Ah, yes, that's the drains, sorry about that,' sighed Tony, a tall, cheerful Englishman in his early fifties, as he welcomed me to his Portakabin office.

'Phew, thank goodness for that, I thought it was the miso,' I laughed.

'Oh yes, it *is* the miso,' Tony said. 'It's just that we have to hold on to our waste to let the sediment settle before we can release the water into the sewer. The local council doesn't really understand what we do here. Because we use bacteria they don't want us to pump waste directly into the sewer. I try to tell them it's good bacteria, but they don't listen.'

There are, Tony explained, three basic types of miso – one made with soybeans, salt and rice; one made with soya, salt and barley; and one made with just soya and salt. They range in colour from deep reddish brown, to light sandy beige. Light coloured miso tends to be slightly sweet, while the red has a richer, more powerful flavour, 'Red's got more amino acids so it is better for you. They say one bowl a day keeps cancer away. You know, in Japan we don't say that you "drink" miso soup, you "eat" it – because it is usually full of vegetables, tofu and fish.'

With over two thousand miso producers in Japan, there are also a huge number of regional variations. Around eighty per cent is kome miso, made with rice and beans; on Kyushu they often use barley and beans – this is mugi miso; while miso from Nagoya is made with beans only, this is mame miso. Tokyo miso is traditionally dark, rusty coloured, sweet and powerful; while sendai miso, from Miyagi Prefecture, is salty. Predictably, Kyoto miso is refined and subtle, and a pale cream colour. Tony, meanwhile, also produces Osaka's unique sweet, white miso. The ingredients; whether or not they are steamed or boiled; fermenting time (some stand for two to three years) – all of this can affect the colour and flavour of miso, he said.

Of course, making top-quality miso requires experience and an empathy with mouldy rice and beans – you need to judge the amount of salt to add; the proportion of beans to rice or barley if they are used; and at what point optimum fermentation has been achieved. When the koji starts devouring the rice, it heats up but must be kept below 40°C as the koji's enzymes first turn the starch into sugar and then break the beans down into amino acids. The sugar is important for white miso, and the amino acids give flavour to red miso.

Tony showed me round the factory, a fairly basic warehouse with various pipes and valves, tanks and dials about the place. It all looked rather rudimentary; then again, to make miso you basically need a big barrel, a grinder, a rice steamer, bean cooker and koji room – that's it. As with sake and soy sauce (which was originally a by-product of miso manufacture), the magic ingredient with miso is a koji, a highly-prized type of fungus, specially bred for use in miso-making. It is grown onto steamed rice, barley or beans and acts as starting agent to get them fermenting. Salt is added, and when the beans and koji are mixed, the mix is left with a heavy weight on top and with minimum contact with air, for two to three weeks, for white miso, and one to two years for red. 'You can speed the process up,' Tony told me. 'But it doesn't taste so good. We do it the proper way. Natural fermentation.' After fermentation, the beans are usually ground to a paste (although in some parts of Japan it is used as it is, or minced) and steamed to stop them fermenting further. Once you've bought it, miso can then last up to six months in the fridge.

For all its simplicity, the resulting product – a solid brown paste not unlike peanut butter – is a complex substance. As well as amino acids it contains lactic acid, which helps balance the glutamate flavour and preserve the miso. In terms of health benefits, as well as being a good source of protein and minerals, it also contains cholesterol-lowering compounds, while the fermentation process appears to boost the antioxidant levels already present in the soybeans. There has long been an association between miso consumption and reduced rates of cancer, in particular breast cancer – due, it is believed, to the presence of isoflavones, an antioxidant unique to beans. When news came to Japan of the Chernobyl nuclear disaster, their response was to send miso, for instance. A survey of 270,000 people also indicated an association between miso soup and reduced gastric cancers – thought to be because miso purges the gut of various toxins – and some scientists believe that it slows ageing by suppressing the oxidisation of cellular lipids. Used as a seasoning, miso is also lower in sodium than salt and soy sauce.

Ironically, just as the rest of the world is waking up to the miracle powers of this remarkable paste – exports have doubled over recent years – Japan is turning against it. Miso's appeal appears to be waning with the Japanese, who are increasingly adopting Western-style diets and finding they have less time to cook from scratch. Consumption has dropped to less than 500,000 tons a year compared to 580,000 tons in the eighties.

I asked Tony about natto, another fermented soybean product. Natto is a traditional healthy breakfast dish in Japan. It is made from only partially fermenting soybeans, which turns them into a deeply unappetising, stringy, lumpy vomit-like substance, with a taste that subtly blends soil and old cheese. I'd had my first and last taste of natto at the hotel breakfast buffet in our hotel in Sapporo. For me, perhaps the most off-putting thing about it was the determined mucus strands that clung to each bean as I tried to pick them up. Along with the foul-smelling durian fruit and truffles it has to be one of the most polarising foodstuffs on the planet. 'That's made with a different fermenting bacteria,' Tony said. 'We don't make it. Actually, they say that you should never make miso and natto in the same premises because the natto bacteria is stronger and can affect the miso koji.'

What were his tips for cooking with miso? 'Oh loads. You can mix it with mirin and mustard and use it as a dip. With dengaku you mix red and white miso and put it on tofu then grill it. I use it in chilli con carne instead of chocolate. It is great as a seasoning, instead of salt, in a Western-style stew. You get a real, natural MSG boost – just remember that white miso has five to six per cent salt and red has ten to twelve. Red miso apple cake is nice, and a gratin with white miso works well. I've heard some London restaurants are serving pork with miso, which is a classic combo. We even made a miso ice cream once.' Experimenting back home, I found a dessert-poon or so of miso works really well in tomato sauces. You can use it instead of a stock cube in many dishes to enrich the flavour of a dish, and miso mixed with vinegar, water, sugar, garlic and sesame makes a great salad dressing.

I asked Tony about his story. He has lived in Japan for twenty years, having moved there originally as a TEFL teacher. He speaks the language fluently and is married to a Japanese woman; it was her family who founded the Osaka Miso Jyozo company a hundred years ago. The miso industry is very traditional and, originally, his in-laws were against even the idea of their daughter marrying a foreigner. How did he win them over? 'I guess when they realised I wasn't going to run away with her there was a slow thaw. Anyway, her dad's a boozer like me. We got on. In Japan before the son takes over a company he is sent off to another company to get some training, so I did that. After ten years the old man grew weaker and I started taking on visiting clients. He died three years ago and I took over fully.

'Actually I was always interested in fermentation. I made ginger ale when I was twelve – I found out if I put lots of sugar in I could make it more alcoholic! [Tony also used to help run a major annual beer festival in Osaka.] I taught English in Kuwait for a couple of years and used to make wine in my basement, then made yoghurt, now I make bread.'

How did the the company's clients react to him? 'Well, I suppose the people who were offended were too polite to say anything, but it still causes a stir I suppose. It is seen as a very tough profession. It didn't help that we got hit by the Kobe earthquake [the Great Hanshin quake of 1995]. Even though it was across the bay, there was a lot of damage here. We lost the original factory which was where the car park is now. I was on the thirteenth floor at home at the time and all the crockery was smashed.' Apparently, the ground where the factory stands is still rather unstable. 'Every time there is a concert in the Osaka Dome over the way there it is equivalent to a force three earthquake!'

Tony brought out a plate with some different misos for me to taste. The white was yeasty and sweet; the one-year fermented red paste saltier, with a slight Marmite flavour. 'Yes! You're right. You know I have thought about making a miso spread for bread. That'd be good, don't you think?'

I agreed. If people will eat Marmite, they'd definitely go for miso. We tried a two-year-old red miso. It had an astringent, burning flavour. 'Well, we are eating it neat. It goes very well in a broth. It clears the palate well, which is what miso soup is supposed to do, of course. You should only eat miso after a meal. Often it is served with the other dishes but meant to be left until the end. In kaisekei places, they will serve it alone at the end.' A white barley miso was next – it was sweet, with a hint of pineapple. 'That's very popular in Osaka. They have a real sweet tooth here.'

Tony and I chatted more generally about Osaka and life in Japan. He generously offered to introduce me to his contacts at the fish market – the second largest in the country – so that I could get to see the pre-dawn tuna auction. 'Let's go right now, I can show you around,' he said.

The market was on the other side of town so Tony drove me there in his Toyota estate. After making the introductions, he invited me for lunch at his favourite market restaurant, a dingy place on the first floor filled with stevedores and traders. They greeted him as an old friend, and we sat at the counter in front of a large, square steel vat filled with a murky brown liquid in which floated several unidentifiable foodstuffs.

'What do you mean you haven't tried oden!' Tony said, interpreting my grimace correctly. 'It is delicious, you have to try it.' Oden is the Japanese equivalent of a good stew; a lucky dip winter warmer in which you can find bricks of tofu, various meats, burdock root, daikon, potatoes, fish cakes, seaweed and boiled eggs. You might also chance upon the curious konnyaku – a flavourless, rubbery meat substitute made from the flour of the konjac, or 'devil's tongue', root. Pretty much anything the chef has to hand goes in and it is said that a really great oden is eternal – the vat literally never stops simmering with each day's serving merely a top-up of the previous day's.

The chef fished out a few choice morsels – some deep-fried tofu, spoon tender pork, daikon and a hard-boiled egg. It was delicious, although I did wonder if my impression had more to do with diminished expectations than the inherent qualities of the dish.

Osakans are a hospitable and generous people, even adopted sons (Tony had insisted on paying for the oden). This was underlined the next evening when I hooked up with a couple of friends of friends, local food lovers who had promised to show me some of the addresses from their little black gourmet books.

We met outside the National Bunraku theatre. Hiroshi, in his early forties I'd guess, was wearing a Kangol flat cap and surfer shirt. With him was Chiaki, a pretty, petite woman around the same age. They introduced themselves with customary Japanese diffidence, but as we began to talk food, the shyness soon disappeared. 'Osakans like to eat at lots of different places in one night,' Hiroshi said with the hint of a wicked grin. He wasn't kidding. We must have eaten in half a dozen places over the course of the evening. And we're not talking tapas.

There was a stunning okonomiyaki, cooked in front of us in a grimy old-school joint, on a hotplate caked in black grease. Hiroshi said it was the very best in the city, and I didn't doubt it. 'Osakans eat it straight from the spatula said Chiaki, as she divided it up with her metal spatula. 'We are always in a hurry you know.' The waiter was keen to engage me in rugby talk as England were playing Japan in the world cup that night but I was more interested in the sauce he brushed over the okonomiyaki. 'Secret recipe,' he whispered, laughing.

Let's be clear, this was not healthy eating. The Japanese know how to comfort eat as well as, I would argue even better than, the rest of us.

Next stop was Daruma, the most famous kushikatsu restaurant in Japan. As with okonomiyaki, it is inexplicable to me why kushikatsu – breaded, deep-fried skewers of meat, fish and vegetables – has not already taken the world by storm. This is another of the great Osakan fast foods, and deserves to be right up there with tempura and yakitori – to which it is closely related – as a globally known Japanese style of cooking. Kushikatsu uses a unique batter and yet another special, meaty-sugary, ebony coloured sauce to envelop morsels of vegetables, seafood and meat.

The secret is in the batter, which in Daruma's case is made with puréed yams, flour, eggs, water and a unique blend of eleven spices. It forms a thin, crisp crust around whatever is being deep fried – we had beef, shrimp, quail's eggs, cherry tomatoes, asparagus, chicken and scallops. The skewers are cooked in beef oil at 190°C. The dip is served in a communal pot on the counter bearing a 'No double dipping' warning in English.

Daruma is right next to Osaka's 1960s telecommunications tower (another compulsory Japanese big city landmark, along with the aquarium and Ferris wheel) although it is far older than its prominent neighbour having been founded eighty years ago. We took our place at the counter our feet splashing down in water spilled by the kitchen staff as they ducked and swooped around the tiny open working kitchen. It may have been shabby, but I couldn't have wished for a finer introduction to the art of kushikatsu – the quail's eggs and tomatoes were standouts, the thin crunchy batter with its fine sandpaper finish cracking to unleash a meltingly delicious interior. The skewers cost less than fifty pence each and it was only the risk of hospitalisation through over-eating that held me back.

'Are we planning on going anywhere else, because if we are I had better stop,' I said to Hiroshi at one point. We were, but I couldn't. The skewers and the beer kept on coming. By the time we left, at around six, a long queue was already forming outside. 'They queue here for miles every night,' Hiroshi said. Ferran Adrià – who, by now, I felt I was stalking through Japan – had eaten there recently, the chef had told him.

The evening started to blur after the fifth or sixth beer, but I do remember going to Shinsekai market, the city's main food market, and then on to a standing bar, a current Osakan trend. Here we chatted a little more about the character of Osakans. 'Osakans are friendly, they have a sense of humour, they like cheap, good food,' said Chiaki. 'You can see the history of the city in their character. We are a mercantile people, outward looking, tough at business, but fair and adventurous. We are down to earth, not pretentious like the Kyoto people. We are blunt and to the point. And we do not wait for anything!'

My new friends were beginning to open up a little now. Hiroshi, it turned out, had been an actor but now wrote scripts for TV variety shows and a weekly TV food programme. Chiaki, a music producer, said that her husband was the third best mandolin player in the world.

They told me that in Osaka everyone from heads of corporations to the men that mend the roads eat side by side, standing up in these kinds of bars. We ordered hamo, fluffy and mealy; and then garlic miso with sea bream. Then came a sizeable triangle of deep-fried tofu with ginger and spring onion.

The drinks took a turn for the worse at this point. A large tumbler of sweet potato shocku appeared first – which was nice, but made everything go that bit more blurry – but then came an awful, milky sake full of sediment (I think this must have been nama-sake, or unpasteurised sake).

Hiroshi had written an article for a local newspaper on this particular bar which was almost a hundred years old and run by the third generation of the same family. The article was framed on the wall behind us and included a photograph of the chef's father. He had died the week before, the chef told us. His mother emerged from the kitchen, tiny and sad but with a brave face that said 'life continues, people must eat'. His ten-year-old daughter pulled a beer for another customer, while the chef peeled a huge daikon in front of us, gently teasing off its outer skin with an equally gigantic, but obviously razor-sharp knife. The technique is known as katsuramuki, meaning 'column peel', and is considered a basic test of a good Japanese chef, rather like being able to crack an egg with one hand, or flip a pancake.

Next up was an udon noodle place chosen by Chiaki. I had tried to protest against this last addition to our itinerary. I really was stuffed, and more than a little drunk, but I am glad she persuaded me, for at Chiaki's favourite udon restaurant I tasted heaven.

It was just a simple dashi broth with small, crispy, deep-fried gyoza floating in it. The discussion had taken a more personal slant. 'Michael-san,' Hiroshi asked me. 'Your favourite food? What would your last meal be?'

I paused. Would it be elaborate tasting menus at Ducasse and Robuchon, or a great British roast? I did consider fresh oysters, lobster, pan-fried foie gras, and I had already eaten so many memorable meals in Japan that any one of them would suffice. But the truth was, right at that moment, I had eaten nothing more delicious than that dashi. It was sweet as fresh peas, yet complex with the tang of sea and, when you bit into the gyoza, a satisfying porky punch with a zing of spring onion and herbs. I may have been dribbling drunk, but I remember it as being as good as anything I had tasted up until that point and said so. Chiaki and Hiroshi beamed; I only hope they didn't think I was just being polite.

I had to know how they made it. To alarmed looks from my dining companions, I stood up from the table and tottered into the open kitchen. This absolutely is not done in Japan, but as is often the case, being foreign and presumed both ignorant and ill-mannered, is a passport to all sorts of forbidden territories. I eventually managed to communicate my enquiry and was shown the blend of three dried fish they used to steep in the konbu broth: katsuobushi, sardine and mackerel.

It had been the food crawl to end all food crawls. I had eaten more in ten or so hours than I would usually consume in a week. (OK, a couple of days.) I don't know how I got back to the hotel that night, I certainly don't remember the journey, but I do remember that, true Osakans that they are, Chiaki and Hiroshi never let me pay for a thing.

Chapter 27

The Forest of Lost Souls

This has to be the most unsettling place I have ever visited, but I am having to put on a cheery face as the children are beginning to sense something isn't quite right. As we walk further into the heart of the forest I glance across at Lissen. She has the same brave face, but in the flicker of the candles that light our way I can see her eyes darting into the pitch-black undergrowth. The stony, blank faces of dead children peer back at us, bathed in the dancing lights.

It is at this moment that I realise Emil is no longer with us.

There is a place at the foot of Mount Fuji where a number of Japan's thirty-four thousand annual suicides go to die. It is called Aokigahara Forest and the very air itself there is said to be congested with the spirits of the tormented. Twice a year a squad of clean-up guys fan out through the forest and harvest the corpses, usually finding well over seventy in various states of decay.

We are not there – what, do you think I am, *insane?* – but Aokigahara is on my mind as we take what was supposed to be a pleasant early evening stroll into the cemetery amid the forest of lost souls on the top of Mount Koya.

We had arrived earlier in the day on the sacred mountain plateau, encircled by cedar and cryptomeria conifer forests 2,800 metres above sea level. Koya-san, as the Japanese deferentially call the mountain, is the spiritual heart of Japan. It is also as good as the geographical centre of the country, located a three hour train ride south of Osaka followed by a short, vertical ride up the mountain in a clunking old funicular. The journey is grindingly slow, deliberately so I suspect to allow decompression from modern Japan, for

Koya-san is most assuredly not modern Japan. It can come as something of a shock.

Koya-san is the resting place of the great spiritual leader, scholar and polymath Kobo Daishi. In 804AD, aged thirty-one, Daishi – then named Kukai – travelled to China where he studied esoteric Buddhism, known in Japan as Shingon, or 'True Word' Buddhism. Shingon is a kind of fast-track Buddhism. It teaches that one can attain enlightenment during a single lifetime, which has the obvious appeal of allowing you to circumvent all those tiresome stages of reincarnation as bugs and cattle and so forth. Daishi founded the head temple of the Shingon order on Koya-san on his return from China in 816AD: legend has it that he threw his trident to determine where to build the temple, went looking for it, and met a hunter with a two-headed dog who told him it had landed on Koya. The mountain's popularity as a pilgrimage destination for the upper classes of Kyoto and Osaka grew from the eleventh century, surviving anti-Buddhist movements and, eventually, the admission of women in the late nineteenth century. It remains an important religious site to this day.

Prior to the arrival of Buddhism in Japan, the country's main religion was Shintoism which, despite its drastic subsequent decline, remained the official state religion until WWII. Shintoism is a complex yet in many ways primitive ritualistic belief system based on the worship of gods (kami-sama), believed to be present throughout the natural world. Shinto's equivalent of Genesis tells us that the sibling gods Izanagi and Izanami made love and created humans (not sure what that makes us), which explains those giant penis shrines the TV travel shows always visit when they come to Japan. Today, less than two per cent of Japanese practise Shintoism but Japanese Buddhism incorporated many elements of Shintoism to the extent that, for many, the two still blur somewhat.

There were once around 1,500 temples on Koya-san. Today there are a little over a hundred but the town, which has a permanent population of just 7,000 people, is busy year-round receiving over a million pilgrims.

I was not one of them. I am not going to bore you with an existential journey to my spiritual core, largely because I suspect I don't have one. I do sometimes find myself thinking elevated thoughts while enveloped by the aromas of tempering Valhrona Jivana, say, or at that glorious moment when you break the caramel on a really good crème brûlée, but that's as far as it goes. We had come to Koya-san for a different reason. I wanted to try the local vegetarian cuisine, a highly refined multi-course meal called shojin ryori, featuring, among other things, a special way of preparing tofu, called koya-dofu – freeze dried, legend has it, after a monk left some tofu out during a cold night and observed how it turned interestingly spongy when reconstituted (apparently even more nutritious than regular tofu). Over the centuries shojin ryori has developed into a sophisticated, refined form of dining in which great effort is made to make the most out of relatively humble ingredients to express three key tenets of sincerity, cleanliness and presentation. Kaiseki ryori evolved in part from shojin ryori, but perhaps more interestingly, as far as I was concerned, shojin ryori was almost entirely fat free.

The funicular was the highlight of an otherwise slow and tetchy journey. Asger and Emil were impatient to meet the 'monkeys', having somehow concluded – admittedly following some misdirection from me – that they would be our hosts rather than monks. Imagine, then, their dismay when they discovered that, not only were there no monkeys, but that they were going to have to be quiet and contemplative for two whole days. Not even the bear warning signs on the busride to the town of Koya-san could cheer them up after that bombshell.

As with the Christian Franciscan brotherhood, Shingon Buddhism has a tradition for hospitality and around half of the temples on Koya-san have rooms, some of them boasting flat screens, private baths and minibars. Judging by the signs at the gates, most take MasterCard too. Though charming, our shukubo, as these religious hostels are called, wasn't one of the luxurious ones and the traditional tatami room we had been shown on arrival was virtually empty apart from a low table, some cushions and an electric heater as, even in summer it can get chilly at night.

'Where's the TV?' Emil asked, after some few frantic minutes searching.

'I'm afraid there isn't one,' said Lissen. Asger frowned, then laughed, thinking we were joking.

'Hey, why don't we go out exploring. Maybe we can find some monkeys!' I joked. Lissen gave me a look.

'. . . or some other funny things instead,' I added, then more desperately, 'Chocolate! Pokémon?'

On Koya-san there were none of these things. It is, for Japan, a rare Pokémon-free haven. The town is divided into the Garan, or Scared Precinct – the main temple district centred on a short high street with a few restaurants and tourist shops – and Okuno-in, the forest cemetery where Kobo Daishi is interred, supposedly not actually deceased but merely sleeping. Apparently local monks bring him lavish dinners every night.

We had to be back in our room for dinner by 5.30, so we didn't get as far as the Okuno-in during daylight, when I am sure it isn't nearly so spooky. But even in the bright afternoon sun there was a palpably weighty atmosphere about the place, something oppressive and claustrophobic. Perhaps it was the smell of incense, the occasional maudlin ring of a gong, or the glimpse of shaven-headed, black robed monks clip-clopping down the street in their wooden sandals. Piety is never easy company.

The monasteries are extraordinarily graceful though, with stunning gardens, each with a precise, painterly quality, and arranged in multiple layers of frilly verdant foliage interspersed with theatrical explosions of red maple. At ground level the gardens were dotted with moss-covered boulders ringed by precision-raked grey gravel, prompting chilling flashbacks to Emil's Kyoto misadventure. Elsewhere ancient pines leaned at perilous angles, propped up by wooden posts like elderly pilgrims.

Back at our monastery we left our shoes at the door and transferred to the complimentary red vinyl slippers. There were about five sizes too small for me with the result that they made me totter like a low-rent tranny. At 5.30 on the dot, our paper door slid open and a monk silently placed a lacquered tray filled with an array of colourful dishes on the low table. We knelt around the table and began tucking in to lovely, light vegetable tempura; kamaboko (steamed fish paste, pressed into colourful cakes and served in slices), udon noodles, salad, fresh tofu, crunchy pickles, miso soup and fresh fruit.

Afterwards I wandered down to the kitchen to say thank you. I met a shaven-headed Mexican woman, a nun, called Veronica who told me she had lived in the monastery for eight years, making dinner for around fifty people every night. Did they ever eat meat? I asked. 'Not really, but if we are given meat we have to eat it,' she told me, before hurrying off with more trays for other guests.

We decided to go out for an evening stroll which, it soon became clear, was not a typical Koya-san pastime. The main street was deserted and I later found out that the Japanese, who for all their superficial modernity are a deeply superstitious people, rarely if ever venture into the Okuno-in after dark. We walked down the hill passing the point where we had turned back earlier in the day. At the entrance to the forest we passed two elderly ladies selling pine sprigs and satsumas as offerings. They seemed alarmed to see us and looked away when we smiled. They would be the only sign of life from hereon, but I wanted to see Kobo Daishi's tomb which lay at the far end of a stony path deep in the forest, so onward we went.

The atmosphere amid the tall pines was airless and still. Koya-san's thousand-year-old forest is said to be full of the kami-sama, the Shinto gods who inhabit everything that is natural, from animals to trees and rocks, and, after dark, with only lanterns to light our way, it was all too easy to imagine this was true.

Entering the forest we came upon an astonishing sight, row after row of stone shrines, stupas and pagodas nestled among the trunks of the pines. In between them were eerie little statues of figures, like children, each with a small, red cotton bib hung around their necks, some with knitted hats. Many had offerings of sweets or coins placed before them; others sat leaning, as if they were dozing, in their own wooden huts, like lazy car park attendants. Some of their faces had been worn away by the weather, with others the rain had made the dye in their bibs run pale pink. The statues are called jizo. They are memorials to babies and infants who have died. We didn't tell Asger and Emil this for obvious reasons, but they had sensed a mood change regardless and stopped singing a song they had made up about monkey monks. Deeper into the forest we came across a giant ziggurat made up of even more jizo, perhaps five metres high, standing sentinel, waiting.

Koya-san has been the burial place of many of Japan's notables over the centuries and in recent years there has been a trend for Japanese corporations to build small memorials to deceased employees here. Living employees visit these memorials – many designed to represent the companies' products (one is shaped like a coffee cup, another is like a space rocket) – and leave their business cards.

It was while we were photographing the rocket that we realised Emil was no longer with us. We started to retrace our steps, calling out – more 'whispering out' – for there was something about this place that inhibited shouting. I was growing anxious. Emil often goes missing, that wasn't unusual, but he had never done so in a haunted forest cemetery, at night.

Eventually we found him. It seemed an age, but was probably less than five minutes. He hadn't gone far. He was crouching beside a jizo, his hand on its head, talking.

Lissen picked him up and told him, softly, that, if he wanted to wander off, he should always tell us.

'What were you saying to the statue, Emil?' I asked, trying to sound cheerful.

'We were just talking,' he said. 'She said she was lonely.'

Finally we crossed the Mimyo-no-hashi bridge, where pilgrims ladle water over a statue in memory of babies who drowned or were aborted, and then came to the Toro-do, or lantern hall, where Kobo Daishi still awaits the next Buddha. The hall was lit by ten thousand oil lamps, two of which, it is claimed, have burned since the eleventh century – one of them originally lit by the then emperor. The only sound was of the stream outside. We took a quick glance, and hurried back, trying hard not to run.

Back at the monastery I met up with a Swiss monk called Kurt, who I had been told acted as a kind of unofficial ambassador for Koya-san, giving talks around the world on Shingoism and the mountain.

'I came here for enlightenment,' Kurt told me, as we sat in his office drinking rough Italian wine. 'I came to Japan for the first time twenty-seven years ago to research spiritual design. I was an artist – performance, installation – I took a kind of holistic approach, anything to express my thoughts: speech, writing . . .'

I asked him about shojin ryori. What does it mean? 'It means pure food. A Buddhist monk must eat what is given to him; he must not order the killing of another animal, but if someone gives him meat he must eat it. Here at the monastery of course we only do vegetables. And no onions or garlic because they stimulate sexual desire. Some foreign guests don't like the tofu, but I have noticed they are neurotic.'

But wine is OK? 'In Buddhist terms, no drugs are allowed because they take away consciousness. You must be conscious and present in what you are doing, that is why Buddha suggested meditation because that way you can understand your own mind. I drink it to boost blood pressure and because you are here. Actually, many years ago I was a specialist dealer in beer, spirits and wine. But luckily Buddhists don't judge people. We are not missionaries. While Christians say "this is right and this is wrong", Buddhists are tolerant, they don't judge one way or the other. There are as many ways to reach liberation as there are sentient beings. We respect them for who they are. We know people are not perfect.'

It sounded like an appealing approach to life, until he explained to me that he rose each morning at four for prayers and offerings. Would I like to join them the next day?

'Maybe,' I said.

I asked about his beliefs. 'No, I am not a believer. I doubt. Everything is energy. This gives you a liberalistic outlook because attachment causes misery – to ideas, to concepts, to notions of perfections. I am always surprised, for example, how many people fight to keep with their partner. You know suffering comes from attachment. Buddhism requires that you look within your own mind as it really is. Once you discover the mechanics of your own mind you can reach a liberation and just be present. Happiness is in the moment. The moment you lose your ego, you are free'

'What, like with the first bite of a crème brûlée?'

'More like an orgasm.'

'Ah, yes,' I said.

Chapter 28

The Beef Delusion

After the dainty yet insubstantial vegetarian cuisine of Koya-san I had a yearning for some meat, lots of it, preferably rich, red, bloody beef. If the stories are to be believed, the Japanese accord their cattle a greater reverence than the Hindus do theirs – at least up until the point of slaughter. They are pampered to a degree that Paris Hilton's chihuahua might find excessive, enjoying beers and massage, sake rubs and relaxing piped music. This, we are told, is why their beef – which we in the West know, variously, as Kobe or Wagyu beef – is so extraordinarily tender, its flesh patterned with river deltas of creamy white fat, and, of course, why it is so costly and desired. Unicorns aside, there can be few more heavily mythologised beasts than the Japanese cow.

Cows have also played an improbable but important role in defining the Japanese's self-image as devout, self-controlled and abstemious vegetarians. It is said that when Buddhism came to these shores in around 730AD, the consumption of meat was outlawed. Not another shred of beef passed Japanese lips until, one morning in 1872, the Emperor woke up and decided he fancied a little beef for his dinner, made a public pronouncement to that effect, and the Japanese became meat-eaters overnight. Even then, the historical blame for the Japanese's loss of carnivorous innocence is typically placed at the feet of the mercantile barbarians from the West. As Shizuo Tsuji writes in *A Simple Art*: 'The first cows slaughtered in Japan were for the tables of Western residents.'

Unusually, Tsuji is quite wrong. Let's get this straight: the Japanese have always eaten meat. The 730AD decree which is generally held

211

to be the vegetarian watershed, was in reality as much a pragmatic solution to the problem of over-consumption of animals that were needed for farm work; it was intended to stop everyone eating the cows and horses that pulled the ploughs, for which reason pigs were never included.

As I have mentioned before, being partial to wild boar, the Japanese promptly re-named them 'mountain whale' to circumvent the 'no meat' edict. Samurai in particular remained particularly keen carnivores. As noted historian Ishige Maomichi writes in *The History and Culture of Japanese Food*: 'The main purpose of the ban was to prohibit the eating of beef and horse meat and protect the livestock population as well as to prevent drought, insect damage and famine. Moreover, it was limited to the spring and summer months which constitute the paddy farming season.' In fact, the only real concession to the Buddhist principle of avoiding needless bloodshed was to outlaw the indiscriminate trapping of animals and fish.

The truth is, the Japanese kept on eating meat using the same excuse that my grandmother employed for her nightly eggnog: that it was for 'medicinal purposes'. They realised the health values of meat and cloaked their love of game with the term *yakuro* or, 'medicinal hunting'.

Increasing contact with Westerners in the sixteenth and seventeenth centuries also alerted the Japanese to the fact that they were physically smaller, a situation they attributed to the Western traders' meat habit. Around this time, according to historian Katarzyna Cwiertka, so-called 'beast restaurants', serving horse, wild boar and venison, became popular.

By the second half of the nineteenth century, as the trading ports of Nagasaki, Hakodate, Yokohama and Kobe opened up to the West, eating meat became yet more popular – even the Emperor was at it and the floodgates opened with his 1872 announcement (and public meal of beef on 24 January 1873) that meat was permitted. Within five years, Tokyo was consuming twenty-five cows a day, and within ten years hundreds of restaurants serving meat sprang up across the country.

Beef consumption increased dramatically in the post-war period for much the same reason as in the latter part of the nineteenth century: the Japanese saw their American conquerors were bigger and stronger and attributed this to their meat intake. In 1955 the Japanese ate an average of 3kg of meat per year. Today, according to some estimates, they eat over 30kg.

Those open ports were also the starting points of a more general craze for Western food and dining practices, such as the use of tables and chairs. Improbable as it may sound, initially at least, the Japanese adopted British cuisine as their favourite foreign food, because it was simpler and cheaper to produce than French – hence the otherwise perplexing rise of Worcestershire sauce and 'curry rice', both still popular in Japan today. The Japanese had seen how the British suppressed India and they didn't want it happening to them. The solution? Get with the meat programme!

And this is where the misnomer 'Kobe beef' stems from. Of all the nineteenth-century international trading ports, Kobe was the most cosmopolitan. These days there are still said to be over a hundred different nationalities living in the city, and visiting ships always knew they could rely on finding a good steak on arrival. Kobe was the birthplace of one of the most popular ways of eating beef in Japan, which helped cement its position as a recognisable global brand. The dish was teppanyaki – in which cubes of beef are briefly seared on a hot plate – invented in the 1950s by an okonomiyaki chef who wanted to offer American diners a dish they might recognise.

But not all Japanese beef is Kobe beef, in fact, since most countries had until recently banned beef exports from Japan since the BSE crises of 2001, anything purporting to be Kobe beef that you might have encountered in, say, one of those outlandish burgers with foie gras and truffles in New York or London, has probably come from the American Midwest, Australia or China. Even in Japan, Kobe accounts for only a small percentage of beef production. It is, after all, a city crammed onto a small stretch of land between the mountains and the sea. There ain't much room for grazing.

A better name might be Wagyu beef, but that too is a little broad (it means, simply, 'Japanese beef'). The main cattle raising districts of Japan are Maesawa, Yonezawa, Yamagata, Kobe and Matsusaka. Over eighty per cent of cattle raised in these areas today is black-haired, short-horn Tajima-gyu cows or 'Japanese Blacks', many of which start their life on the southern islands of Okinawa before coming to mainland Japan to be reared. The consensus among the chefs and foodies I had spoken to so far was that, of these, the best beef came from those raised in Matsusaka between the Kumozu river in the north and the Miyagawa river to the south. The beef here is said to be more beautiful, tender and tasty than any other.

We'd seen this extraordinary meat, which looked like inverse raspberry ripple ice cream, with the branches of fat – called sashi – lacing extravagantly through the red flesh, on sale in supermarkets everywhere, but our first chance to taste it came in Kyoto, in a shabu shabu restaurant in the city's famous Pontocho nightlife district.

Shabu shabu is half dinner, half performance art in which bacon-thin escalopes of beef are wafted in a small charcoal-heated samovar – a hoko nabe – full of a very light, simmering konbu dashi. Shizuo Tsuji says that the name shabu shabu comes from the supposed sound this wafting of the beef makes in the water but it is not a traditional Japanese dish at all; it only arrived in Japan in the early twentieth century and is generally considered Mongolian in origin. The meat is wafted for mere seconds, and then dipped either in ponzu or a sesame-based sauce, or sometimes raw egg. After the precious meat had been eaten – with great enthusiasm from Asger and Emil, these kind of theatrical cooking techniques might have well been invented for small boys – mushrooms, onions, cabbage and tofu – less enthusiastically received, it must be said – went into the pot. As with the chanko nabe experience in Tokyo, just as we thought we'd conquered the whole lot, the waiter brought us noodles to add to the broth, which had by now become lightly flavoured by the ingredients.

We tried another way of eating Japanese beef, sukiyaki, the next day. Sukiyaki uses slightly thicker escalopes of beef fried in beef tallow on a hot skillet, then dipped in a sugary soy-mirin sauce (Japanese Food Schism No. 286: In the east they cook the meat in the sauce; in the west, they use it as a dip.). It was a little too sugary for my taste although the children devoured it like wolves: but then again, it is no great leap from sugary beef to a Big Mac, is it?

On both occasions the beef itself was a vivid pinky red and webbed with veins of fat to the extent that it was a split decision as to whether we were eating fatty meat or meaty fat. Its texture was akin to the most tender milkfed veal, as unctuous as Brylcreem and it lingered on the tongue for just a few moments before melting away like butter in a hot pan. Alone it had a creamy, indefinably savoury flavour, like uncommonly tasty fat.

I wanted to get to the bottom – the rump, if you like – of this extraordinary meat. How could they breed beef that was so rich and fatty without the cows keeling over from heart attacks? Could all the rumours concerning the beer, the music and the sake rubs be true?

The rumours are to be found in the most reliable of sources: Japanese food writer Kimiko Barber says, for instance: 'The beef is marbled because the cattle are massaged with beer to distribute the fat throughout the meat.' I had seen this claim made for Japanese cattle-rearing in newspapers and books countless times. But could massage actually *move* fat around in this way, I wondered. And did beer really add to the fattiness of the meat as others claimed? Could there be a farmer on earth who played music to their animals?

If all the rumours were true, I had a very clear vision of what I wanted to achieve with my research. Since I'd started reading about Japanese beef, I had formed a shameful, childish ambition. I hadn't mentioned it to anyone, not even Lissen, for fear of that she would dismiss this entire Japan project as the self-indulgent folly of a crazed and immature man.

I wanted to give a massage to a cow.

It was partly the absurdity of it that appealed, but also, I'll admit, the cheap kudos of participating in the production of one of the word's greatest gourmet products. I became fixated on capturing the money shot of me, standing next to a cow, giving it a meaningful rub. And if Matsusaka was where the best beef was raised, this was where my cow groping would have to take place.

Matsusaka is a historic castle town in central Mie Prefecture, about three hours by local train south-east of Osaka. Figuring that out had been the easy part. The rest – finding people from the cattle industry in Matsuzaka who were willing to talk to me – was less straightforward.

Initial confusion on the part of the various local authorities I contacted – 'Sorry, we don't export' – was soon replaced by mistrustful suspicion, then stalling, with endless emails bounced back and forth. Which magazine did I write for and when would the article be published? Could I send copies of articles I had written about beef before? Tell us again what was your interest in Japanese beef? What did you say your name was? And so on, round and round in an endless polite holding pattern. And I hadn't even dared mention the real reason why I wanted to visit a Matsusaka cattle farm.

Eventually, through sheer persistence, some dates and meetings were set up at the renowned Wadakin ranch, but I was not allowed to bring anyone apart from a translator. So instead of being accompanied by Lissen and the kids, I set off from Osaka station for Matsusaka with my new friend Sasha the ponytailed Serbian (who spoke Japanese), from my cooking demonstration in Kyoto.

The three-hour train ride gave us a chance to get to know each other and for Sasha to expound upon Serbia's benign role in the Balkan conflict and the glories of Serbian cuisine – which he claimed was the motherlode of all European cooking.

This probably sounds as if Sasha was boastful or deluded, but he was actually quite a modest man. His dream, he told me, was to return to Serbia to open an authentic Japanese restaurant. 'It will be over many floors of the same building,' he told me. 'The ground floor will be common people's food like ramen and curry rice, then the higher you get the more refined the food will be until, right at the top, you will have kaiseki.' It wasn't a bad idea, actually.

Arriving by train in Matsusaka, the nature of the town's main industry is immediately obvious. Advertising hoardings promote beef restaurants, butchers shops and ranches wherever you look. As we arrived at the Wadakin ranch – which looked more like a well-manicured country club – I had my strategy all planned out. I would listen attentively as the farmers explained their methods, taking assiduous notes and asking serious questions in order to appear a proper cow enthusiast. At no point would I be so crass as to ask outright whether or not they massaged the cows or, heaven forbid, if I might give one 'a bit of a rub.' I would bide my time until I judged the moment was right, then I would ask, casually, if I might, you know, perhaps just take a quick peak at some actual cows, for 'research purposes'. Then, lingering by the stalls, I hoped to catch a glimpse of their secret husbandry techniques; to try and see any massage-and-beer action going down; and perhaps even get Sasha to distract the farmers while I nipped under the fence and, under the pretence of just, you know, patting a cow, give it a surreptitious knead. At least then I could honestly say that I had massaged a cow.

What was the worst that could happen if they caught me? Sure, I would have to leave in utter ignominy, heaping shame upon my family and country, but if I got to rub a cow it would be worth it.

Imagine my surprise, then, upon arriving at the farm to find a field with four horned, black-haired Tajima-gyu cows with yellow rings through their noses loitering in it, and two cow hands standing by with giant, four-litre bottles of shochu, a crate of beer and two woven straw rubbing mats.

I was barely out of the car and shaking hands with my hosts before one of them was showing me how to take a mouthful of shochu, then spray it over the side of the cow before rubbing it into his hide with a bundle of woven straw, and then egging me on to try it for myself!

My prime ambition for this entire trip was about to come to fruition, without even having to demean myself any more than usual: I was going to give a massage to a cow.

I heaved the huge shochu bottle up to my lips, thought about wiping the rim but decided it was best not to blow this chance of a lifetime by insulting my hosts' oral hygiene, and took a mouthful of the burning liquor. I summoned all my lung power, puckered and pointed at the side of the cow, and let rip with a messy, dribbling spurt, much of which ended up down my shirtfront. The Wadakin ranch hands looked on with broad grins. I half expected a hidden TV crew to emerge, perhaps from the back end of the cow, but the handler urged me on with the straw, showing me how to rub vertically to ensure the shochu permeated the animal's coarse black hair. He then offered me a large, brown bottle of beer. The cow, seeing this, started swinging its head around excitedly. I plunged the bottle into its mouth although in the gnashing of teeth and flailing of cow lips much of its contents fell to the floor as the animal desperately tried to suck the bottle dry.

The farm hands looked on approvingly and I felt a chapter of my life had drawn to close. I had done it. I had massaged a cow. I felt empty, shallow and not a little foolish, but somewhere there was also a perverse sense of achievement.

Not having had much practice at spitting at cows, I had managed to swallow a good proportion of the spirit, so the interview with Kinbe Matsuda, the founder of Wadakin and one of the most respected cattle breeders in Japan, was not as coherent as I would have wished. Here is what I could decipher from my notes.

The cows are raised to the age of ten months in Hyōgo prefecture, another of the main cattle breeding areas of Japan, before being brought to the Wadakin ranch. They are bred only for meat, never to produce milk and not for breeding, and are slaughtered, virgins, at three years and ten months. By this stage a diet of mostly rice stems, with some corn, soybeans and grain will have brought them to a weight of six to seven hundred kilos. After slaughter, one hundred grams of their meat will sell for ¥4,800 (almost £20) in Wadakin's restaurant, which is the only outlet for Wadakin beef in the world.

'Why the beer?' I asked.

'If one of them isn't eating as much as they should it helps give them an appetite,' Mastuda, who is the fourth generation of his family to run the farm, told me. 'We don't do it every day.'

And why shochu? 'Because it is cheap and high in alcohol which is good against insects.'

And did they really play the cows music?

'No, that's ridiculous.'

On the subject of exactly why Wadakin massages its cows, Mastuda-san was a little more vague. 'We massage to stop the fat building up,' he said, or at least that's how Sasha translated it. 'The fat is very important for the flavour,' he added. 'It is very healthy. Not much cholesterol, like olive oil.'

We got to taste some Wadakin beef at the farm's lavish five-storey restaurant and hotel complex back in central Matsusaka. The restaurant's speciality is sukiyaki, but I wanted to try Wadakin beef in its purest state, as sashimi. It was served with just a dipping sauce of ginger and soy, and was sweet and creamy and lacking in that metallic, bloody flavour that rare beef has back home. It was also actually a little tougher than the other Japanese beef I had eaten, which was no bad thing.

So, all in all, a triumphant day. But on the train home something was still nagging me. I had the feeling people had been telling me things I wanted to hear, that I hadn't really found the definitive answers I had been looking for. So, a couple of days later, following more delicately negotiated phone calls, I headed back to Matsusaka, this time alone.

I was met by the manager of the local beef research centre. We drove in his none-too-fragrant Honda to a group of cow sheds which were home to a couple of hundred Herefords and black Tajimas.

Along the way I bombarded him with questions. Why was Japanese beef so expensive? And why was it so tender? What did they feed the cows? Was it true about the massage and the beer? Was Wadakin for real, or is that just something they lay on for tourists?

'Raising cows here is a very labour intensive process,' he explained. 'It takes so long. We don't slaughter them until thirty months and they don't produce milk during that time. Look,' he pointed to a concave indentation in the back of one of the cows as we arrived at the sheds. 'that's how we judge when to slaughter – when that indent reaches about the size of an egg, they are ready.'

Wadakin was for real, he continued, the beer does stimulate appetite but he didn't really agree with its use. The real secret to Japanese beef, he told me, is the breed and the feed, that and the fact that most of their herd were females, which were more tender than the males. 'The black Japanese cows are the only ones that you can get this marbling with. We feed them only grass to start with,' he gestured to a couple of big-eyed black cows munching lazily in their stalls. 'Then they get rice straw, which is one of the most important factors in creating the marbling. After ten months we only feed them rice straw with a little green straw or grass because this helps to create the fat cells. Green grass stops the production of fat cells because it is rich in Vitamin A. They still need a little Vitamin A though, otherwise their legs get swollen and they go blind, so they get some green stuff.' He claimed, perhaps less plausibly, that the Japanese prefer these kinds of ultra tender meats because their 'jaw muscles are not so strong because we are used to eating a traditional diet of rice'.

He led one cow out of its stable and offered me a metal-toothed brush. 'You can have a go if you want.' Being by now an old hand at Japanese cow husbandry techniques I began giving the animal a vigorous brushing.

And the massage? How did that affect the marbling? 'It doesn't have any direct effect on the fat, but the cows like it, it keeps them relaxed which might mean they eat more. But we usually only do it before they are slaughtered to calm them.'

I stopped brushing. So, *that* was the secret. Massaging was essentially a relaxation regime – happy cows make for good meat – it was a complete myth that it created the marbling.

But you know what? The truth is, I think when all is said and done, Japanese beef is nice once in a while, but really it is too tender and fatty for me. It's not the health consequences that bother me so much, it's more that I like a bit of resistance in my meat. Should beef really melt in the mouth? It's not ice cream, it's an animal.

Chapter 29

Ama Divers

On the train back from Matsusaka I browsed through some brochures from the local tourist office. In one, on the history of Mie Prefecture, my eye was caught by a strangely haunting, sepia photograph of two women dressed from head to foot in white hooded jump suits and wearing goggles. They looked like uncommonly stylish welders, but according to the brief paragraph underneath these were the fabled female divers, or ama, who have swum in the waters off the easterly Pacific coast of Mie for almost two thousand years.

The next page was about Mikimoto Pearls, the first company to cultivate pearls, founded by Kokichi Mikimoto, the son of a noodle maker, in 1893. Mikimoto was based in the city of Toba. Looking at the map on the back of the brochure I saw that Toba and Sugajima, one of the main areas for ama divers, were about an hour's drive from each other on the Sakishima Peninsula.

Drawing on a decade of professional experience, I did what all journalists do when presented with two small snippets of possibly related information, I fashioned them into a dramatic story. By the time I arrived back at the house in Kyoto I was able to tell Lissen and the boys heroic tales of female divers who dressed in white to scare killer sharks and could hold their breath for half an hour while diving for pearls worth as much as a house.

The next day, I contacted the Mie tourist board to find out more. Were any of the lady pearl-divers still alive? Yes, absolutely, but they didn't dive for pearls, the tourist board official told me. All the pearls produced in the region were farmed. Of course, if I had thought about it for a moment, I would have realised that you don't need to dive for cultivated pearls – that's the whole point of cultivating them. The ama divers dive instead for abalone, scallops, sea cucumbers, seaweed and sea urchins. Was there any chance I could meet them, I asked. No problem, she said. How about tomorrow?

So, the day after that, 1 October, we caught the train to Toba. We were met at the station by two representatives of the tourist board who whisked us off on a spectacularly scenic minibus ride around the Ago Bay to the village of Osatsu, where most of the thousand or so ama divers live.

We drove along precipitous roads through forested hills high above a cobalt sea dotted with rocky islets. In the West the only images we tend to get of Japan are overwhelmingly urban, but this was a potent reminder that once you break free of the concrete and the malls, Japan has natural beauty to match anywhere in the world.

We eventually came to a ramshackle fishing village on a horse-shoe bay, and parked on the beach. A narrow path hugging the side of the cliffs led, at a startling height from the crashing waves below, to a small hut a couple of hundred metres away at the mouth of the bay. Here, we were told, our lunch would be prepared. As we walked further out towards the ocean we started to hear an eerie whistling noise, then, as we arrived at a wooden hut at the end of the path, two figures emerged from the sea up a ladder to meet us.

And there they were, the sepia-toned ladies brought to life: two real-life ama divers, Tamie Kosaki and Kayo Kosaki, sisters in their early forties. They were carrying wooden tubs in which were a handful of intriguing shellfish.

They showed us into the wooden shack where an open fire – or robata – had already burned down to hot ash in the middle of the floor. We sat around it as the women grilled their catch – sazae sea snails and scallops, as well as some pre-bought squid and clams – and began to unravel the story of the ama divers.

Thirty years ago there were four hundred divers living in Osatsu alone, they said, but the numbers were declining everywhere and now there were only three thousand in the entire region. There were two types of ama divers, those who swam out from the shore and fished around ten metres from the beach, and those – usually husband and wife couples – who sailed further out, around thirty metres, to dive. Both types of divers are highly respected in the community, like village elders.

The women dive almost every day for about an hour at a time, while the husband stays on the boat. I made some lame joke about marital relations at this point but apparently women have always been the divers in these parts because the locals believed their extra body fat meant they were better insulated to dive into deeper, colder waters, and – slightly less plausibly – that they have larger lungs, and so could hold their breath longer.

'We use about ten kilos of weights to go down and as we are pulled back up we whistle to control our breathing. If we breath too fast it is dangerous,' said Tamie. They demonstrated. It was the eerie, breathy whistling sound we had heard as we arrived, deeply evocative for the Japanese, apparently.

'We start usually at around twenty years old but the oldest ama is eighty-one, and she is still diving. We dive for shellfish but also seaweed, it depends on the time of year. In March we dive for seaweed, now the number-one thing is sea cucumber.'

What was their most prized catch? 'Abalone, but it is so difficult,' said her sister. 'They stick to the rocks very firmly and it takes time to get them off. We don't have much time because we hold our breath.'

'How long can you hold your breath?' asked Asger, who had been practising his own breath-holding on the train ride there. 'I can do it this long.' He puffed out his cheeks and began to turn pink, exhaling dramatically after about ten seconds.

'About a minute and a half,' Tamie said, laughing. 'Of course, if we are still we can hold it much longer, but we have to use a lot of energy swimming around on the seabed looking for the shells.'

I could understand why ama divers hadn't used oxygen in the past when the technology hadn't existed, but why didn't they use it now?

'Today we have to be careful about over fishing,' said Kayo. 'Without oxygen it limits how long we can search for the shellfish so we don't catch so much. We have to check their size with this [she held up a forceps-style measure] so that we don't catch the young ones.'

Lissen asked about the white suits. Were they really originally worn to frighten off sharks? 'No, it is more to protect against jellyfish and sunburn. We do see sharks though, about one metre long, but they are not dangerous. What we do is dangerous though. Last year one diver was hospitalised when she got trapped in the rope. We wear this symbol,' she pointed at a star-shaped badge. 'It is our charm against the sharks'.

As Kayo spoke she turned one of the sazae on the grill. Its juices spat across the hut. Asger and Emil looked on with horror and fascination, recoiling with wide eyes when offered one on the end of a fork.

As the guest of honour I didn't have the privilege of refusal, even though my experience of snails is of a great deal of chewing with not much flavour by way of reward. I once visited a snail farm on a Finnish island. The woman running it explained that before you eat snails you have to starve them so they – and there is no delicate way of putting this – expel all their waste matter. These snails, though not the same species, had clearly not undergone this purging, having just been wrenched from the sea, which probably explained the bitter aftertaste from their dark green intestine. I had to eat five.

Was this one of their favourite dishes, I asked. 'Oh no,' they both shook their heads. 'Uni [sea urchin] with rice. Very simple: rice with lots of rice vinegar and seaweed and vegetables with uni on top.'

Back in Toba we had some time to kill before catching our train to Kyoto. As the home of Mikimoto, Toba is famous for its pearls. The surface of its beautiful rocky bay is covered with the wooden rafts used to suspend the oysters to grow the pearls. In the middle of it all is Pearl Island, a theme park built by the mighty Mikimoto company. Inside, lavish exhibits explained how they cultivated pearls within the shells of Akoya oysters: 'A portion of the internal organs is parted with a spatula and a small incision is made in the surface of the body of the oyster with a scalpel. Then, very gently, a path is made through the incisors into the gonads.' Something to think about the next time you reach for that twinset.

In a rash moment of holiday euphoria I encouraged Lissen to buy anything she wanted from the row of pearl shops along the seafront (I should also add that it was nearly her birthday). But panic set in as soon as I saw the prices and I spent the rest of the afternoon making disparaging comments about the various strings of pearls that caught her eye. 'Ooh, no, they're terribly vulgar,' I said, sucking my teeth. 'Those make you look fat.' Unfortunately, Lissen is a trained jeweller and can tell a good pearl from fifty paces. She sent me and the boys to look at the massive waterfront aquarium while she got down to some serious bargaining.

Chapter 30

The Greatest Soy Sauce in the World

The next day, alone, I travelled by bus across the Akashi Kaikyo suspension bridge to an island in the inland sea; an island so beautiful I regarded it from the window in a kind of blissful trance. There were gentle mountains and gorges packed tight with tombstones; distant glinting seas; giant wheeling tombi hawks, silhouetted against a crisp, blue sky; rice-straw wigwams drying in the sun; and ceramic-tiled wooden houses, as seen in dozens of samurai movies.

I was travelling to Shikoku Island to taste the world's greatest soy sauce, the soy equivalent of cold-pressed, extra virgin, single-estate olive oil, or fifty-year-old Modena balsamico; a true gourmet rarity produced in the traditional method by, in fact, an ancient samurai family.

But first, the supermarket stuff.

The single most important ingredient in Japanese food is not rice – which is more than a mere ingredient, it is virtually a spiritual element to a meal – but soy sauce. Though the Japanese do use salt in their cooking – and, as I was to discover on Okinawa, they produce some of the greatest salts in the world – the majority of their seasoning comes from this fabulously savoury, ebony brown, viscous liquid.

They consume on average over eight litres each per year of various types: light and salty usukuchi, traditionally associated with the west of Japan; less salty, dark koikuchi, traditionally favoured in the east of Japan and accounting for eighty per cent of the market; another soy made with equal parts wheat and soybeans; one made with added amazake – a fermented rice drink – as well as saishikomi, shiro and tamari soy, the latter thicker and richer and made using little if no wheat.

One soy company dominates both the domestic and global soy markets. Kikkoman's distinctive little squat-bottomed bottles with the double spouted, brittle red plastic screw tops are ubiquitous the world over, found on every table of every Chinese and Japanese restaurant from Washington to Wolverhampton, and in most domestic kitchens too. The company has plants in Holland, China and the US, producing over four hundred million litres per year. It is the Coca-Cola of the soy sauce world. And the Pepsi Cola, come to that. Well, can you name another soy brand?

Japanese soy has traditionally been made in Chiba Prefecture, in either Choshi or Noda, and sent down the river to Tokyo. They have been exporting it further afield to France since the seventeenth century – Louis XIV was said to have been a fan. Kikkoman started in Noda three hundred years ago, where it still has its base. Back when we were still in Tokyo at the beginning of our journey, almost two months earlier, I took an interminable train ride there twenty miles north across the endless expanse of Tokyo's suburbs.

Noda was very clearly a one company town. The air was thick with the meaty smell of soy sauce – a kind of sweet, beefy, wheaty aroma, but Kikkoman didn't appear to have brought great wealth to Noda which was a rather bleak, ramshackle low-rise place, dominated by the giant, rusting hulks of wheat storage tanks.

I had hoped to visit Goyogura, the exclusive brewery dedicated to making soy sauce for the Imperial Household, but that was undergoing renovation. Instead Hiroyuki Yano, a nice man from the PR department, showed me around the visitor's centre, starting with the dreaded corporate video ('Defying the passing of time and national boundaries, since times of old, that's Kikkoman!'), before we followed the process of turning soybeans into soy sauce, or shoyu, via windows into the factory itself.

It is a surprisingly straightforward process, which probably explains why home brewing of soy was commonplace in Japan until the war.

The main ingredients are steamed soybeans and roasted, crushed wheat, in Kikkoman's case non-GM and grown in the US and Canada (the Emperor's soy sauce is made exclusively with domestic ingredients). These are fermented using the Kikkoman aspergillus bacteria, a koji, which is mixed with brine to make a mash called moromi, and left to develop for six months. Sugar and amino acids combine to create that deep caramel colour while yeasts and lactic acid create the aromas – there are three hundred different aromas in soy, apparently, a figure comparable to wine. The moromi, an unpleasant looking orangey-brown mash, is churned and then pressed in 2,800 metre long nylon sacks, before being pasteurised.

What was the difference between this and how the Chinese make their soy, I asked Yano-san. 'The fermentation process is different. Some of them are made by chemical process,' he sniffed. 'They can use acid to take the protein from the beans, for instance.' Some companies add corn syrup and artificial caramel, or even hydrolyzed vegetable protein and hydrochloric acid, but not Kikkoman.

Until thirty years ago Kikkoman made its soy sauce by fermenting the moromi in traditional wooden trays, a method originally devised because it allowed the temperature to be easily regulated by lifting the trays to control the circulation of air. These days they use giant, glass-lined, temperature-controlled stainless steel tanks. There are 2,000 of them in the Noda plant alone although this isn't the biggest Kikkoman factory – that is in Wisconsin. This vast scale of production enables the company to sell its soy sauce for less than the cost of bottled water.

I was impressed by the straightforward, relatively 'slow food' brewing process at Kikkoman, but a chance tasting of another, far more subtle, rich and soft artisanal soy in a restaurant in Kyoto sent me off on the trail of a rather more refined soy sauce, made at the Kamebishi Brewery on the island of Shikoku.

Kamebishi is the only soy company in Japan still making soy sauce the old-fashioned way, using the mushiro method, in which the fermenting beans are spread out on woven straw mats placed on top of bamboo trays. The resulting mash is left to mature for a minimum of two years.

Kamebishi was founded over two hundred years ago and is still run by the seventeenth generation of the Okada family, originally of samurai stock. The factory remains in the small rural town of Higashikagawa, in the original samurai house, a sprawling, single-storey, red stucco farmhouse with a heavy, ceramic tiled roof.

The current head of the clan is Kanae Okada, a single mother who returned from a high-flying career in the travel industry in Tokyo to rescue the family firm some years ago. 'When I was growing up I never wanted to be a part of it and my father didn't force me,' Kanae told me. 'I went off to work in the US, worked in Tokyo and had a child. I worked at the Japan Cultural Centre and many of my colleagues there had a cultural speciality, like kabuki or sumo and I felt so ashamed that I had neglected this part of my heritage. In the States it was the same, everyone was so interested in my family but I couldn't answer any of their questions. So I returned fifteen years ago to start running the company.'

Kanae recognised the cultural and commercial importance of her family's product and was determined to save it from the brink of bankruptcy. This she has done with a mix of shrewd business sense, a respect for traditional methods and some remarkable new product innovations, including freeze-dried soy for use as a seasoning, and a soy sauce that she ages for – so far – twenty-seven years.

'We are very different from Kikkoman,' Kanae told me as she showed me around. 'We roast our wheat on hot sand to 200°C. We use whole soybeans; they use dried beans with the oil removed. We ferment the moromi on straw mats on top of bamboo slats at between 28°C and 30°C. We age it for a minimum of three years in cedar barrels. It is very intensive, very intuitive.'

Kanae is the first woman in Japan to run a soy company. What about her sixteen-year-old daughter? I asked. Will she take over the company one day? 'Actually, she isn't like I was when I was growing up. She is really proud of what we do. She comes with me on business trips and explains things to clients. Many young Japanese are fed up with being white collar, they want to make things. We used to have a real problem getting workers – you know, we are quite a way from anywhere here – but we get many young people coming to work here now. Only a few can cope with the hard work, but I think they will come back to the old ways. Ten years ago we were having a real crisis. Sales were dead, but now they have doubled.' Perhaps the traditional sectors of the tofu and sake industry could benefit from a similarly dynamic, innovative approach.

We clambered up into the dark, cobwebbed loft where they keep the hundred-year-old cedar barrels containing the slowly fermenting soy – all the better to control the flow of air and, thus, the temperature. Every surface – walls, floor, old pipes, ceilings – was caked with a thick, tar-like crust. We gingerly tiptoed across the top of the barrels – essentially large wooden tanks, set into the floor. It reminded me of Fagin's London, and I must have pulled a bit of a face as Kanae said: 'You know it isn't dirty. It is decades of fungal growth but, actually, the whole process is extremely hygienic. We never clean it. Someone from the government's hazard analysis department came and said we had to clean everything, but I had to explain that this environment is exactly what makes our soy taste so special. The mould here is more than two hundred years old! We did tests and found two hundred and thirty different types of bacteria, yeast fungus and microbes – all of them are part of our fermentation process. These micro fungi produce lots of alcohol so in the summer it gets above 40°C and really smells of booze.' In other words, the entire building was alive with fertile microorganisms, a giant fermentation chamber.

The floor was slippery, and the barrels about two metres deep. Has anyone ever fallen in? I asked. 'Yes, I did once, when I was four. It was full of soy, too. Luckily there was someone to fish me out, or I would probably have died.'

The result of all this effort (for the first two nights of fermentation, someone has to babysit the mash, stirring it and maintaining the right temperature) is a soy that is richer and smoother tasting than

233

supermarket soy. It sells for roughly twice the price, but that is still, to me, ridiculously cheap for an artisanal product.

We retired to Kanae's office to talk about the future of soy. 'I started to make soy salt for the French and Italian chefs because they couldn't season their food with soy sauce because of the colour. Now lots of Italian chefs are using it. It is packed with umami. You can think of it as natural MSG. Pascal Barbot and Alain Ducasse are very interested in using it.'

Then she brought out the special stuff. 'And this,' she said proudly brandishing a bottle whose contents were pitch black and syrupy, 'is the twenty-seven-year-old aged soy. The only aged soy in the world. I got the idea when I visited a balsamic vinegar producer in Modena who had a hundred-year-old balsamic, which tasted incredible. We are not going to sell this until it is fifty years old, but you can taste it now if you like.' It was rich and deep, with a powerfully lactic taste, hints of sherry, cedarwood and grilled steak, like a refined, complex Marmite but without the afterburn.

They also sell a ten-year-old soy for around £100 a bottle – presumably the most expensive soy sauce in the world – which, though not quite as intense, is wonderful drizzled over carpaccio, just like balsamic. Even more exciting were Kanae's plans for the future, which include soy maple syrup for ice creams, chocolate soy flakes, caramel soy and balsamic soy salt. 'The chocolate isn't quite ready – it needs more of an umami boost.' (Since my visit, the chocolate has been perfected, and is now on sale.)

Wandering around after our meeting, while waiting for my bus, I chanced upon another ancient, artisanal food producer, making wasanbonto sugar. This is the so-called King of Sugars – primarily sold as ultra-fine sugar bonbons, little balls the size of peas wrapped in tissue paper, and made by hand from sugar cane for over two centuries. Legend has it that a pilgrim from Southern Kyushu, at that time the only place allowed to grow sugar cane in Japan, walked all the way to Shikoku smuggling a chikuto sugar cane plant, and upon arrival collapsed and died. They planted the sugar cane and, it turned out, the soil and water were perfect for its cultivation. The cane flourished and when processed by squeezing then boiling the juice, then stone pressing the syrup to refine it, it produced much smaller, powder-sized crystals than the same plants grown in Kyushu. At ¥3,000 per kilo it is, today, the most expensive sugar in Japan. I just had time, as my bus came in to view, to buy some of the company's bonbons, which were extraordinarily fine. They dissolved quickly on my tongue, leaving a faintly flowery, sweet aftertaste.

Chapter 31

A Tale of Two Cooking Schools, Part II

We had been settled in Osaka for a over a week. It was time to meet the other contestant vying for the culinary papacy of Japan, the man hoping to replace Shizuo Tsuji as the leading authority on Japanese cuisine. You'll remember that in Tokyo I had met Yukio Hattori, famous for inventing the TV cook-off show *Iron Chef* and head of the Ecole de Cuisine et Nutrition Hattori in Tokyo. He had staked his claim with his in-depth knowledge of the health issues involved in Japanese food, his involvement with the Japanese government's Shokuiku programme, and the fact that he had promised to take me to dinner in the best restaurant in Japan.

Now I was to meet his chief rival, Yoshiki Tsuji, the son of Shizuo and, since his father's death in 1993, the President of Japan's largest cooking school, the Osaka-based Tsuji Culinary Institute (TCI), bastion of the Kansai method of cooking.

I had emailed the school before we left for Japan and had been surprised to receive a reply from Tsuji himself, inviting me to visit, which is how I found myself waiting in the TCI's grand conference room, surrounded by French antiques at a vast oval oak table beside a bust of Shizuo Tsuji. I awaited the arrival of his son.

Assistants entered first, offering tea and informing me of Tsuji's imminent arrival. Soon after their boss arrived. With a smooth, handsome face, and dressed in a sleek grey sports jacket and dark trousers, Yoshiki Tsuji, forty-three, looked like a Japanese Richard Gere. He later told me he was an enthusiastic triathelete, which explained his trim physique and perhaps, too, the sense of coiled, latent energy.

He spoke softly, with the minimum of projection, as if used to people hanging on his every word.

We moved into a lounge area, part of his private office, where he explained a little about the school. There were over five thousand students in various buildings here in Osaka, he said, as well in two chateaux the school owns in southern France – Chateau de L'Eclair (found for Tsuji senior by his good friend Paul Bocuse), and Chateau Escoffier – and a smaller school in Tokyo. There was, he said, a roughly equal male:female split among the students, who come mostly from Japan but also from South Korea and Taiwan and are aged from graduate level to over sixty. They are taught Japanese, French and Italian cooking, as well as patisserie and baking.

I asked if Tsuji-san felt at all papal. 'No, no, but I do feel extremely responsible,' he said. 'We are creating craftsmen here. We do have fewer and fewer students wanting to learn Japanese cuisine because it is so demanding, but we are one of the first schools to realise the danger of this.'

Can he cook himself? 'Only breakfast. I have had training since the age of twelve, but stopped cooking once I turned eighteen.' His father wrote over thirty books – not just on food, but on various other passions including music and Tsuji has so far written two of his own – *The Theory of Evolution of Epicurism*, and *An Introduction to the Food Industry*. But his business training in the US has helped him find new ways to develop and expand the school, taking advantage of the economic slowdown in Japan to take over a neighbouring bank, for example. The TCI is now a mini-town in its own right, having spread through several neighbouring tower blocks in this part of Osaka.

'Would you like to see them?' Tsuji asked. I would, I said, expecting a PR flunky to take me on a brief tour. 'Then let's go,' he said. Tsuji was clearly proud of his school and wanted to show it to me personally. It soon became apparent why. It was not merely the most impressive culinary school I had ever seen – making my alma mater, the Paris Cordon Bleu, look like a Ugandan bush primary school in comparison – but one of the most impressive educational establishments one could imagine.

The first room we visited was a state-of-the-art kitchen-TV-studio built specially for filming and photography. It bustled with students working beneath arc lights, prepping dishes for the cameras. Next was the main lecture auditorium, twice as large as the one at Hattori's school, Tsuji pointed out, with highly polished mahogany writing desks and a gigantic stainless steel work station decorated with twelve copper pots hanging from the front, each sparkling beneath spotlights. It was designed by John Morford, the man behind the Park Hyatt Hotel in Tokyo (the *Lost in Translation* hotel) and, as with the rest of the school, it was clear that no expense had been spared on materials. Throughout, the decor was elegant and expensive, like a posh health farm, in grey slate and sophisticated beige and wherever we went, all the students were in crisp white uniforms with blue aprons and grey trousers. The chefs, meanwhile wore single-breasted white jackets, ties and tall toques.

All of the four hundred and ninety teaching staff are Japanese, Tsuji explained, and most of them are specialists, including one who has spent over thirty years perfecting the art of the tamago, or Japanese rolled omelette. 'We have the highest quality of teaching. There is huge competition to become a teacher here and many can't keep up with the standard once they come.' I had heard various stories about the brutality of Japanese chefs. How did they prepare students for the punishing regime of working in a real kitchen? 'The teachers aren't allowed to hit with their hands or with utensils, or use psychological bullying, but within those limits, they are extremely tough. They have to be,' said Tsuji.

Students pay upwards of £15,000 a year to attend, 'It is the most expensive cooking school in the world,' he told me proudly. 'Even though Dorothy Cann Hamilton still insists it is the Culinary Center in New York. I argue a little with her about that!' (Tsuji now has a foot in New York himself as the co-owner with David Bouley of a new Japanese restaurant called Brush Stroke.)

There was an entire building dedicated to French and Italian cooking, as well as another for advanced patisserie. In the administration block Tsuji pointed out the offices of the school psychologists, employed to help students assimilate into school life and solve personal problems, something they consider extremely important.

We sat in on a demonstration in a large, sparklingly clean kitchen. The chef was running through a 'sun'-themed menu, showing students how to tackle an entire sack of salmon roe, followed by a salmon filet dish in soy and yuzu. The chef pin-boned the salmon, deftly sliding the bones between his index and middle finger as he went like an expert seamstress. Then he marinated some salmon strips in soy, mirin, onion and vinegar together with a little dried chilli. The students sat attentively, the only noise the low thrum of the air conditioning.

In Europe and America the catering industry still relies on apprenticeships whereby keen youngsters work, often for nothing, in professional kitchens, starting on the lowest tier. The system is often abused to the extent where you might as well call it slavery but in Japan things are slightly different. 'It used to be that young chefs would literally have to sit outside in front of the restaurant they wanted to work in for a week, hoping to be allowed to join the kitchen – I am talking about the really famous restaurants – but that system has pretty much collapsed now. We don't have the culture of *stages* in Japan. We do have apprenticeships, which start at sixteen, but instead of getting paid they get accommodation, food and travel costs, but that is also declining now.'

In contrast, TCI graduates, are eagerly sought by the top restaurants in the country – fifteen thousand restaurants send requests to the school for one of their three thousand graduates each year.

When the demo finished Tsuji invited me to lunch. I followed him to one of the canteens, whose kitchen is entirely run by the students. At the Cordon Bleu, we would watch the chef demonstrate three courses, then adjourn to the practical kitchens to make the main course. Here, though, students were making ten courses for a dining room that would soon be filled by fifty or so very picky guests.

We were early, so Tsuji invited me to spend some time watching in the kitchen. I was astounded by the students' skill, organisation and the complexity of the dishes they were preparing. In one corner one male and one female student were putting the finishing touches to some exemplary sashimi plates, elsewhere another was deep frying somen noodles to use as decoration for and to add bite to tempura.

The meal was superb – elegant, colourful, fresh and inventive; I would have been hard pushed to distinguish it from a meal in a good local restaurant. We sat with some students. I asked one – with Tsuji translating – why he had come to the school: 'Because I love Japan and want to learn about Japanese culture,' was his Miss World-ish reply. 'Japanese cuisine is the coolest and most beautiful in the world,' said another. Right.

Over lunch I mentioned that I was looking forward to eating in one of Osaka's best restaurants, Kahala, that evening.

'Oh, yes, it's wonderful,' said Tsuji. 'How did you find out about it? Who are you going with?'

'Kadokami-san [Takeshi Kadokami, one of Kansai's leading food writers, whom I had met the previous day] recommended it. I am going alone. He says it's not really a place to take kids.'

Tsuji looked pained. 'You're going alone, but . . . no, no, we can't have that.' He reached inside his jacket and took out his diary. 'Let me see, well, would you mind if I accompanied you?'

'That would be great, yes, but I doubt you could get a table now, could you?' (The restaurant only seats eight and is booked up weeks in advance.)

'Oh, don't worry about that,' said Tsuji, beckoning a minion and speaking to him in Japanese.

A few moments later the assistant returned, and nodded once to indicate that it was all taken care of.

So, that evening Tsuji and I met once more at Kahala, the celebrated counter restaurant run by Yoshifumi Mori, a short, stout, grey haired chef in his early sixties.

Tsuji-san told me that Mori-san had run this chic, low-lit restaurant in the Kita Shinchi nightlife district of Osaka for thirty-five years. He is self-taught, and his often wildly imaginative cooking blends the most exquisite Japanese seasonal produce with French and contemporary 'molecular' techniques. Some have called him Japan's Ferran Adrià, which seemed appropriate as far as our first 'dish', a sparkling sake with wasabi, was concerned. His signature beef *millefeuille* followed – five ultra-thin, exceptionally tender layers of beef briefly seared on the hotplate in front of us by Mori-san himself – along with a glutinous shark's fin with matsutake mushroom, and hamo served with gigantic mustard seeds on a bed of soft konbu.

There were over ten courses in all, and I later discovered that the meal must have run to over ¥100,000 (£500) with the really quite serious bottle of vintage bordeaux that Tsuji ordered to go with it. He insisted on paying, and had in fact done so before I even realised the bill had been presented, but that was not the end of his hospitality.

'Do you have time for a drink perhaps?' he asked as we left.

A couple of doors further down the street, he turned, smiled, and led me into a basement entrance, his private members club, he explained. We were met by a heavily made-up middle-aged woman in a glamorous frock, and shown through to a long, narrow, brightly lit lounge.

My first thought – and this is honestly true – was 'Ah, isn't it nice that all these men have brought their wives out for the evening.' It was only when one of the 'wives' slinked over to our table and proceeded to sit next to me, so close that our thighs met, that reality dawned.

Before we had even sat down, Tsuji's personal bottle of single malt whisky had been retrieved from the club's storage and was waiting at our table. He poured glasses for me and the two women who had by now joined us. They were good friends he said. 'I often come here when I am alone in Osaka. My family lives in Tokyo you see. They really are friends of mine, sometimes I'll take one of them out to lunch or something.'

I smiled, suddenly a bashful teenager again, at the girls. The idea of paying for female company, even platonic, has always seemed self-defeating to me. If you are paying someone for their company then, by definition, their interest in you is insincere and meaningless, like the friendship of the dogs in the Bow Wow café. But within seconds I had completely fallen for the hostesses' charms. I was putty in their hands.

They were exceedingly good at their job, spoke a charming, broken English, and all too soon I grew utterly convinced that they really *were* interested in me for myself, that I had somehow seduced them: yes, they were that good. No matter that one looked like a young, Japanese Ava Gardner and the other had Renee Zellweger dimples, I genuinely believed they fancied me.

As the evening wore on, the conversation became more personal. I asked Tsuji where he had learned his impeccable English. At the age of twelve, his father sent him to Fettes boarding school, Tony Blair's alma mater. That must have been tough. 'Well, put it this way, I was the only Asian boy at boarding school.' It struck me as curious that a man with such a finely honed sensitivity to food as Shizuo Tsuji would send his son to live in Scotland. 'I tell you,' laughed Tsuji, 'it took ten years for my palate to recover!'

I mentioned that I had discussed Tsuji and Hattori's rivalry with chef Murata in Kyoto. When I'd asked him about Tsuji he had sniffed. 'Tsuji flies first class between Japan and Europe, and stays at the Ritz.' I mentioned this to Tsuji. Curiously, he took issue with Murata's choice of hotel. 'Pfh, I would never stay at the Ritz,' Tsuji said, affronted. 'I always stay at the George V!'

Chapter 32

Fukuoka

And so onwards the Booth family caravan rumbled, south the next morning by Shinkansen, the bullet train, to the island of Kyushu and its capital Fukuoka.

An efficient train system is often cited as a symbol of a well-functioning society but the Japanese rail network makes Switzerland's look like, well, the one I grew up with in Britain. It is the paragon for paragons of efficiency. Not only are trains punctual to within seconds (and are judged late if they arrive more than a minute after their allotted time), but when they arrive their doors line up exactly with corresponding markings on the platform so that, if you have an allocated seat, you know precisely where to wait on the platform. There are even 'queue' lines painted on the platform to guide you into the precise position for your quasi-reverential attendance.

The arrival of a Shinkansen is a show-stopping moment, its great white snout slowly gliding to a perfectly damped halt accompanied by various satisfied exhalations. This was the first time on the bullet train for Lissen, Asger and Emil. I had been building it up for days and was extremely excited in their behalf. In the end, Asger and Emil were fairly nonchalant about the whole thing, and all efforts to draw their attention to the aerodynamic shape of the train, the speed at which the landscape blurred by, and so on, fell on deaf ears and otherwise occupied eyes (with yet more new Pokémon figures).

Fukuoka is the end of the line for the Shinkansen, 1,175km from Tokyo. The line actually terminates in two cities: the smart castle town of Fukuoka, and the more mercantile Hakata. The two which merged in 1889 and are now home to 1.3 million people.

Fukuoka/Hakata-ites like to think of themselves as cultured and cosmopolitan – the city has high-speed ferry links to South Korea and it takes around the same time to fly to Shanghai as it does to Tokyo. Perhaps because of this, the city has a unique food culture centred on its yatai, or street-cart food stalls, which we found by chance while wandering through the city centre that evening.

We felt at ease in Fukuoka immediately. Of all the places we visited in Japan, this was the one we could most see ourselves returning to live in. Small enough to be manageable, but large enough to be interesting, Fukuoka also has a special atmosphere – relaxed, welcoming, fun loving and unpretentious. Throw in a great climate, excellent shops, museums and music venues and a buzzing nightlife district, and you have everything you could ever wish for in a city.

The yatai contribute their own casual-festive ambience to the city. On our first evening wandering in the city centre we turned a corner to see the Naka river lined with these chaotic food stalls, many of them on wheels, some of them swathed in plastic sheeting and looking like the camps I used to build with my brother in the woods, with bare light bulbs, steaming pots and crowds of diners queuing for a place at their trestle tables. Some were open, others were curtained. We were turned away from one of the latter as soon as the cook spotted the children, deducing, probably correctly, that their food wouldn't meet with Asger and Emil's approval. Others were more welcoming and soon we were all seated overlooking the river in the balmy evening air on small folding stools at a communal table each with a bowl of ramen before us.

Hakata ramen is based on a white-ish broth made from pork bones. It's a little spicier than other ramens, but thoroughly delicious. The next day we went in search of more and found a famous ramen shop, Ichiran, where diners eat in individual, curtained-off booths, as if at a peep show. Again the ramen was superb and the children were particularly proud to dine in their own private zones, although the waiters did rather tire of being summoned repeatedly by buzzer-happy fingers. The booths ran both sides of a small serving corridor behind which staff scurry around accommodating diners' needs. And, even without a four- and seven-year-old to test the waiters' patience, theirs is clearly a demanding clientele. Each diner gets a small questionnaire-type form to fill in where they can customise virtually every aspect of their bowl of noodle soup – the firmness of the noodles (extra firm, firm, medium, tender, extra tender), the strength of the onion, the fattiness of the broth, and so on. The 'no mobile phone' and, next to it, a 'no talking to your neighbour' sign, served notice that this was a place for the serious ramen aficionado, which brought to mind an extraordinary man I had met back in Tokyo.

Emi, my researcher friend, had taken me to the Ramen Museum in Yokohama to meet the World Ramen Champion, Mr Tahamiton Kobayashi, but before we enter his esoteric but fascinating world I should take a second to clarify the bewildering array of noodles available in Japan.

The traditional noodle division in Japan is that between soba and udon. Soba – thin, mottled noodles made from buckwheat flour (or more often a blend of buckwheat and wheat) – are supposedly preferred in eastern Japan, while udon – thick, soft, slippery, white flour-based noodles – are eaten in the west. This was originally because buckwheat grew well in the meagre soil around Tokyo; now, of course, you can eat all kinds of noodles throughout Japan, but still the gourmands of Kanto and Kansai cherish their differences. Toshi had made clear to me that there is a certain snobbery associated with eating zaru-soba: cold, cooked soba, served on a bamboo draining mat with a little dipping sauce. Eating warm soba in a large bowl of soup – a dish called kake-soba – is thought common (although he did admit to doing this in the privacy of his own home). Soba has an earthy, almost metallic grain flavour not unlike a French *galette* – both are made with buckwheat flour. If you can find the 100 per cent buckwheat variety, you can be confident you are doing your body a world of good as they are packed with vitamin B1 and B2 and have more protein than rice. Buckwheat is also rich in bioflavonoids, which are good for blood pressure, and antioxidants, thought to help ward against cancer. As buckwheat is a slow-release carbohydrate, you don't end up feeling zonked out half an hour after eating soba noodles as you do with pasta. Udon, meanwhile, is largely empty calories and probably the best thing to be said for it is that it fills you up and has a pleasing soft/firm texture. It is eaten mostly in a warm, dashi-based soup although it can also be served with a cold dipping sauce as kama-age-udon.

Udon and soba are thoroughly Japanese noodles, while ramen is a Chinese import (the word comes from the Cantonese word *raomin*). Despite this, the Japanese eat far more ramen than soba and udon combined, mostly because of the extraordinary popularity of instant ramen noodles. Ramen only came to Japan in the early twentieth century, but its relatively high levels of fat appealed in a similar way to meat to a post-war populace looking to 'bulk up', and it was a useful rice substitute during times of shortage. Shizuo Tsuji dismisses ramen noodles altogether as being Chinese, and they are not included in *A Simple Art*, although he grudgingly concedes of yakisoba, which despite the name are fried ramen noodles, that 'they are part of the ambience of every Japanese festival (as is cotton candy)'.

Somen noodles, meanwhile, are thin and fine – the imperial noodle. Made with wheat flour and sesame oil they are essentially just thin udon noodles, as are the marginally thicker hiyamugi. Harusame noodles are made from potato flour and are similar to shirataki noodles, the clear 'glass' noodles made from the same root as konnyaku (these are the noodles that turn pleasingly frazzled when added to tempura batter). And then you have the unfortunately named wanko-soba, served in Iwate Prefecture in mouthful-sized portions – wanko waitresses fill your bowl the minute you empty it and you are expected to consume around fifty bowls. These are the noodles most commonly served in eating competitions (the record is 350 in one sitting).

But of them all it is ramen that fuels this nation. Forget sushi or tempura, which are largely treat foods, when they are short of time, when they need a meal-in-a-bowl, when they want an umami hit, crave carbohydrates and porky protein, when they want warming and filling, and to lose themselves in slurping contemplation of a bottomless bowl of sustenance, it is to ramen that the Japanese turn, whether it be instantly rehydrated in a polystyrene bowl, guzzled standing up at a bar on the way to catch a train, or lovingly served by a conscientious ramen master.

Today a whole industry has grown up in appreciation of ramen noodles, with specialist ramen magazines, and countless websites and blogs dedicated to detailed discussion of specific restaurants. In terms of chefs, you have your ramen purists, and the innovators desperate to create the hot new ramen style. Right now food industry analysts are talking up a 'ramen boom' with over two hundred thousand ramen noodle restaurants in Japan.

Essentially, ramen is a dish of yellow, chewy, curly Chinese wheat noodles served in deep bowl of soup with toppings – usually including a slice of roast pork. But as anyone who has seen the cult Japanese film *Tampopo*, about a young female ramen chef shown the ways of the noodle by a mysterious outsider, will know, there is a whole lot more to it than that. The potential for variety – in terms of the recipe for the noodles, the soup and the extras is limitless, as the Ramen World Champion, Takamitsu Kobayashi, explained:

'There are four basic types: soy ramen from Tokyo; shio ramen, seasoned with salt, and miso ramen, which are both from Sapporo; and Tonkotsu or Hakata ramen, which is served with a white pork broth and comes from Hakata and Kyushu generally. I fell in love with ramen at this museum, actually,' he continued wistfully. 'It was a pig-bone soup ramen. I never thought anything could taste so good.'

I had assumed Kobayashi, thirty-two, was the world champion in *making* ramen, or perhaps the winner of a speed-eating competition (which used to be popular in Japan until the economic bubble burst in 1991 and such conspicuous consumption came to be considered a little unseemly), but he won the competition through his arcane know-ledge of the techniques, chefs, restaurants, regional varieties and sheer, endless trivia that has grown up around this dish. He had gone head-to-head against twenty-four other ramen connoisseurs for a prize of ¥500,000, identifying different types of ramen and individual restaurants from photographs; and even identifying a restaurant just by listening to a recording of ambient noise from it.

What did he do with the prize money, I wondered? 'I ate it all. Actually I spend more than three times that on my ramen obsession in a year. I have to visit over a thousand ramen restaurants a year.' Did he ever get sick of ramen? 'Never, because every ramen is so different. The soups are different – there can be pork bone, chicken bones, katsuobushi, konbu, other dried fish, it is limitless. You know, I once ate eleven bowls in one day. Come, I'll show you.'

We had met in the lobby of the Ramen Museum in Yokohama, the city with the largest Chinese population in Japan. Beyond the entrance was a small display on the history of ramen noodles featuring three hundred different ramen bowls, and a shop selling various ramen-themed souvenirs. There was another display showing twelve different types of noodle, each, to me, identical, but the real draw, the reason the museum has been packing them in since it opened in 1994 (a million and half visitors come each year) and has spawned several imitators elsewhere in the country, awaited us downstairs.

Here, in a perfect recreation of 1950s Yokohama, permanently lit as if at dusk with old street lamps, dark alleyways, peeling period advertising, rusty drains and old-fashioned shop fronts, were ten or so ramen restaurants, each run by tough looking chefs serving a different type of regional ramen.

The first we tried was the Tokyo ramen, with a dashi-based soup. It was stunning, with a deep, deep umami richness and sharp, dashi tang. I only meant to taste it but in what was now a familiar pattern I simply could not stop slurping until the entire bowl was sloshing around inside me. The white miso Hakata ramen from the Fukuchan shop was a little thin by comparison, but lighter in colour and with a long-roasted pork flavour. We tried a Sapporo miso ramen next, made, as the name suggests, with miso. As we entered the shop the chef was examining his ramen broth with a microscope.

'What on earth is he doing?' I asked. 'Oh, that's quite normal. He is assessing the density of the soup. Many do this.'

To me the Sapporo ramen tasted a little 'high', a result of the noodles which, in this case, were fermented and unusually chewy. It was also too salty by far. Kobayashi agreed, and I felt a small swell of pride. Might I, too, have the right stuff to become a ramen champion? I doubt it, seeing as, after just three, I felt like a ramen-filled balloon.

But Kobayashi continued eating, noisily. He explained why the Japanese slurp their ramen so loudly: it helps cool the noodles and brings out the flavour and aroma better. And boy did he slurp, he might as well have been tasting a great burgundy.

How could he tell a good ramen from an also ran? 'The al dente texture of the noodles is an essential way to judge a good ramen. The Japanese emphasise texture in their food, in China they don't care so much, but we add carbohydrated sodium and natural water to make the noodles chewy and sticky. Also the Japanese love the taste of umami so we use dashi in the soup – the Chinese do not. And of course our soy sauce is different.'

I wondered if there was such a thing as a gourmet ramen restaurant, a poshed up version. 'No, ramen is common food for the people. The most you will pay is a thousand yen. But you know the real craftsmanship of the ramen cook is that he creates this meal, his best meal, always within this limited space. I call it the Art of Ramen. It is practical food. This what I really love about ramen!' In a country where space is at a premium and everything from cars to mobile phones was designed to fit in the smallest space possible, I could see the appeal of an entire meal in one bowl. 'Yes, exactly! You've got it!' Kobayashi said.

I asked what kind of physical effect eating so much ramen has on him. He was large by Japanese standards but didn't look too chubby. Were there consequences to a life of ramen dedication? 'I am OK. Ramen is not as bad as McDonald's. It has vegetables you know.' And his wife, what did she think of him travelling (for two hours that evening, it turned out) at least once a week to the museum and throughout Japan in pursuit of the perfect noodle soup? 'She shows some understanding. But then, I did meet her through a ramen website and she was working in a ramen shop.'

We parted with an exchange of business cards, Kobayashi's proudly proclaiming him a Ramen Champion. 'I am glad you are going to introduce ramen to the world!' he said, waving goodbye from the entrance of the Yokohama museum.

Chapter 33

Once Upon a Time in Shimonoseki

I'll admit, I actually was a little nervous when I left Fukuoka that morning. For all the absurd misinformation bandied about, people have, and still do, die from eating fugu and there genuinely was a slight chance that I might never return from my trip to taste the world's most notorious fish dish (although, admittedly, my inability to decode a Japanese bus timetable would be a more likely hindrance).

The fugu is a type of puffer- or blowfish; actually, several types of similar-looking blowfish are served as fugu in Japan, but all contain varying levels of poison. Their ovaries and liver – called the kimo – contain a deadly neurotoxin called tetrodotoxin which is thirteen times more toxic than arsenic. Each fish contains enough to kill thirty people, particularly in the summer when they are at their most potent. If you are unlucky enough to ingest too much kimo, the first sign will be a dry mouth. Difficulty breathing might follow, then you will start to lose focus. There is no antidote, although some people do survive. Others have died painful and horrible, paralysed deaths, eventually through asphyxiation. Captain James Cook, discoverer of Australia, once had a lucky escape from eating fugu fish, but the famous kabuki actor, Mitsugoro Bando, was not so lucky. In 1975 he unwisely requested several servings of the kimo and died as a result; the chef who served him went on to serve an eight-year prison sentence. The Emperor of Japan is forbidden from ever eating it.

Though they are starting to breed non-poisonous fugu, most are still toxic and I had read that around six or seven people continue to die from eating wrongly prepared fugu in Japan each year. Many dozens more have lucky escapes and pull through after intensive care (if you make it through the first twenty-four hours on life support, you ought to be in the clear), and all this despite tight regulations concerning who can prepare the fish. Famously, you need a special fugu licence to serve it in a restaurant, which takes two or three years to earn and these days, following some unfortunate incidents with restaurant bin foragers, chefs must store all the poisonous parts in a locked box. Civilians can only buy a fugu to cook at home if it has been prepared properly with the risky bits removed, and the majority of the deaths are from people who catch the fish themselves and try to prepare them at home, or from thrill-seekers who want to feel their tongue go numb or even experience a temporary coma. But, still, some deaths are genuine accidents from fish prepared by professionals in restaurants. The latest fatalities came in January 2009 when seven diners in a restaurant in Yamagata Prefecture fell ill after eating fugu sashimi and testes prepared by an unlicensed chef. One of them, a 68-year-old man died almost immediately, the rest experienced numbness and tingling in their hands and legs for some days afterwards.

(I think it is worth pausing here to revisit the famous Simpson's episode in which Homer eats some fugu prepared by an apprentice chef at their new local Japanese restaurant, the Happy Sumo, and is told by Doctor Hibbert that he has twenty-four hours to live. In fact, he survives. Marge realises he is alive the next morning because his dribble is still warm. Homer vows to cherish life in future by eating diet pork rinds instead of full fat, and then watches some bowling on television.)

The acknowledged fugu capital of Japan is the harbour town of Shimonoseki, two hours north of Fukuoka beside the Kanmon Channel, a narrow stretch of turbulent water which separates Kyushu from the next island north, Honshu. I could have eaten fugu virtually anywhere in Japan – you see the fish swimming in tanks in the windows of specialist restaurants in most Japanese cities – but I had heard that the best fugu chefs and the freshest fish were to be found here. More fugu are caught and processed in this small city than anywhere else in Japan, a total of three thousand tons a year, over half the annual haul. Some come from fugu farms, some are caught wild. I figured that if anyone was likely to be a safe bet to prepare me a safe piece of fugu sashimi, it was the fugumongers of Shimonoseki. Rather disappointingly Lissen and the kids were untroubled by my mission that day. They were fast asleep when I left early in the morning.

Fukuoka's bus terminal is on the third floor of a gargantuan shopping mall, which caught me out. In the end I had to run for a prolonged period, something I hadn't done for some years, including up two flights of steps. Remarkably, I managed it without too much agony. There was none of the usual lung burn or dizziness I usually experience on the rare occasion I have to run for something. It did sap my energy for the next couple of hours, but at least I wasn't the hospital case as I might have been some months earlier. Could my Japanese diet of the last two months really be making me healthier?

The bus terminal was clean, quiet and ordered. Each bus stop was attended by a conductor in a grey polyester uniform who went out of his way to tour the hall rounding up passengers so that they didn't miss their ride. Several conductors politely rebuffed my insistent advances to board what I thought were the buses to Shimonoseki, but weren't. Eventually, like a fly repeatedly battering a window pane, I gave up and awaited death. Some minutes later, one of the conductors found me and helped me onto the correct bus, his white gloves gently shepherding me on board without ever actually making contact.

Its fugu riches do not appear to have bestowed great prosperity on the town of Shimonoseki, that much was apparent within moments of arriving. It has a weary, run-down look with rusty prefabricated buildings, stained concrete walls, overgrown vegetation and a general air of neglect. But Shimonoseki is still proud of its claim to fame, which it pronounces 'fuku'. The manhole covers are embossed with a cartoon fugu fish, I noticed, and the seats in the local busses had been upholstered with fugu-print cloth. The shops were full of cuddly fugu, fugu key rings, mugs and the fugu-themed mobile phone chains. On my way from the bus to the fish market down by the harbour, where you might have expected to see a statue of a local dignitary or literary hero, I passed a large, bronze fugu, instantly recognisable by its pursed lips and rounded boxy shape. I noticed a crowd of people. Getting closer I realised they were gathered around a giant inflatable fugu. It turned out that, by serendipitous coincidence, I had chosen to visit the town on the day of its annual fugu festival.

As kids bounced happily outside, inside the market a large crowd had gathered around a fish tank. I squeezed my way to the front to find several children dangling fishing lines trying to catch one of around two dozen fugu swimming despondently around the tank. Anyone could have a go for ¥2,000 (about £15). The unfortunate fish, about the size of a house brick, were being pulled from the water with hooks through their skin, or their eyes or tails – any method seemed fair game for the young crowd, egged on by their parents.

I noticed that the fish, once caught, were being whisked away, still alive, somewhere backstage by the market staff. After looking around to see no one was watching, I followed one of them. Here, in scenes that would make Sweeney Todd's head swim, they were being dispatched and prepared to be sent back out to the customers in plastic bags. I watched mesmerised by the slaughter unfolding before me as four men stood around their metal work station in blood- and guts-spattered aprons and white gloves. I had wondered whether fugu had spines like other types of puffer fish, but as this would probably have been as appropriate a time as any to deploy them – what with their faces being sliced off and their innards being ripped out and everything – I concluded from their absence that they have none.

I am not a complete girl when it comes to working with meat or fish: I have plunged live crayfish, crabs and lobsters into hot oil and boiling water, prepared still-warm wild ducks by pulling off their heads, ripping out their feathers and cleaning their innards out, but I must admit to some queasiness as I watched the fishermen hold each wriggling fish on the chopping board in front of them, before stunning the fish with a swift blow of the knife handle to the back of the head. Next they chopped off their faces and fins – the latter set aside to be fried and served in warm sake as a snack – and pulled off their skin – also potentially poisonous – in one swift movement. The fish were still gasping for oxygen at this point, their tongues bulging from the newly opened orifice in the front of their head, their gills ballooning. And they were still moving as the fishermen plunged fingers inside them and pulled out their toxic guts, tossing them into a bucket on the floor. So much for a padlocked box. Finally, the eyes were gouged out and the rest of the fish chopped into large pieces, its hollow carcass included, before being bagged and sent back out to the customer. I timed it: the whole thing took just thirty seconds – not quite the level of meticulous care one might wish for in the preparation of a deadly fish, but I am sure they knew what they were doing.

I stepped closer, smiling at the men. They smiled back apparently untroubled by having a witness to all this. I pointed at the bucket of innards. I wanted to make sure it was the poisonous stuff. I had an idea, a really, *really* stupid thought that had popped into my head just at that moment, circumventing all rationality and common sense: I was going to try to taste the liver. After all, until it became illegal, people did actually used to eat small amounts. It is said to induce a pleasurably tingling, numb sensation on the tongue.

I pointed at the bucket, I mimed choking to death with my hands around my neck, my tongue sticking out and my eyes rolling, and finished with questioning upturned palms. They nodded. It was indeed a bucket of fugu toxin.

I loitered for a few moments more as the filleters returned to their work, then knelt down next to the bucket to tie my shoelace. I wasn't going to take a big bite of the stuff, just touch it with the tip of my finger, and lick the residue – not enough to kill me, that was for sure. But just as I was stretching out towards the bucket, one of the filleters spotted me and waggled his finger. I pulled my hand back and smiled sheepishly, he returned to his fish, and I immediately shot my hand back out, touched a piece of liver and quickly licked my finger.

I stood up, feigning innocence. Almost immediately the room began to go all swimmy. My vision went slightly foggy and speckly. I started to panic. What had I done? How stupid can one man be? Was my tongue that dry before? This was it: the cramps would be next, and soon I would be a writhing, frothing heap on the floor, one more notch on the fugu's kill chart. But the sensation stopped almost as quickly as it had started. I was fine. Panic over. It was getting up so quickly that had made me dizzy, not the liver. I neither felt nor tasted anything on my tongue. Maybe it wasn't even the liver I had touched. I'll never know.

Back in the market I began my search for breakfast. A drum troupe was entertaining the crowds. I was the only Westerner. Plates of fugu sashimi – each wafer thin, transparent slice arranged in a petal around the plate in a style called fugusashi – were fetching from ¥1,000 to ¥20,000 depending on size. I bought a small plate and took it outside onto the boardwalk where more crowds were gathering for their own al fresco breakfast taking in the views across the roiling currents in the harbour and to the mighty suspension bridge above.

Fugu could never really live up to its dramatic reputation, and I have to say it was an anticlimax – chewy with a watery flavour, a little bit squid-ey, a little bit bream-ey. No wonder they slather it with chilli sauce and ponzu.

Deep-fried cubes of fugu were a different matter altogether – crisp, meaty, moist and delicious. I used to think that turbot, or perhaps halibut, were the perfect fish for battering and deep frying, but fugu is superior even to them. Its robust texture and meaty flavour holds up especially well to the batter, keeping its shape but turning tender in the heat of the oil. I'd love to see it on the menu on Brighton seafront.

Still famished, I started a tour of the astonishing sushi stalls, about a dozen in all, each selling a fantastic array of sushi, all super fresh, expertly made, and in some cases, of varieties I had never seen before. Most was about ¥100 (50p) per piece. It was among the best sushi I would eat in Japan – the scallops fat, fresh and creamy-sweet, the tuna nigiri topped with huge tongues of red flesh. I ate so many pieces I began to get stomach pains. In the end, my own greed had succeeded where the deadly fugu fish had not.

Chapter 34

Okinawa

Urban Japan offers enough outlandish distractions to occupy even the most demanding visitors, but after more than two months of travelling with only glimpses of countryside from fast moving trains and planes, we were yearning for the beach and some sub-tropical sea.

We arrived late at night on the main island of Okinawa Honto on a flight from Fukuoka. We drove in darkness in our little rented car to a hotel we had booked online some weeks earlier. The hotel's website had shown sea views and sandy beaches and we woke with high hopes the next morning. Unfortunately we drew back the curtains to find ourselves surrounded only by a sea of concrete, the turquoise water a tantalising mirage in the distance.

Okinawa is an archipelago of 159 islands, historically known as the Kingdom of the Ryukyus. It lies midway between Japan and Taiwan, 685km from the southern tip of Japan proper. Thirty seven of the islands are inhabited, but the majority of its 1.31 million people live on the main island, Okinawa Honto, which is also the home of the largest US Air Force base in the Western Pacific with 20,000 military personnel. This is a, these days, largely unwelcome legacy of some of the most devastating battles of WWII which left a third of this hitherto peaceful people dead. More died on Okinawa than in Nagasaki and Hiroshima combined, and much of the main island was levelled by bombing.

So we didn't like to complain that our first hotel wasn't quite as pretty as we had hoped but checked out quietly and headed over to the north-eastern side of the island in the hope of finding something a little closer to the beach.

We rolled up – with our dishevelled clothes and mismatched luggage – at the Busena Terrace Beach Resort. It looked just the ticket – a winning lottery ticket unfortunately. The desk staff looked at us as if the Beverly Hillbillies had just rolled up and told us that they were afraid they had no rooms. They looked a little afraid actually.

So we checked into something that had a *view* of the Busena Terrace Beach Resort but cost roughly a million pounds a night less, and resigned ourselves to sneaking onto their beach instead. Even though it was October, the water was still just about warm enough to swim in, although the various signs on the beach warning of the myriad creatures that might cause us injury if we went into the water diminished our enthusiasm somewhat. We made do with burying each other in the sand and building castles.

As usual, I grew restless with this after about fifteen minutes and managed to drum up some enthusiasm for a day trip to Naha, the capital. I had heard there was an excellent market on Heiwa Street and wanted to take a look.

On our way the next day we stopped off in an awamori shop. Awamori is the local distilled liquor, similar to shochu, made from rice. The bottles in this shop, however, had an unusual ingredient: snakes. Okinawa is infested with habu snakes, and this is one use they find for them, drowning them in the liquor and leaving the corpses to infuse – the ninety-five per cent proof alcohol neutralising the venom. You can't really taste the snake, by the way, in fact, as you might expect, you can't taste much apart from the alcohol.

The market itself, though smaller than ones we had seen elsewhere in Japan, was fascinating, its produce different from anything you find in mainland Japan. As with Tsukiji, a fish market lay at its heart, but there was plenty to divert our interest on the way in – more snakes, for starters, some two metres long, dried, coiled and hanging from the ceiling like Gothic Catherine wheels; a preserved shark's head for ¥135,000; sturdy-looking Okinawa doughnuts; vacuum packed pigs' heads (pork is very popular on the islands, a legacy of uninterrupted trading with China over many millennia); a large konbu and katsuobushi shop, an indication of the central role dashi plays in Okinawan food (they eat more konbu per capita than anyone else in Japan), and intriguing, lilac-coloured sweet-potato cakes. The fishmongers' stalls were filled with the most extraordinary tropical fish: some orange and yellow striped, other blue like a Hockney swimming pool – and not just fish, but crustaceans: monster crabs; strange clawless lobsters; smaller purple crabs; massive conches; and sea snails.

One of the stallholders explained that we could order anything we liked, and it would be sent upstairs to a restaurant to be cooked for us. I had to be physically restrained by Lissen from ordering a giant conch but not before I had ordered numerous other fish, along with a serving of irabu-jiru, or snake stew, for us all.

Upstairs, in an enjoyably chaotic bus station-style atmosphere, at a ramshackle restaurant (one of several in an informal food-court) with mismatched chairs and paper napkins, we awaited our snake. We were slightly taken aback to see that it still looked very much like snake, black skin and all, but, to their credit, both Asger and Emil tucked in, picking the flesh from the hundreds of small bones. I could hardly baulk at it myself now, so took a deep breath and a small nibble. It was a little like a slow braised oxtail, tender and gamey and really full of bones, but I couldn't see past the fact that I was eating a serpent and quietly moved the bowl aside to attack the whole grilled fish and astonishingly good sea urchin. The latter was locally caught and ferociously expensive, but simply one of the most sensuous and transcendents foodstuffs I have ever tasted. If some mermaids were to open a small, artisanal ice cream parlour specialising only in vanilla flavour, this is how that ice cream would taste.

That night, for the first time in our whole journey, one of our number became ill. Emil started to complain that he felt 'funny'. His arm hurt, he said. We rolled up his sleeve, or at least we tried to but couldn't as it had swollen up. We gave him an antihistamine tablet but that had no effect. I would have to take him to hospital.

The nearest was in the small coastal town of Nago. The hospital, high up on a hill overlooking the bay, took an age to find and I drove around in thickening darkness and growing panic, lost in this strangest of lands with a sick (snake-poisoned?) child and no sense of direction. Emil had started to make wheezing noises and I was terrified he was having a severe allergic reaction to something and that his throat was closing up.

Eventually, by sheer fluke, I found the hospital. It was in a bedraggled building, not what you would expect from one of the richest nations on earth. The waiting room was half full, almost all of those waiting elderly. They looked at Emil and I with fear in their eyes, and Emil shrank behind me in mutual terror. I smiled weekly to the desk staff, and spoke in slow English pointing to Emil's arm while gripping my throat. He was looking dreadfully pale with dark lines beneath his eyes. What on earth was wrong?

Rather embarrassingly we were given preferential treatment and after just a couple of minute's wait we were ushered through into the doctor's surgery. The doctor, a shy, young man, looked as startled to see us as his patients and, for a moment, the panic in his eyes had me worried that he would simply flee and leave us there.

Quickly, to grab his attention, I rolled up Emil's sleeve. Emil winced.

The doctor examined the arm in a vague, distracted way, then listened to Emil's breathing with a stethoscope. 'Don't worry, I can still whistle,' Emil told him (he had recently learned, much to his non-whistling elder brother's irritation). He then tried to demonstrate, but he didn't have the puff.

At this point the doctor walked out, which wasn't encouraging, but he soon returned with an older, female doctor who spoke good English. She said that they were going to give him an injection. Of what, she did not say, but she did ask if he was allergic to anything. I wanted to say, well, yes, clearly, but that would have raised more questions than I could answer, so I said no, not that I knew of.

To this day, I have no idea what it was that bit him. Maybe Emil is allergic to snake (not that easy to test for where we live), perhaps it was one of the tropical fish we ate or more likely some kind of insect bite, but the doctor gave him the injection and his arm deflated over the course of that evening. By the end of it, Emil was whistling like a kettle.

Chapter 35

Who Wants to Live For Ever?

Some people have a peculiar attitude towards mortality. They accept they are going to die, live with it and get on with their lives. There are even people – and I have met some – who are perfectly at ease with the fact that one day they will no longer exist, that their heart will stop, and they will plunge headlong into an insensible, eternal void.

And then, of course, there are those who would willingly end their own lives in the event of impending infirmity, be it mental or physical; people who embrace the idea of euthanasia, and are ready to terminate themselves the moment they start to forget why they went into the kitchen. My father, for instance, used to insist – only half joking – that if he ever started to lose his mind we were under strict instructions to take him out into the paddock and shoot him (thankfully he departed with his marbles intact – which was just as well as we didn't have a gun, or a paddock). I, on the other hand, think about death – by which I mean whole proper minutes spent staring vacantly into space wrestling with the bitter truth of my own mortality – several times a day. If I had a pound for every time someone had said 'Cheer up , it might not happen!' . . . But it will! That's why my face looks like this.

I can tell you exactly when this all began: I was at school staring out of the classroom window one sunny afternoon, when I suddenly realised that I would one day die, AND THE WORLD WOULD CONTINUE WITHOUT ME! If I hurled myself through the first-floor window and plummeted onto the basketball court below, cars would still drive, people would still watch TV and, after the school caretaker had administered a pile of sawdust, Miss Weddick would quieten the class down and continue to explain why water goes the other way round down the plughole in Australia.

Already, a few months prior to that, I had ruled out the likelihood of the existence of God after he had allowed the noble Borg to lose to the petulant McEnroe at Wimbledon. I think I must have been nine. I should make clear that in no other way – academically, socially, physically – was I precocious. It was just my luck that the only sphere in which my development outpaced my peers was in my premature acknowledgement of the brevity and futility of existence. Which is why, as I limp towards middle age, my body and mind slowly disintegrating in ever more humiliating displays of decrepitude, I have vowed to cling to life for as long as I can. Never mind that I may become an incontinent, gibbering wreck and everyone will be sick of the sight of me, my liver-spotted claws shall grip the hands of my nurses insistently as they tend the life support machine beside my bed. I intend to be a burden to my children as long as I possibly can. A 'good innings' isn't going to do it for me, I can tell you, and as for 'three score years and ten', five score and then some, is more like it.

Gerontologists believe that the human body ought in theory to be able to last until well past one hundred and twenty years – the oldest person ever was a French woman who lived to the age of one hundred and twenty-two and a half. They say, too, that only around twenty-five per cent of the causes of death and ageing are found in your DNA, the rest is within your control. Hence, I am a sucker for all of those health-scare stories that the papers run every day; I lap them up as gospel, stressing over my diet, my lack of exercise and my stress levels. Only my insatiable gluttony, a susceptibility to addictions, inherent indolence and a fundamentally weak character have stopped me from becoming a vegan. No, instead of making radical changes to my life, I am on a constant quest for some kind of healthy-living magic bullet, the secret foods and lifestyle tips that will prolong my life and somehow, against all rational belief, keep my knackered old body going for another seventy years or so.

So while Lissen and the boys had been dreaming of Okinawa's idyllic sandy beaches and tropical seas, it was in fact my desperate fear of a godless death that had brought us to the paradise islands of southern Japan.

Okinawans, you see, know the secret of eternal life, or at least the secret of living a healthy, active life well into three digits. They live longer than anyone else on earth, and unlike others who claim this title – the people of the Hunza Valley in Pakistan, or the Ecuadorian Andes, for instance – they can prove it, having kept meticulous official birth records since 1879. And they don't just cling on to life courtesy of expensive medicines and machines that go 'ping', elderly Okinawans are active, live alone, contribute to society and remain healthy and mobile up to and beyond 100 years of age, into the realms of the so-called 'super-centenarians'. In Okinawa, if you meet an octogenarian, there is a good chance they are still someone's child.

The three leading killers in the Western world are heart disease, strokes and cancer but the Okinawans suffer from them less than any other people. Out of one hundred thousand, only eighteen a year die from heart disease compared to over a hundred in the US. Of course, the Japanese in general are world leaders in terms of life expectancy: Japanese women have a life expectancy of 85.99 years, the highest in the world, while the men are second in the world with 79.19 years, after Icelandic men who just pip them with 79.4 years. And Japan has over forty per cent of the world's so-called super centenarians, aged 105 and over, including, as I write, the oldest man in the world Tomoji Tanabe (111). (The oldest woman, who was also Japanese, died a few months before we left for Tokyo.) This in itself would be reason enough to look more closely at the Japanese diet and lifestyle – at why, for example, only three per cent are considered obese, compared to thirty per cent in the US – but the longevity of Okinawans is a special case indeed. They have over two and a half times as many centenarians per capita as the mainland. Okinawan women live, on average to 86.88 years. As I write this, there are over

800 centenarians resident on Okinawa out of a total population of 1.31 million, the highest ratio in the world (Japan as a whole now has 30,000 centenarians out of a population of a little over 127 million).

The Okinawans are clearly doing something – several things – right. For someone with a morbid fear of death (is there any other kind?), there was no better place to go in search of tips.

The longevity of the mainland Japanese is a fairly recent phenomenon; until the seventies, the Swedes held the record for long life, yet the Okinawans have a reputation for healthy living that dates back centuries, perhaps millennia. The Chinese, who have traded with the Kingdom of the Ryukyus since the third century BC, referred to it as the 'Land of the Immortals'. Some even claim that the ancient Chinese myth of Shangri-La is about Okinawa.

But still it is an unlikely place to find the world's longest-lived people. For a start, Okinawans are the poorest people in Japan, thus undermining all conventional wisdom correlating health with income. Okinawa has always been beset by typhoons and famine, its people forever picking themselves up, dusting themselves off and starving all over again. Periodically, outsiders have invaded and brutally subjugated what was an avowedly non-military, peaceful country where, for a time, all weaponry was banned and guitars took the place of swords. The Japanese Satsuma clan came in 1609, imposed harsh taxes and used the islands as a trading route to China at a time when the country was supposed to be closed to the outside world. In the mid-1850s Commodore Perry – hardly barbaric, but still an aggressive outsider – based his fleet in Okinawa, before sailing on Japan with the intention of opening it up like a reluctant oyster. And then, of course, the Americans came again during WWII. Over a quarter – some say as many as a third – of the population died, a large proportion of them having been persuaded to commit suicide by the Japanese rather than surrender (tragically this happened only some weeks prior to their traumatic surrender when Emperor Hirohito reluctantly conceded that 'the war has not necessarily developed to Japan's advantage'). And last but very much not least, the place is absolutely infested with poisonous snakes, as testified by the various puncture marks several locals were to show us during our stay.

The reasons behind the mainland Japanese's longevity are more obvious. After the war, rampant economic growth improved healthcare immeasurably, stamping out deadly diseases such as tuberculosis. They started to eat more protein and animal fats. They bulked up. The average height increased by three inches. But perhaps the biggest single contributing factor to the improved health of the nation was a reduction in their salt intake in the early seventies. The Japanese had always had low rates of death from heart disease, but they died in virtually as many numbers from strokes due to their salty diet. They still continue to consume more salt than we do in the West (the Japanese government recommends twelve grams per day, Western governments tend to recommend six grams) but in 1970 the Japanese government imposed reductions on levels of salt in soy sauce. After that, there was no stopping them. Incidents of stroke declined dramatically and it has only really been their recent enthusiasm for Western fast food trends that has seen obesity and cholesterol levels begin to rise. But what made the Okinawans so exceptional?

I had made contact with one of the leading experts on Okinawan longevity, a Canadian gerontologist called Dr Craig Willcox, who lives in Okinawa. Together with his twin brother Bradley – now based at Harvard – and local gerontologist, Dr Makoto Suzuki, who was the first scientist to spot Okinawan longevity and started the government funded Okinawan Centenarian Study in the mid-seventies, Willcox has been studying Okinawan longevity for over a decade.

A few years ago the three of them published *The Okinawa Program: How the World's Longest-Lived People Achieve Everlasting Health and How You Can Too*. It had gone on to become a *New York Times* bestseller, and the brothers had even been on *Oprah*.

One morning, a week or so after arriving on Okinawa, I left Lissen and the kids to various beach-themed activities (crab goading;

purposeless digging) and drove back down south to the capital, Naha, where the Okinawa Research Center for Longevity Science is based in Okinawa International University, to meet Dr Willcox.

Dressed in a Hawaiian-style shirt, with thick, shoulder-length hair and clear, tanned skin, Willcox was a persuasive advert for his own programme. I asked how old he was. He glanced at the students working behind us and whispered mock conspiratorially, 'Forty-six, but don't tell anyone.' I'd be lying if I said he looked ten years younger, but he did at least look a very good forty-six, which was frankly all the hope I needed.

After a brief introductory chat, we decided to continue our discussion over lunch. Willcox knew just the place, a small wooden shack a few hundred metres from the campus. There, we ordered some classic Okinawan dishes, and got down to the nitty gritty.

Just how healthy were the Okinawans? 'They have low cholesterol and suffer less from heart disease than anyone else, they are not big smokers or drinkers and they have among the lowest levels of homocysteine in the world – homocysteine causes at least ten per cent of heart disease deaths,' Willcox said, tucking into a plate of goya champaru, a classic Okinawan dish featuring stir-fried goya – a kind of knobbly, bitter cucumber which has been shown to lower blood sugar in diabetics and has also been used to treat AIDs. 'They have a low risk of arteriosclerosis. They have low instances of stomach cancer, which the rest of the Japanese suffer from. The Japanese have also historically had a high rate of strokes, but Okinawans have never eaten as much salt. They have a very low risk of hormone-dependent cancers, such as breast and prostate cancer. They eat three servings of fish a week, on average. They tend to use canola oil to fry with, which is even healthier than olive oil. They eat plenty of whole grains, vegetables and soy products too. And they eat more tofu and more konbu seaweed than anyone else in the world. Squid and octopus, which they also eat a lot of, are rich in taurine which is believed to lower cholesterol and blood pressure.'

I was scribbling furiously at this point, so Willcox paused to let me catch up and take a few mouthfuls of the goya champaru. I had tried to eat some goya earlier in our trip in Kyoto. I'd picked one of these weird, gnarly cucumbers – some call them a melon – out of the vegetable section in the supermarket and taken it home to give to the kids in their daily mid-afternoon, raw fruit and veg snack. Asger had taken a tentative bite before spitting the entire mouthful out into my hand. I had tried it and also found it impossibly bitter, consigning it to the 'What are they thinking of category?' of unpalatable Japanese foodstuffs. But here, fried with egg and pork, its bitterness was subdued and helped cut through the fattiness of the dish.

Dr Willcox continued: 'They have strong bones, from the fish they eat and, of course, they get lots of sun, plus more vitamin D from soy products. They have low dementia rates, which might be linked to the gingko nuts they eat, or it might be the sweet potatoes.'

Ah yes, the Okinawan sweet potato. I had tried these striking vegetables the night before at a restaurant across the street from our hotel. Okinawan sweet potatoes, while looking essentially like the orange variety we get at home from the outside, are the most extraordinary deep purple inside, the kind of colour, almost artificial in its intensity, that you rarely find in nature. It is the colour of a bishop's mitre, or a 1976 Morris Marina, or Prince's knickers – very, very purple. It is to me the most beautiful-coloured vegetable in the world. And they taste sensational, particularly as tempura, which is how I had tried them – not too sweet, and with a pleasant, flowery aftertaste and soft, almost creamy texture. I had also tried sweet-potato ice cream, another Okinawan speciality. Emi had introduced it to me back in Tokyo when we first met, and I had declared it there and then the best ice cream in the world. I still stand by that statement: as ice cream it loses its potato-ishness, and the floral sweetness comes to the fore. (Lissen had tried it too, and we were now both locked in a battle over who could claim it for their list of 'top ten things we would like to export from Japan to make the world a better place.')

The Okinawan sweet potato – called 'beni imo' – was introduced to the islands on 1605 by a man called Sokan Noguni. Noguni is revered to this day as a local hero, the 'Imo King', for bringing this miracle vegetable to the islands. 'Since the sweet potato came here from China via South America, Okinawans have eaten pretty much nothing but that, along with fish. At one point in their history they were getting sixty per cent of their calories from sweet potatoes,' enthused Willcox. Complex carbohydrates are an important part of the Okinawan diet, contrary to several current Western diet fads. Willcox guffawed loudly when I asked about the Atkins diet. 'Of course you lose weight with Atkins at the start, but you lose water and lean muscle. You actually increase body fat percentage.

'Sweet potatoes are high in flavanoids, which are antioxidant and a hormone blocker. Okinawans consume more flavanoids than anyone else in the world, up to fifty times more than we do in the West. They [the potatoes] are also rich in carotenoids, vitamin E, fibre and lycopene, which is a carotenoid that has been shown to help prevent prostate cancer.' In fact, one imo contains four times the daily vitamin A and half the vitamin C requirements of an adult. Recent research has also indicated that they help stabilise blood-sugar levels and lower insulin resistance.

Of course, what the Okinawans eat is only part of the explanation for their remarkable longevity. As far as Willcox was concerned, what they *didn't* put into their mouths was as important. In his view calorific restriction – in other words, not eating very much – was the key to a long life. 'Calorific restriction has been shown to work in all other animal species including primates so I'd be very surprised if it didn't work with humans,' he said. 'There are so many connections to obesity and health.'

'So, what kind of restriction are we actually talking about?' I asked, a note of nervousness entering my voice. 'Well, back in the 1960s a study showed that Okinawan children were consuming almost forty per cent fewer calories than other Japanese children, so you can imagine how that would compare to the children in the West. At the same time Okinawan adults were eating more than ten per cent fewer calories than the normal, healthy recommended level.' On average, Okinawans eat 2,761 calories per day, compared to 3,412 in the UK and 3,774 in the USA. Of course, they are physically smaller than us, but I'd say there was room for cutting back wouldn't you?

Eating less is deeply ingrained in both the Okinawan psyche and quite possibly their genes too. Typhoons, disease, poverty and their geographical isolation have meant that Okinawans have endured frequent famines. They have adapted accordingly, eating what we in the West would consider emergency ration quantities on a day-to-day basis. They even have a phrase to describe this philosophy: *hara hachi-bu*, meaning 'eat until you are eighty per cent full'.

It is said that the three words that have earned more for the beauty industry than any other promotional or advertising strategy are 'rinse and repeat' on a shampoo bottle. Well, here are two-and-a-half words that could wipe out the entire health, beauty, diet and exercise industries in a trice. *Hara hachi-bu* could transform the health of the entire world, if only we could all find the self-control. It is based on the simplest of physiological principles – it takes your stomach's stretch receptors twenty minutes to tell your brain you are full, so if you eat until you feel eighty per cent full and just wait twenty minutes, you will feel properly full. Try it. It works. (It also explains my confusion at the discomfort I always feel after being allowed near all-you-can-eat buffets.) In the course of our evolution as a species it is only in the last century or so that a large proportion of the human race has been in the position of having a surplus of food, but our bodies are still physically attuned to having far less.

I'd go as far as to say that *hara hachi-bu* has revolutionised my life and helped me lose four stone. Except it hasn't because my greed receptors generally override my stomach capacity and I live just across the street from an awfully good patisserie, but I am sure most people would have the modicum of self-control required to implement it in their lives.

This got me thinking about diet fads. For the last decade or so in the West we have been brainwashed into thinking the

Mediterranean diet was best. 'It is also good,' said Willcox. 'Sardinians, for example, tend to live long, but there is perhaps too much dairy still.'

Usually, when a group of two or more people are gathered and the talk turns to how healthy the Japanese are, someone will confidently assert that osteoporosis rates are much higher than in the West 'because they don't get enough calcium because they don't eat dairy' (it's like if you are out walking and you see a swan, someone will invariably say, 'They can break your arm, you know.'). This is a myth. 'Osteoporosis rates are actually lower in Japan,' Willcox told me. 'They get more exercise and vitamin D. Smoking is a problem though, lung cancer rates are increasing. That's a problem now because it can take twenty or thirty years for the cancer to appear and if you look twenty or thirty years ago to the 1980s, eighty per cent of Japanese men were smoking.'

Willcox, Willcox and Suzuki have a great deal to say about fat in their book too, mostly negative. 'Really, less than ten per cent of your calories should come from fat, but a little pork is a good addition for the protein,' Willcox said. And guess which meat the Okinawans have traditionally eaten more of than any other? That's right, pork. In fact, they are renowned for their pork cuisine, and have a famous saying, 'With a pig you can eat everything except the "oink".'

So even when Okinawans are eating bad stuff it's doing them good. The same goes for the famous (in Japan at least) Okinawan black sugar, a dense, malevolent looking cane sugar called kokuto that tastes wonderfully rich, like molasses or muscovado. 'It is true, their sugar is much better because it isn't processed or bleached. It also has more iron in it. But as with the salt, you still want to stay away from sugar if you can,' he said.

But dietary and medical factors were only part of the secret of Okinawan longevity. The improved post-war healthcare eventually trickled down to Okinawa at a time when those who had endured the war – by definition the most resilient of their generation – were entering middle age. Yet they still ate the traditional Okinawan diet, and this, combined with modern healthcare, proved to be a potent longevity tonic for a specific demographic which is now reaching, and flying past, the century mark.

According to Willcox the fact that they appear to be the least stressed people on earth plays a role too. The Okinawan concept of time pays scant regard to the tyrannies of the clock, which makes it difficult ever to be late. He also believes their supportive localised social structures – called uimaru – are immensely important to their longevity. One aspect of this is the *maoi*, or local 'people's banks' where around a dozen or so friends meet and contribute a small sum to a kitty, then each month vote to decide who gets the money. Meanwhile, their healthcare systems incorporate both traditional medicines and healers – called yuta – and t'ai chi is widely practised. Interestingly, one of the reasons given for the superior longevity of Okinawan women in particular is that they are more likely to practise a religion – a belief in a higher power supposedly giving them a greater sense of ease and contentment than godless heathens like me.

Oh yes, and there is no word in the Okinawan dialect for 'retirement'. Many of the centenarians Willcox and his team have interviewed continue, if not to work in full-time jobs, then at least tend their gardens, grow vegetables and even have part-time jobs. So while in the West there is growing concern, a resentment even, that people are living longer and being a burden on public healthcare finances, the centenarians of Okinawa are more of a boost than a burden.

It is usual for the elderly – even those aged 103 and over – to live in their own homes. In his book, Willcox describes his centenarian subjects' 'youthful glow' and 'sharp, clear eyes, quick wits and passionate interests'. They don't suffer from 'time urgency', he writes, they are very self-confident, self-reliant, optimistic and easy-going but also stubborn.

What about . . . you know . . . ?' I raised my eyebrows. 'What? Their sex life?' he laughed. 'Now that would be an interesting area of research. We do know that Okinawan centenarians have higher levels of sex hormones, and we do know that some of our centenarians are sexually active, but I don't think we could really get away with asking them about that.'

Sadly, Willcox told me that it looks like the age of Okinawan longevity is coming to an end. The next generation are unlikely to last much beyond eighty as they have embraced the American fast food, sugar-rich diet with gusto – young Okinawans are eating twice as much meat as their parents, for instance – with the result that Okinawans aged fifty and below have the highest rates of obesity in Japan, with, inevitably, the highest rates of heart disease and premature death. The last few decades have seen Okinawans go from being some of the leanest people in Japan to having the highest body mass index among the Japanese. Lung cancer rates are on the up too. Apparently Nagoya is about to overtake them as the prefecture with the greatest longevity.

By now the restaurant owner was starting to clear up in preparation for dinner. I had one last question of urgent personal import.

'I have a friend, not me you understand, but a friend, who is having a slight problem with hair loss,' I said. 'I can't help noticing that Japanese men do seem to tend to hold on to their hair pretty well. What's their secret? Is it the seaweed?'

Willcox, who I had long ago noted was blessed with an impressively thick head of wavy brown, lustrous hair, laughed. 'Well they do say konbu is good for hair loss and perilla too, but I am afraid you'll have to tell your "friend" it's more along the lines of folk advice than scientifically proven.' I would just have to settle for eternal life then.

As I drove back up the coast road, past the vast, razor-wired US military base, I reflected on our conversation. Willcox had described the health of elderly Okinawans' as being due, in essence, to a balance between four factors – diet, exercise, spiritual well-being and psychosocial factors such as friendships and social support systems. As a misanthropic nonbeliever I couldn't do much about the spiritual and psychosocial elements in my life, but I vowed to start drinking jasmine tea (I had never as much as tasted tea until Mrs Shikobu's ceremony in Toyko, so this was a major life decision), which Willcox claimed was even better than green tea for lowering cholesterol, and to up my intake of vegetables and fish. Willcox took turmeric supplements every day too, as do many Okinawans: it is thought that turmeric might help prevent cancer and gallstones.

Recently, Okinawan products such as the black sugar, the local hirami lemon (thought to have anticarcinogenic properties) and Okinawan sea salt had become popular 'longevity produce' on sale in mainland Japanese cities. It can only be a matter of time before you see them in chic health stores in London and New York.

'Eat as low down the food chain as possible,' Willcox writes in *The Okinawa Program*. The notion of man as a hunter-gatherer is misleading, he continues. Gathered produce has always far exceeded hunted food in the human diet. Willcox told me that we in the West eat far too much protein than we need, we ought only to eat an amount the size of two decks of cards – around a hundred grams – a day. Perhaps I could start adding a little bit of MSG to my meals to trick my body into believing it is getting more protein than it is, and start eating more tofu of course. Seaweed is also clearly important; the Okinawans eat more konbu than anyone else in Japan. But you have to eat the real stuff; dried is fine, but supplements aren't nearly as good apparently.

All that remained was for me to see for myself the benefits of healthy Okinawan living. I had to bag me a centenarian.

Chapter 36

The Oldest Village in the World

The best place to find a centenarian on Okinawa, perhaps in the world, is the village of Ogimi, in the north-western part of the island. Over a third of its 3,500 residents are aged over sixty-five with a dozen or more centenarians among them – the highest proportion in Japan and most likely the world.

Lissen, Asger, Emil and I drove there along a coast road of dazzling beauty, the East China Sea glittering in the sunshine. We arrived in time for Sunday lunch having made a reservation at the village's only restaurant, specialising in longevity food.

Just outside Ogimi we passed a stone marker on which was written: 'At seventy you are but a child, at eighty you are merely a youth, and at ninety if the ancestors invite you into heaven, ask them to wait until you are one hundred, and then you might consider it.'

The village itself was just a single, poorly-made street with small, low-rise houses, most of them wood, all of them with immaculately tended, lush gardens. In some of them elderly men and women tended their flowers, fruit and vegetables. Only a passing funeral procession put a dampener on the idyllic atmosphere.

The restaurant was a simple, open-fronted place with a corrugated plastic roof and bare wood tables and chairs. Above the entrance there was a large vine loaded with freakish pink dragon fruit. Before we ate, I asked the owner, Emiko Kinjyo, if she might afterwards be able to introduce us to a centenarian.

A few minutes later she returned and beckoned us to follow her down the high street. We came to a dark, wooden, traditional open-fronted Okinawan house, essentially a large living/bedroom with a small, neat garden surrounding it.

An elderly lady walked slowly out to meet us, smiling at Asger and Emil. We all smiled back, not really knowing the etiquette when dealing with someone who was born before talking pictures were invented and had lived through two world wars. The woman's name was Matsu Taira. She moved with grace and ease, her face exuding a fragile radiance. She smiled again and beckoned us to sit beside her as she knelt on the wooden veranda of her house (without a single knee crack, I might add). She was extraordinarily thin with thick grey hair swept back Don King-style. Her face was weather-worn but serene. She lived alone in the house, she told us, but was visited by her family daily. She still tended her garden, where she grew goya and potatoes. She ate little, but it was fresh and mostly from her garden or the gardens of her friends. Her only vice was the occasional piece of Okinawan black sugar. She offered some to Asger and Emil, who had been standing some distance away eyeing this extraordinary woman warily, but now approached shyly.

I asked her about the war. She said she had hidden in the hills with her mother and sister for many weeks during the fighting. Her father had not survived. It struck me that perhaps this generation of Okinawans, the generation that had survived the war, really was unique. I was reminded of something Willcox had said to me about how impressed he had been by the strong will, the sheer stubbornness of many of the centenarians he had met. Of course, to have survived when a third of their number had perished must have taken astonishing levels of resourcefulness. Surely that will to survive had played an intrinsic role in their longevity in later life.

Emiko explained that the Okinawans don't in fact consider 100 to be the big milestone we do in the West. Instead they celebrate the ninety-seventh birthday with a public party called kajimayaa. Taira-san had recalled hers with a smile. All her family came and there were pinwheels, she said, toy windmills that are always used to decorate a kajimayaa to symbolise a return to the youthfulness that

Okinawans believe comes with age. The government gives them a lump sum too.

Taira-san looked calm, then, slowly, tiredness crept across her face and Emiko quietly suggested we should think about going.

Back at the restaurant we ate rice and tofu, bamboo shoots, seaweed, prawn tempura, pickles, small cubes of braised pork belly and a little cake and ice cream for dessert. The seaweed was especially remarkable – Okinawans call it umi-budo, or sea grapes, others call it sea caviar on account of its tiny pods arranged around an edible stalk like a DNA helix. The pods pop in your mouth, just like caviar releasing a flavour of the sea.

Emiko explained that Okinawans differentiate between kusui-mun, which are foods with medicinal benefit, and ujinimun, which have nutritional value. She tried to blend the two she said, offering us a traditional Okinawan dish called tofuyo, or fermented tofu (similar to the Chinese sufu, which is most likely where the Okinawans got the idea). The tofuyo was an evil-tasting, dark red tofu and served in small cubes with toothpicks. The idea is that you are supposed to nibble the cubes tiny morsels at a time, but no one explained this to me, so I stuck a toothpick in one and ate it whole. The effect was instant and involuntary. I gagged and spat it out onto my plate.

Emil made a 'See?' face, remembering only too vividly his experience with the dried scallop. 'Oh my god, ugh, ugh pfttcht, that is disgusting!' I said, desperately gulping down water. My mouth was burning. It was as if I had eaten a cross between Roquefort and nuclear waste, but apparently it is good for you. The Pharmaceutical Society of Japan did some research into tofuyo and came to the following conclusions:

Spontaneously hypertensive male rats at eight weeks of age were fed a diet containing lyophilized tofuyo for six weeks. At thirteen weeks of age, the systolic blood pressure of rats in the tofuyo group was significantly lower than that in the control group. After feeding the experimental diets, the ACE activity of kidney was significantly lower in the tofuyo group than that in the control group. Total cholesterol in serum in the tofuyo group was significantly lower while the ratio of high density lipoprotein (HDL) to total cholesterol in the tofuyo group tended to be higher than that in the control group.

Given the choice, I think I will take my chances with high cholesterol.

Chapter 37

Healthy Salt

If my insatiable, neurotic fretting over the health pages of women's magazines has taught me anything it is that conventional dietary and health advice is based on the demonisation of three substances: salt, sugar and animal fats. Salt causes hypertension and strokes; sugar makes you fat and gives you diabetes; and as for animal fats – see all of the above, and add geopolitical agricultural Armageddon to the mix.

On Okinawa, however, things are rather different. We have already heard mention of their sugar, called kokuto – an unrefined, dark brown, almost black sugar made with all of the cane plant. Relatively unprocessed, it is packed with minerals, potassium in particular. In terms of animal fats, the Okinawans traditionally eat very little meat but the one exception to this has been pork, which they have always eaten more of than the mainland Japanese. Pork is a relatively lean source of protein, and is also abundant in other useful substances such as iron, zinc, vitamin B6, riboflavin and niacin.

And then there is the salt. Gourmet salts have been a fashionable larder accessory for some years; none of our kitchens is complete without a box of Maldon or a little tub of Sel de Guerande. The Japanese make some of the most renowned salts in the world, most famously the Red and Blue Label salts of Oshima – but no matter how prettily packaged or expensive, it is still salt and salt, we are told, is a killer.

But not in Okinawa, at least not if Masakatsu Takayasu of the Nuchi Masu salt company is to be believed. Okinawa is famous throughout Japan for the quality of its salt and several top chefs

I spoke to used Okinawa salt in their kitchens. But it was Emi who told me about Takayasu. He had recently opened a new, cutting-edge salt-processing plant which, she said, used a new method of harvesting sea salt that produces a salt that actually helps *reduce* blood pressure, as well as offering more minerals – mostly magnesium and potassium – than any other salt in the world. Healthy salt? Was that possible? Could it be the solution to the world's hypertension?

There is more than a hint of Bond villain's lair about the Nuchi Una factory. It is located in Uruma, on Henza Jima island, which you approach across a causeway flanked by an extraordinary rocky seascape. A road takes you round the eastern side of the island, climbing up to wooded cliffs high above the Pacific. There perches a startlingly white, modern salt refinery and visitor's centre complex.

Takayasu-san is a physics graduate and, he told me as we sat in his cluttered office, also an expert in evolutionary theory. With his plaid shirt and trouser top rolled over his belt, he looked more like an imo farmer but he had some fascinating things to say about salt.

'Think about it like this,' he said, sitting forward in his chair and resting his elbows on his desk. 'Life was created four billion years ago from the ocean. We have only spent four hundred million years on land which means for three point six billion years we evolved in the ocean salt, living from ocean salt minerals. The first amniotic fluid was sea water, still today amniotic fluid is salty. How could it not be good for you to still eat those minerals?'

OK, that much I could follow: I knew too that Ringer's solution which is used in intravenous drips has a similar composition to sea water. But following that theory wouldn't all salt, even the salt mined on land, still be good for you? 'No, because to refine salt, you must heat it and in that heating you make it more difficult for the body to take in those minerals because they stick together. But here we have devised a system that harvests the salt using only natural temperatures and an instant evaporation technique. The minerals remain separate and when dissolved in the intestine become ion and so can be absorbed easily by the body. In fact, because it retains so much potassium, thanks to our special system our salt *reduces* blood pressure because it helps the body to expel sodium from the body via our urine better. It has all the minerals of sea water – zinc, iron, copper and manganese. It's pure.'

It took almost ten years to develop the system – Takayasu-san calls it the 'room temperature, instantaneous vacuum crystallisation process' – which, in essence, extracts the salt from sea water by turning it into an extremely fine spray directed at a 'reverse osmotic membrane', a kind of fine netting. Takayasu-san got the idea when, in a former career running an orchid nursery, he observed the way the flowers were watered using a fine spray mist. He showed me where they do this. We peered through a porthole into the spraying room at an amazing snowscape with salt cascading over every surface. The air was thick with it, like an Arctic blizzard, as a warm air fan turned the sea water into an ultra-fine mist, vaporised it, separating out the minerals, which accumulated just about everywhere else in the room.

There are other salt spray systems like this Takayasu-san explained, but they dry the salt at a high temperature. Nuchi Masu uses low temperature. The result is a salt containing twenty-one minerals, including potassium, which is good for reducing blood pressure and, apparently, has a much lower level of artery-hardening sodium nitrate. But you would surely also have to eat an awful lot of salt to have any effect – I mean, we usually only eat about, what, ten grams a day?

'Listen,' he said avoiding the question like a skilled politician. 'Why do you think Okinawans live so long?' 'Diet,' I replied. 'Plus the climate, exercise, good healthcare . . . oh, come on, you aren't saying it's the salt, are you?'

'Exactly, yes it is! You know Okinawa has the most typhoons of anywhere in the world? Well, because of the typhoons Okinawan soil is constantly soaked by sea water. That sea water is full of minerals which enter the soil and then the fruit, vegetables, grasses and animals raised in Okinawa. Everyone says Okinawans live so long because of the konbu they eat or the weather, but no. They play just a small part, and anyway, the pork is so good here because their feed is so full of minerals. In Okinawa all our soil has all the minerals.'

This sounded plausible. Perhaps that explained the superb quality of the cows that are raised on Okinawa before being sent to Matsusaku or Kobe, but, hold on, don't other places get lots of typhoons? What about Florida? He had a simple answer to that: 'They don't grow things in Florida. Listen, for many years Okinawa had no choice, it had to grow its own food. People here say typhoons are our enemy, but now I call typhoons good! If it weren't for typhoons I would have died at age fifty [he is sixty], so I say to people, what would you prefer, no typhoons and die young, or typhoons bringing goodness to our soil and live to one hundred.'

Though he had skilfully avoided the question of just how much benefit was to be had from something we ate so little of as salt, his argument was still fascinating. Could Okinawa's regular salt-water saturation be the reason for its inhabitants' longevity? The islands are surrounded by coral which is, of course, rich in a variety of fundamentally important minerals, some of which would end up in the soil after each typhoon. I thought back to the magical Okinawan sweet potato – it was the only crop that had flourished on the islands for centuries; it must have acted like a sponge for all the sea minerals that washed the land. It clearly wasn't the only reason for Okinawan's longevity, as Willcox's research has so effectively detailed, but Takayasu's argument had a logic, and he had a good deal of scientific research to back his claims.

He told me that Nuchi Masu is even planning to remove the sodium chloride from its salt to leave just the sea water minerals. 'I am going to market it as a health food – a "Sea Supplement".'

It all sounded fantastic, I said. Could this be done anywhere? 'Everyone should eat salt produced like this but people just haven't recognised the value of this system yet. You can use it any place where the ocean is not polluted, as long as the ocean is clean you can harvest clean salt. But I do have the patent on the system of course.'

But what about the flavour? Is that better than other salts as well? (I knew the answer to the question even as I was asking it.) 'Yes, yes,' he enthused as he led me to the factory shop and restaurant, all tastefully decorated in a modern Scandinavian style with gorgeous views over the aquamarine sea. Jazz tinkled in the background as lovely young assistants guided other guests to their tables and around the shop. 'I have commissioned research into its umami profile that has shown that it has much more umami flavour than normal salt. It is ultimate umami salt.'

Takayasu-san showed me a book he had recently published entitled: *Salt: Health Revolution to Rescue Modern People*, subtitled *Miracle salt that doesn't cause high blood pressure to say goodbye to diabetes and dry skin*. Close by were various bath and massage products made from the salt; salt caramels; and elegant 250g plastic sachets of the salt itself, on sale for ¥100 – less than 50p. I bought a packet to try at home. It was extremely fine and soft, like powdered sugar, and as far as I can make out it does have a slightly milder taste, milder even than the other Okinawan salts I tried, like Aguni and Ishigaki. It lacks the textural interest of French marsh salts or Maldon, but is perfect as a dipping salt for tempura or just to finish off meats at the last minute, as it dissolves quickly and evenly.

Nuchi Masu is currently producing around eight tonnes of salt a month, but capacity is set to ramp up to thirty tonnes. Takayasu-san had begun exporting it to Germany as 'Life Salt' a month earlier, and in 2007 it won a Best Gold at the Monde Selection, a major food produce show held in Brussels. Kamebishi, the company that made the superb soy sauce on Shikoku Island also used Nuchi Masu salt, and top chefs are following suit throughout Japan.

Now, if they could just managed to develop fat-free foie gras and French fries, I need never buy another woman's magazine as long as I live – which would, of course, be well into three figures.

Chapter 38

The Restaurant at the End of My Universe

We flew from Okinawa back north to Tokyo the next day just in time for my dinner date with destiny at Mibu, the restaurant Yukio Hattori had said was the best in Japan.

Mibu, you'll recall, was the place that made Joël Robuchon weep and humbled Ferran Adrià. It is what the Japanese call an *ichigen-san okotowari* place, meaning 'entry by invitation only'. Hattori was allowed to dine once a month with seven guests, and this month I was to be one of them.

On the flight I stared down once more at the snow-capped Mount Fuji passing slowly below, yet I was feeling anything but serene. I was wracked with anxiety. Lissen will tell you that is my default setting, but I was working myself up into a proper maelstrom of anticipatory angst. What was expected of me? Why had this rich, powerful and influential man extended this remarkable invitation? More troubling still, would the food live up to the billing, and even if it did, would I be able to tell? Mibu had no website, in fact there was no mention at all of it on the Internet. I had absolutely no idea what to expect, what to wear or how to behave. Was I expected to pay, or at least offer to pay? Or would that cause offence? Who would we be dining with? Just how many ways were there for me to disgrace myself with some oafish breach of etiquette?

Emi, who had also been invited, tried to assuage my fears when we met that evening in Ginza, the heartland of Tokyo's lavish, high-rolling dining and nightlife scene. Ginza is home to some of the most expensive restaurants in the world. During Japan's extraordinary economic rampage in the 1980s, this was where you came if you wanted to eat gold leaf-wrapped sushi off the belly of a naked woman – a style known as Nyotaimori – or spend an average annual salary drinking rare single malts. Today, Ginza, with its red-brick grid of broad avenues and tree-lined side streets, originally developed by the British in the early twentieth century as an area for silver minting, still generates more wealth than many small nations and could easily lay claim to being the planet's retail flagship.

Emi had rung Hattori's secretary and been told he would be paying and that we would be accompanied by a couple of food writers and three chefs from Hattori's cooking school.

By the time we arrived outside one of Ginza's best-known land-marks, the Sony Building at six-thirty in the evening Hattori-san was already waiting, dressed in his customary deep black silk Mao jacket and rimless glasses, together with three men in dark suits and ties – the chefs – and two women dressed for the office in pencil skirts and white shirts – the food writers. We all chatted briefly making introductions.

Hattori led us down a side road and around a corner to an anony-mous building whose open front led to a strip-lit staircase. It looked more like the entrance to a multi-storey car park than a restaurant but we followed him up two flights of stairs.

We were greeted at the entrance by the chef's wife, an imposing woman in her late sixties dressed in a magnificent dark kimono, a glossy black crest of hair crowning her cherubic face. Mibu has but one small, low lit, windowless dining room, given over to the member and his guests each evening. As we were shown through from the entrance I looked down at the floor. The flagstones had recently been dampened – a Japanese custom intended to express hospitality. Inside the dining room the pale clay walls were timbered with honoki wood, the most luxurious and costly panelling you can get in Japan, as used for the coffins of emperors. But Mibu was neither glitzy nor osten-tatious, far from it. The room was very simple, decorated in a Zen style with just a scroll and a vase – both, it turned out, priceless.

We sat at tatami-covered tables, not on the floor, which was some relief. I sat across from Hattori, with Emi on his left, the journalists to my right, and the chefs, who remained silent throughout the evening, taking assiduous notes and photographs, on my left.

Chef Hiroshi Ishida has run Mibu for over thirty years, his wife explained as she offered us sake from a pot with an unusually long spout. She poured it from a height, as you might ouzo. 'This is the ancient way,' she explained. 'When there was a risk of poisoning, if you poured like this the oxygen would mean the sake was less acid and there was less danger.' The pot was worth a million yen apparently. She drew our attention to the scroll on the wall. It was of a dancer. 'This is seventy years old. See how she is drawn with one unbroken line.' I imagined the decades of study that had led to the point at which the artist was able to create something of such purity. 'We get power from art,' the chef's wife said quietly, almost to herself, as she left the room.

When she returned with the first course, she introduced the flowers that were the only other decorative feature of the room; they were hamagiku, or white beach chrysanthemums, representative of the autumn festival period and a celebration of the countryside – the theme of that evenings meal.

The first course was a clear dashi with a fan-shaped gingko leaf floating on the surface. Beneath was a ginko fritter – chewy, nutty and bitter – and a slither of poached gobi fish. It was an elegant, refreshing start to the meal. 'Eat the gingko leaves too,' advised Ishida's wife. 'They are very good for vitamins against dementia.'

'The chef has a real appreciation of the four seasons,' Hattori said. 'I have been coming here twelve times a year for sixteen years, and every time is an evocation of the month we are in. You have to eat food in season, that's the only time you can enjoy the moment. It has to be fresh every day.'

Ishida's wife brought some grilled ayu, a seasonal river fish. 'It goes well with sake. Note the bitterness of the guts,' said Hattori.

The fish, famously caught by fishermen using trained cormorants, had been grilled whole, including the innards, and was served in a plain paper cone. Mrs Ishida showed me how to pinch the flesh on the tail together to release it from the bones, and then eat around the spine.

'This is Ochiayu time, the time when the ayu fish return down the river fat and pregnant. Her life is finished. The fisherman prayed all day and asked the ayu to be medicine, so we appreciate it,' she said.

The oily saltiness of the fish went perfectly with the chilled sake while the bitter aftertaste from the guts of the fish was a welcome challenge to the palate, just lifting it from a complacent comfort zone. Shizuo Tsuji writes of the ayu that it is, 'the *piece de resistance* of Japanese grilled foods and one of the few Japanese dishes in which the bitterness is meant to be enjoyed.' While it is the least employed of the five tastes in the West, bitterness is an interesting element of Japanese cuisine. The gingko nuts, too, had a bitter aftertaste that helped cut through their chewy, cloying texture.

'I could see you were getting hot,' Mrs Ishida said returning with a plate of sashimi. It was bonito, a rainbow of purple and red, and below that, beneath a layer crushed ice, sashimi of gobi fish. Was it the greatest sashimi I had ever had? No question. This was properly fresh bonito that had never been frozen. Unlike the bonito or tuna I had eaten before, whose flesh had so often been coloured and degraded into a soft, sometimes mushy mass, this required effort to chew. It had texture and flavour.

Aubergine was next. Often, Mrs Ishida said, chefs reject fruits and vegetables late in their season, thinking they are past their best, but her husband realised that late crops were full of flavour. Indeed he relished working with vegetables that other chefs might discard. The aubergine we were about to eat, for example, was at the Nagori stage of the season, the end (the other two stages are Hashari, the baby vegetables, and Sakari, the ripe stage).

'We enjoy very much the end of the vegetable's life, we take care

294

of it. It is a principle of our cooking. These vegetables are with us only for three or four months of the year, then they are gone. We won't be able to eat them again, so we celebrate them until they have gone.'

The aubergine was slippery and fall-apart tender; I had never experienced such an intense aubergine taste before. Aubergine can be watery or, when cooked, often just a sponge for oil and other flavours, but this one, which I guessed had been gently steamed, had not only retained its flavour but intensified it. It was served with tiny, soft yams the size of marbles.

Until now the meal had been fascinating, revelatory and delicious, but things took a turn for the transcendent with the next course, hamo, or pike conger eel, served in a dashi scattered with yellow chrysanthemum petals.

I took a sip of the gently steaming, dashi – thickened with kuzu, or arrowroot, which gives body without tainting the flavour in the way that conventional Western thickeners like flour, butter or cornstarch do – and literally convulsed with pleasure. Hattori saw my reaction, smiled and nodded to himself.

'You see, I really wanted you to try a proper dashi,' he said. 'Now you know what I was talking about. This is the number one dashi in Japan. Usually restaurants prepare dashi in the morning, but here it is prepared right at this very moment, the katsuobushi is shaved at the last minute. The smell of dashi evaporates quickly so usually there is only a faint trace, but here you get the full flavour.'

My embarrassing shudder of pleasure was involuntary, like a mini-orgasm. Every hair on my body had stood on end. It was as if the chef had found a taste receptor I never knew I had, some kind of palate g-spot, and performed a kind of culinarylingus. It is always difficult describing flavours; using words to evoke taste is rarely effective – as with talking about architecture – but this soup had a deep meatiness, an addictive savoury foundation above which danced teasingly tangy notes of the sea. It was impossible to divide its flavour from its aroma, which I suspect is where the great power of this dashi, of any good dashi, lay. I would give anything to experience it again.

'You know,' said Hattori, 'Ishida just came up with this dish this afternoon. In ten years, I have never eaten the same dish twice. That is almost one and a half thousand dishes, all different.'

'But, but . . .' I stammered, incredulous. 'I don't believe it. It is like this dish has always been around. This dish must have existed before, it is so good.'

'That is just what Ferran Adrià said when he ate here,' said Hattori, triumphantly. 'He said it was like Ishida-san's food must always have been with us. If you really want to experience the core, the fundamentals of Japanese food, this is the place. Much cooking destroys the essential flavour of ingredients, but he makes the most of them.'

As always in a Japanese meal, the arrival of the rice signalled the end of the savoury courses, but this was not the usual bowl of plain rice to 'fill a hole.' Instead we were served exquisite, soft, warm, sticky rice studded with chestnuts from Tamba.

Dessert was a kogyoku apple from Gunma prefecture, cooked in thin slices and as light as a communion host. It was served, Ishida's wife explained, on rare silverware, the only type they could find that could hold perfect droplets of apple juice without them running. It looked like the plate was speckled with Swarovski crystals. 'This is the ultimate dessert!' said Hattori.

Ishida-san brought it in to us himself. He was a short, straight-backed, stocky man dressed in a single-breasted white jacket and dark trousers with a shaved head and the kindest face – a gentle grandfather.

I stood up to shake his hand, but he gestured, smiling, that I should sit. I asked where he got his inspiration from. 'It is very difficult. But I am always looking to get better at what I do every month,' he said.

'He is competing against himself!' said Hattori. 'Nobody can cook like him.'

Where did he get all of his ingredients, from Tsukiji? 'Of course,

I do sometimes go to Tsukiji, but mostly I have direct contact with my suppliers, with my fishermen.'

If you go to eat at the restaurants of one of the great European or American chefs, Alain Ducasse or Thomas Keller for instance, the food is generally a direct expression of the chef's personality or ego; there are other top-class restaurants, Nobu, say, or the Ivy, where you go for the ambience, the decor, excessive fawning from the waiting staff, or to spot famous people; and then there are the celebrity chef joints like Anthony Bourdain's Les Halles in New York or any of the Gordon Ramsay places – to be honest, I am not sure why anyone would go to those as it is about as likely that the celebrity chef in question will be working in the kitchen as it is that a member of the Ford family has built your Fiesta.

But Mibu was something else. It wasn't really a restaurant in any conventional Western sense of the word. You didn't go for the decor, to be seen, or because it was prestigious or a celebrity hangout. You went for the narrative, for what the food told you about nature, flavour and texture, perhaps even about yourself. It was dining as a spiritual experience, as an evocation of history, as philosophy, as a path to deeper mysteries of life, creation, death and nature. Something elemental, in both senses of the word – both basic, fundamental, and of the earth. And I am sure I missed around eighty per cent of the meaning and references.

'Customers are like patrons of artists for us,' Ishida's wife told me. 'This food is not something you can buy with money. God gives you the time to enjoy this moment but you need to have the ability to enjoy the moment, which is priceless.'

It was a seismic moment in my life as an eater. The ingredients were rigorously seasonal – which is one of Ishida-san's abiding principles. The flavours were pure, representative of the ingredients, subtle but intense when required. Somehow Ishida was able to overlay different flavours, different intensities of taste within the same dish, yet with each remaining clearly identifiable. How often do we hear the chef behind the latest hot destination in London, Paris or

New York, say that their food is 'seasonal, fresh, local and simple'? Before being presented with a plate of foam, gelatine, *sous vide* this or puréed that; food in towers; food compressed into ring moulds; sauces smeared to look, as one critic memorably put it, 'as if someone wearing stilettos had slipped in goose shit'. I admit, I spent a year training to make this kind of food, and then worked in two Michelin-starred Parisian kitchens serving it to customers with precision placed chervil leaves, sticky reduced stocks and absurdly turned vegetables, but now I knew better. At Mibu the plating was elegant but entirely without artifice or fuss. The food looked as if it had simply 'arrived' in position.

It was a stark contrast to a meal I'd had a couple of nights earlier, on the thirty-eighth floor of the Mandarin Oriental Hotel. The Molecular Tapas Bar is one of the hottest restaurants in Tokyo, with space at its counter for just six diners. The Japanese-American chef, Jeff Ramsay, served us dishes that were part food, part magic trick: olive oil granita, made by pouring the oil into dry ice; a deconstructed miso soup; and carrot caviar, a classic El Bulli dish made by dropping carrot juice into a calcium chloride solution (as used to make tofu) so that it formed into small, soft spheres. It was the antithesis of Mibu – raw ingredients utterly transformed, unrecognisable. Some would dismiss this as too much 'messing about' with food, and it is tempting to see Ramsay's style of cooking as a kind of corruption, but personally I feel there is plenty of room for both approaches to the preparation of food, and, once in a while at least, I find the invention and theatricality of so-called molecular cuisine absolutely thrilling. At least there are no airs to 'simplicity' and 'purity' with this kind of cooking. And I'll never forget the effect of a 'miracle fruit' (synepalum dulcificum), a small, olive-type berry that grows wild in Africa and which, after you chewed it a little, turned raw lemon wedges sweet.

But there was a poignancy to our meal at Mibu, an elegiac quality which, had it not been such a joyous sensual feast, might almost have been melancholy. The food worked on so many levels: visual, cerebral, in terms of flavour, and viscerally. Ishida-san cooked with his heart and spirit. He and his food were indivisible. The dishes he had created especially for us that evening – never to be repeated – were born of a lifetime's experience and a depth of understanding of Japanese culture that few Japanese chefs could match, and even fewer will attain in the future. There had been around ten courses, but by the end I felt neither bloated, nor hungry, but perfectly, blissfully sated. 'Another good restaurant might manage a couple of courses of this standard, but never be consistent over so many,' agreed Hattori.

As we were leaving, we were each given plastic bags with some more of the apple dessert , some foil-wrapped sashimi and another ziplock bag of some of Ishida's own katsuobushi shavings – his leftovers from our meal, now no longer fresh enough for his exacting requirements.

By the doorway I asked Ishida's wife how old he was.

'Sixty-five', she said.

'Oh, he can go on cooking for years yet,' I said.

'No,' she said quietly, so that he couldn't hear. 'By cooking he is cutting his life short.'

It is only in the last month or so, as I continue to reflect on that evening that the fundamental lesson of my visit to Mibu has become apparent: that to be a truly great chef, to excel in your métier, surpass your peers and create something beyond a meal, you must above all else have humility. Humility regarding your craft, so that you are constantly striving to learn and open to new ways and ingredients; humility towards your peers, so that you never rest on your laurels; but, above all, crucially, humility to the ingredients, because without the produce, without the fruit and the fish, the meat and the vegetables, a chef is nothing. Ishida employed his produce with the greatest respect, allowing their flavours to vibrate with a purity and simplicity that I could work years to achieve but in reality would probably never even dare to attempt because as well as humility, that kind of simplicity takes great courage for a chef. I know that using the word courage in the context of a kitchen – when there are men facing death in Iraq, or the mines of Africa every day – may sound hyperbolic, but to serve a steamed aubergine naked and to present this as your best work takes some front.

When Michelin published their first Tokyo guide a few weeks later to a fanfare of publicity and outrage in both the Japanese and French capitals – Tokyo was judged to be worthy of almost twice as many stars as Paris – Mibu was nowhere to be found. It was not even mentioned among the restaurants that had refused to participate in the inspector's assessment.

Sometimes I wonder if it ever existed.

Epilogue

> Japanese cuisine is deceptively simple, Its key ingredients are
> but two: a rather delicate stock (dashi) made from konbu (giant
> kelp) and flakes of dried bonito, and shoyu, Japanese soy sauce.
>
> Shizuo Tsuji, *A Simple Art*

I think the key word here is 'deceptively' for, of course, Japanese
cuisine is anything but simple. I never for a moment thought I would
discover all there is to know about it during just one journey, no
matter how action- and meal-packed it was, but, equally, I never
anticipated quite how dazzlingly multifaceted, how regionally diverse,
how occasionally befuddling it would turn out to be.

On our last day in Tokyo, in one last, desperate box-ticking binge,
we did get to sample both shirako – cod's sperm, or milt – which
I thoroughly recommend – and chicken sashimi, which was also
rather lovely once I had surmounted the psychological hurdle. Also,
Emil wants it to be known that during a meal later in the day, he
ate an entire fish eye, and enjoyed it. But there were so many things
I didn't get to eat but wanted to, so many cities I wanted to visit
but didn't have the time for and, most importantly, so many *seasons*
of food I wanted to experience. I could spend a lifetime studying
just one aspect of Japanese cuisine – as, indeed, my friend Mr
Koyabashi the Ramen Champion has, or Murata has with dashi –
and still never really find a definitive recipe or perfect my technique.
To hope to master it all was, of course, delusional.

I admitted all of this to Toshi on our first meeting after we had
arrived back in Paris. I suppose I had hoped for a thawing of

temperament, that my conversion to the Japanese cause might temper his bolshiness slightly. But he merely pouted and shrugged his shoulders as if to say, 'This is not news to me, foolish man.'

'So maybe you not cook fish so long now, eh?'

'No, Toshi, I won't.'

'No more cream. Better vegetables.'

'Yes, Toshi.'

'One more thing. You learn. Say, "*Gochisoma deshita.*"'

I repeated, '*Gochisoma deshita.* What does it mean? White men can't cook?'

'It is from Buddha, a thanks to the cooks who gathered and made the food. Now you say it every meal.'

These days I drink jasmine tea every morning, and take my turmeric supplements, as Dr Willcox advises. I beguile guests with my inside-out maki rolls – which are much better now – and by splashing ponzu and miso over everything. I eat tofu, and miso soup, more fish, less meat, more vegetables and less dairy, and I feel all the better for it, not least as I have shed five kilos. My blocks of dried katsuobushi filet in the back of the fridge remain, as yet, unshaved for lack of the correct implement, but with a few ill-judged stab marks following an unsuccessful attempt with a Stanley knife.

Reading through my notes, something suddenly strikes me that I'd better clear up. I am slightly anxious that it might sound as if I spent most of my time dumping the kids with Lissen and galavanting off in search of nice food, but that is only partly true. At least, by the end of our journey, I am happy to say that Lissen was as bewitched by Japan as I was. We talk constantly of returning, preferably next week.

And the children? They still clamour for tempura and sushi on a weekly basis. Recently, at school, Asger's class were offered sushi for lunch by the caterers. None of his friends would touch it but, apparently, he spent the hour touring the tables hoovering up the leftovers. Meanwhile, the Okinawan snake soup is one of Emil's favourite travel anecdotes, along with that time he ate a whole fish eye. He still talks fondly of the Japanese health service and the dead turtle he found on the beach on Okinawa. He remembers the Japanese word for dragonfly, *tombo*, too which he learned in the first ramen restaurant he ate in back in Sapporo. Asger still talks of the time he felled a sumo, and only slightly exaggerates the size of the king crab he was introduced to.

We often look through our photographs but, of course, over time, regrettably, their memories of Japan will fade. I do hope that, subliminally at least, their eyes have been opened to the world of possibilities that exists beyond their day-to-day realm back home. They have experienced for themselves a vivid snippet of the world's variety. I certainly could not imagine having undertaken that journey without them, or of course, without Lissen. To see the world through her eyes is always fascinating. And, having children in tow opened so many more doors, introduced us to so many more people, and afforded us a far greater latitude for appalling behaviour that might otherwise have been the case.

But Japan will always be there, we will return, and the food will awe us once more. Perhaps most reassuring of all is that Shizuo Tsuji's fears of a disappearing culinary tradition seem largely unfounded. Japanese cuisine is changing of course, I don't think Tsuji-san would have wanted it otherwise. Though the worrying trend towards a Western diet continues, and is bringing with it all the health problems we are facing in the West, with people like Kanae Okada at the Kamebishi soy company, Hattori-san or Tony Flenley with his pungent miso, Masakatsu Takayasu and his healthy salt, and of course Tsuji's son, Yoshihiro, I think the traditions and future of Japanese cuisine are in safe, passionate and capable hands.

Acknowledgements and Bibliography

It bears repeating that I owe a significant debt of thanks to my researcher Emiko Doi – not just for her amazing ability to get me into places I might otherwise never even have known existed, but for her warmth and generosity to me and my family while we were in Japan. Asger and Emil are very lucky to have such a special Japanese aunty, and Lissen and I count ourselves similarly blessed to have Emi as a friend.

So many people gave their time to help me in the research for this book and displayed remarkable patience when dealing with my innovative scattergun interviewing technique. Most are already mentioned by name but I would again like to express my sincere thanks for their time and generosity: to Toshi, of course, although I doubt anything in these pages will come as news to him; Yukio Hattori, whose Tokyo Taste event I later attended and much enjoyed; Yoshiki Tsuji, a generous host during my visit to Osaka; miso expert Tony Flenley, who tells me the smell from his drains has much improved; Etsuko Shinobu, the Tokyo housewife whose tatami floor I besmirched with my borrowed red vinyl slippers; Yoshio Ando the wasabi expert; Takahiko Sasaki the konbu expert; Philip Harper and Toko Akira the sake experts who shared their knowledge and enthusiasm; Kanae Okada the remarkable soy revivalist; Shuichiro Kobori the fu expert; Ikuko Uda the wasabi cooking supremo; salt revolutionary Masakatsu Takayasu; master chefs Hiroshi Ishida, Yoshihiro Murata, Yoshifumi Mori, Takamitsu Aihara, Eiji Hayashi and Jeff Ramsay; Osamu the peerless sushi chef who kindly and with great forbearance showed us around Tsukiji; Junko and Sasha in Kyoto;

Chiaki and Hiroshi for their incredible hospitality in Osaka; centenarian Matsu Taira; Ramen World Champion, Takamitsu Kobayashi; our friends at the Onoe sumo stable (congratulations to Sumo Monster and Baruto who, Emil tells us, have gone on to great success since we met); Tamie Kosaki and Kayo Kosaki the ama divers; Kurt, my Koya san guru; gerontologist Dr Craig Willcox; and the people at Fuji TV, the Wadakin cattle ranch, the Yaizu fish processing centre, Ajinomoto and Kikkoman all of whom received with great generosity and kindness.

There are also some who aren't mentioned explicitly in the book but were a tremendous help and inspiration, such as Kylie Clark at the Japanese National Tourist Office in London (a true Japanese food fan, and kindred spirit – go to www.seejapan.co.uk to have all your questions answered about visiting); the renowned Osakan food writer Takeshi Kadokami who gave generously of his time in order to help me understand the nature of Osakan cuisine; and the helpful assistants at the various tourist offices around Japan, particularly in Mie Prefecture and Osaka.

And then there was the woman who politely tapped me on the shoulder while I was on my phone at a crossroads in Ginza and *apologised* for interrupting me to say, did I realise I had dropped a large bank note on the floor? For me, she epitomised the decency and helpfulness shown to us by virtually every single Japanese person we met during our journey through their astonishingly beautiful, endlessly exciting and thoroughly civilised land (I like to think I sent the karma onwards when, later, I found a wallet filled with large banknotes on the back seat of a taxi one evening in Kyoto – perhaps in no other country in the world would I judged it prudent to passed the wallet to the taxi driver, safe in the knowledge that he would hand it in to the police).

Practical travel assistance was very generously given by British Airways (www.ba.com) and Japan Air Lines (www.jal.com); the Japanese National Tourist Office (see above); the Mandarin Oriental Hotel (www.mandarinoriental.com/tokyo – my God, what an amazing place!); and Oakwood serviced apartments (www.oakwood.com which are fantastic if you are travelling with a family).

In London, I am deeply grateful for the continuing support and sound advice of my agent Camilla Hornby at Curtis Brown, as well as the skillful and sensitive editing of Ellah Allfrey, and the faith and enthusiasm shown in my work by the publisher of this book, Dan Franklin.

Finally, to Lissen, in particular, I want to express my unbounded gratitude for your incredible support and patience during this journey. I know that, sometimes there appeared to be precious little method in my madness, but hope that in reading this you will see that there was at least some point to the many hours spent trying to entertain two young, restless boys alone in a strange land. (You can now see just how absolutely essential it was that I visit two cattle ranches, for example.)

One day we'll go back and eat at Kikunoi together, I promise.

Glossary

A–D

ama	Female divers who dive for shellfish and seaweed in waters off the easterly Pacific coast of Mie
Ainu	Indigenous people of Hokkaido
Anime	Japanese animation
aonori	Dried seaweed flakes
awamori	Okaniwan distilled liquor
ayu	Seasonal fresh water fish, typically grilled whole
Bata-kon ramen	Hokkaido-style butter-corn ramen
beni imo	Okinawan purple sweet potato
bonito / katsuobushi	Oily, red-fleshed fish related to tuna / smoke-dried filets of same fish
bunraku	Traditional Japanese puppetry
Burakumin	Oppressed social minority group in Japan
butsukari-geiko	sumo training exercise where one wrestler attempts to push opponent across the ring
cha kaiseki	Original, simple form of kaiseki multi-course meal devised to accompany tea ceremony
chanko nabe	Traditional hotpot prepared and eaten by sumo wrestlers
chikuto sugar cane	Fine-quality sugar
dai ginjo	Exclusive type of sake

dankon	Penis
deba	Triangular knife for filleting fish
dengaku	Skewered tofu coated with miso and grilled
depachika	Department store food hall
dohyo	Clay ring in which sumo wrestling takes place

E–H

engawa	Veranda (also used to describe frilly edges of a flatfish)
enoki	Long, thin, white mushrooms
fu	Type of dough made from wheat gluten
fugu	Puffer fish or blowfish
fugusashi	Sliced raw puffer fish or blowfish
gaijin	Outsider or foreigner
genshu	Undiluted sake
goya champaru	Okinawan dish featuring stir-fried bitter cucumber
gunkan maki	'Battleship' sushi, where a block of rice and topping is wrapped in nori seaweed in the shape of a boat
gyoza	Chinese-style dumpling filled with meat or vegetables
habu	Snake
hamagiku	White beach chrysanthemum
hamo	Pike conger eel
hangiri	Wooden rice bowl used for cooling sushi rice
'hara hachi-bu'	Okinawan expression meaning, 'Eat until you are 80 per cent full'
harusame (noodles)	Transparent noodles made from potato flour or mung bean flour
Hashari	Early season crops

higuma	Grizzly bear
hirami (lemon)	Thin-skinned flat lemon
hiyamugi	Thick noodles made from wheat flour
hoko nabe	Charcoal-heated samovar
honoki	Non-resinous wood

I–L

Ichiban dashi	'No.: 1' basic stock infused with dried konbu seaweed and katsuobushi flakes, used as a base for many Japanese dishes, sauces, soups etc.
'ichigen-san okotowari'	'Entry by invitation only'
'ichigo ichie'	'One encounter, one chance'
irabu-jiru	Snake stew
izakaya	Japanese-style pub-diner
jizo	Statues erected as memorials to babies and infants who have died
junmai ginjo sake	Premium sake
kabuki	Dance drama
kaiseki	Elaborate, ritualistic, formal dinner of up to nine courses, inspired by the passing seasons
kaiten,	Conveyor belt sushi
kajimayaa	Public party held to celebrate the 97th birthday of an Okinawan resident
kakiage no tendong	Scallop fritters (tempura)
kamaboko	Fish cakes made from steamed fish paste
kami	Gods
kanji characters	Chinese characters used in Japanese writing
katsuobushi	Smoked-dried, fermented filets of bonito fish, which are shaved on a special plane and used as a seasoning
katsuobushi kezuriki	Upside-down carpenter's plane used for shaving dried blocks of bonito fish

katsuramuki	'Column peel' – the technique used for peeling vegetables
kimchi	Korean pickled cabbage
kimo	The liver of the fugu fish
kito piro	Ainu mountain vegetables
Wagyu beef	Japanese beef, typically tender and marbled with creamy white fat. Often mistakenly called Kobe beef.
kogyoku (apple)	Japanese apple
koji	fermenting agent used in sake brewing, as well as to make miso and soy sauce, and as a marinade/pickling ingredient.
konbu (or kombu)	Seaweed, dried for use most notably in making dashi; variations include rishiri konbu – konbu laid down and dried for two years to deepen its glutamate flavour; shio konbu – salt konbu; and tororo konbu – konbu soaked in vinegar then dried and shaved
konnyaku	Jelly-like substance made from the 'devil's tongue' root used to add texture to dishes
koromo	Enrobed
koshihikari	Premium-quality, short-grain rice that has been dried naturally in the sun
'kuidaore'	Osakan expression meaning 'eat 'till you go bust' (physically and financially)
kura-gakoi	Method of preserving konbu using a temperature- and humidity-controlled drying process
kushikatsu	Deep-fried breaded skewers
kusui-mun	Medicinal foods
kuzu	Thickening agent
kyo ryori	Kyoto cuisine

kyo yasai	Kyoto vegetables
kyo-kaiseki	*see* kaiseki

M–P

machiya	Historic wooden townhouses found in Kyoto
maki	Sushi roll
makisu	Bamboo mat for rolling maki
maoi	Okinawan local 'people's banks'
matsutake mushroom	'Japanese truffle' – a rare, rich, woody mushroom
mawashi	Loin cloth worn by sumo wresters
meishi	Business card
miora	Flavouring added to rice
mirugai	Geoduck clam
mishiro	Method of maturing fermented soybeans for making soy sauce
miso	Fermented soybean paste for flavouring soups and stocks; variations include kome miso – made with rice and beans; mame miso – made with beans only; mugi miso – made with barley and beans; and sendai miso – salty miso
mochi	Japanese dessert made with rice flour dough
modori	Bonito fish, or katsuo, returning from the north in the autumn
moromi	Koji mixed with brine to form the mash used in making soy sauce
mukkur	Wooden Jew's Harp - a traditional Ainu instrument
Nagari	Late season crops
natto	Acquired taste fermented soybean dish

negi	Japanese-style baby leeks
nigari	Coagulant used to make tofu
nigiri	Edo, or Tokyo-style sushi, in which body-temperature, hand-squeezed blocks of rice are topped with chilled seafood
nikiri	Sushi dip made with dashi, mirin, sake and soy
ninjitsu	Technique for making nigiri which mimics the secret signal of the ninja
Nishiki Ichiba	Kyoto's main market
noren	Traditional restaurant door curtain.
nori	Thin, dried, edible seaweed sheets used for wrapping around sushi rice
obanzai ryori	Kyoto cuisine, largely vegetarian, centring on tofu and yuba
oden	'Lucky-dip' stew containing any combination of meat, fish or vegetables
oishii	Delicious
okonomiyaki	Japanese-style thick pancake with various fillings/toppings; variations include monjayaki – made with a runnier dough than okonomiyaki; and modanyaki – with fried noodles (yakisoba) mixed into the batter
omachi rice	The original sake rice
'Omakase'	'I'll let you decide' (means the chef will choose your meal for you)
omurice	Rice-filled omelette
onsen	Hot springs
o-Toro	Fattiest part of tuna
pachinko	Type of Japanese gaming machine, part pinball, part video game
ponzu sauce	Sauce made from dashi and yuzu juice

Q–T

ramen	Iconic noodle dish served in a meat-based broth with meat and vegetables; variations include Hakata ramen – a white, pork-bone (tonkotsu) broth; miso ramen – a thick, nutty and slightly sweet broth seasoned with miso; and shio ramen – a clear, yellowish broth seasoned with salt
rikishi	Professional sumo wrestler
robata	Charcoal grill
Sakari	Ripe season crops
sakoku	'National seclusion'
sashi	Branches of fat in beef
sashimi	Raw fish
senshu mizu	Kyoto aubergine
shabu shabu	Boiled escalopes of beef
shiitake	Chinese mushroom
Shingon Buddhism	'True Word' Buddhism
shirako	Cod's sperm
shirataki (noodles)	Low carbohydrate, thin, translucent noodles
shisho	Leaf used in salads, sushi and sashimi dishes
shochu	Japanese spirit distilled from wheat, potato, buckwheat or black sugar
shojin ryori	'Pure food' – the vegetarian cuisine eaten by Buddhists
Shokuiku	food and health education programme run by the Japanese government
shoyu	Soy sauce
shukubo	Zen Buddhist religious hostel
soba (noodles)	Thin, brown noodles made from buck-wheat flour; variations on serving include

	kake-soba – noodles served in a large bowl of soup; wanko-soba – white, flour-based noodles served in mouthful-sized portions; and zaru-soba – cooked, chilled noodles served with a dipping sauce
sogi giri	Technique for slicing vegetables
somen	Ultra-thin noodles (at a nagashi-somen restaurant, the noodles are cooked then dropped in a fast-flowing mountain river from where diners, sitting on wooden platforms, pluck them - supposedly)
sudachi	Small, green citrus fruit similar in appearance to lime
sukiyaki	Quick-fried beef dish served with sugary, raw egg sauce
Tajima-gyu cows	Black-haired, short-horn cows known as 'Japanese blacks'
tako yaki	'Octopus balls' – small doughnuts filled with octopus chunks
tamago	Japanese rolled omelette
taro	edible plant root cooked as vegetable or ground into paste or flour
tempura	Deep-fried vegetables or seafood
tenkasu	Cooked flour dough used for tempura
tenugui	Headscarf worn by Japanese chefs
toishi	Whetstone for sharpening knives
toji	Master sake brewer
tokonoma	Small raised display alcove
tombi hawk	Black kite hawk
tonkatsu	Breaded pork cutlets

U–Z

udon (noodles)	Thick, white flour-based noodles; variations include kama-age-udon – served

	with a cold dipping sauce; and kitsune-udon – soft, squidgy udon noodles served in a slightly sweet dashi with deep-fried tofu skin
uimaru	Okinawan social groups
ujinimun	Nutritional foods
umami	The fifth basic taste
umi-budo	Seaweed with tiny pods arranged around edible stalks, sometimes called 'sea grapes' or 'sea caviar'
uni	Sea urchin
ura maki	Inside-out sushi rolls where rice is spread over dried nori sheets
usuba	Rectangular bladed knife
wasanbonto sugar	The 'King of Sugars'
yakuro	'Medicinal hunting'
yanagi	Sashimi knife (with only one bevelled edge)
yatai	Fukuokan street-cart food stall
yokozuna	Highest rank in professional sumo
yuba	Tofu skin
yubari	Orange-fleshed cantaloupe melon
yuka	Wooden platforms
yukata	Short cotton kimono
yuta	Healer
yuzu	Citrus fruit resembling a small grapefruit

Index

www.vintage-books.co.uk